THE HUNGRY TIGERS
THE FIGHTER PILOT'S
ROLE IN MODERN WARFARE

To all fighter pilots, but particularly a couple of close friends: Col. Stan Horne (MIA), and Col. Les Hauer (MIA)—two of the best!

THE HUNGRY TIGERS
THE FIGHTER PILOT'S
ROLE IN MODERN WARFARE

FRANK J. O'BRIEN

AERO
A division of TAB BOOKS Inc.
Blue Ridge Summit, PA 17214

Also by the Author from TAB BOOKS Inc.

No. 2375   *Homebuilts—A Handbook for the First-Time Builder*

FIRST EDITION

FIRST PRINTING

Copyright © 1986 by TAB BOOKS Inc.

Printed in the United States of America

Library of Congress Cataloging in Publication Data

O'Brien, Frank J.
    The hungry tigers.

    Bibliography: p.
    Includes index.
        1. Fighter plane combat.   2. Fighter pilots.
3. Fighter planes—United States.   I. Title.
UG700.027   1986   358.4'14   86-659
ISBN 0-8306-8195-7 (pbk.)

Contents

THE HUNGRY TIGERS
THE FIGHTER PILOT'S
ROLE IN MODERN WARFARE

Acknowledgments

Looking back over many years of flying fighters, I find that quite a few people have shared, in big ways and small, in the formulation of the thoughts and concepts expressed in this book. These dedicated individuals, who were the hard-core professionals of some outstanding fighter squadrons, epitomized the spirit of the hungry tiger. Each one deserves a dip of the wingtip in salute and thanks for his unique contribution to an exciting and fascinating experience. Working and learning with them made flying fighters the best job in the world, bar none.

A special note of appreciation to Col. Richard Sanders, Commander of the 108th Tactical Fighter Wing, New Jersey Air National Guard, for the courtesies and cooperation shown by his unit in helping research certain areas of the book. A pair of tigers assigned to the 108th who were particularly gracious with their time and expertise were Lt. Col. Larry Faison, Air Force Advisor, and Capt. Terry McKenna, Weapons and Tactics Officer.

Two other old pros who also wear the tiger's stripes that helped considerably in this undertaking were Bruce Gordon, Maj. USAF (Ret.), and Jay Dees, Maj. USAF (Ret.). Our many hours in the air together bring back some treasured memories of better times.

Thanks also go to the McDonnell Douglas Corporation, the General Dynamics Corporation, and the Grumman Aerospace Corporation for their generous assistance in providing pictures and information on the F-15, Harrier, F-16, and X-29.

The many hours of proofreading by my wife Marge, the distaff tiger, were greatly appreciated.

Chapter 1

Introduction: What Is a Hungry Tiger?

The fighter pilot's world is populated almost entirely by tigers of one degree or another. The very nature of the job and the characteristics it demands allow only a special breed of cat to gain entry. An aggressive, can-do attitude, coupled with the conviction that he's the best in the business, is what separates the tigers from the rest of the birdmen.

Of course, these essential ingredients of the fighter pilot's image must be backed up by the skills necessary to enable a tiger to prove his right to wear the stripes. It is the acquisition and refinement of these many required skills that is the real measure of the amount of the tiger in the man. The brash and boastful fledgling who has not yet learned his art may sound like and have all the appearances of a real tiger. However, it is not too long before the first few tests of his mettle show that he can't hack the mission, and his facade crumbles.

Being a fighter pilot today in any man's air force is hard work. The dedication and self-discipline necessary to master current weapons systems must be of the highest order. Only those who are willing to put in the time and effort required, and to endure the sacrifices that are a part of the game, need apply. But for those who have the heart—and, as Tom Wolf put it, "the right stuff"—to prevail, the rewards are well worth all the sweat, toil, trouble, and tears. Flying fighters is undoubtedly the best job in the world, bar none. The jock who straps a 10-million-dollar machine to his backside and uses it effectively as a weapon day after day truly represents the cream of the crop in the flying game.

The fighter business, like all others, has its own hierarchy of tigers. Basically, all tigers are equal, but the new guy in any fighter outfit soon finds out that some tigers are more equal than others. The old heads, who have refined their skills over many years and perhaps a war or two, always have a few tricks up their sleeves that the novice never learned at flying school. However, these nuances of the fighter pilot's trade are never kept secret by the old guard. They are passed on as soon as the young pilot's experience and capability prove that he is ready.

Learning these refinements does not occur in one great blinding flash of revelation. It is a gradual process, taught over many missions in the air and innumerable briefings and debriefings on the ground. The latter also includes endless talks over a few cool ones at the club, where a good bit of the conversation is done with the hands to illustrate each move and countermove. There is also a price that almost every newcomer must pay for the acquisition of all this invaluable lore. The dues take the form of a round for all hands, bought by the losers of the day's mock air combat engagement, or those who brought home the low scores from the bombing range.

Despite the frivolity usually associated with learning all there is to know about being a fighter pilot, beneath the surface, the real tigers are deadly serious about the whole thing. The reason for this is the end result of the entire learning process and the years and years of practice: *Can you hack it in combat?* This is where the basics, learned with so much difficulty over so long a time, must become instinctive. Now a different type of learning must occur when the chips are down and the bad guys are shooting back. This consists of finding out everything you can on how to meet and master the highly fluid aspects of each and every combat situation. The combat-ready fighter pilot must be able to perform—and perform well—an imposing number of jobs that go to make up his multifaceted role in modern war. A brief overview of the more important missions in the tiger's domain will serve a dual purpose at this time. Most importantly, it will show the diversity of the tasks and the lack of too many common denominators between them. Each one represents a unique challenge, separate and distinct from the others. In addition, this overview will provide a very generalized outline of how this book will present the details of what it takes to be a hungry tiger.

One point should be inserted here to clarify the difference between *hungry* tigers and all other tigers. As is true in the jungle, the hungry tiger is better at his business than the indolent or the complacent. To bring home the bacon, as it were, his wits must be keener, his reflexes quicker, and his knowledge of how to play the game complete. And so it is with the airborne tiger. The jock who pursues his craft with a zeal, and who constantly works to refine and update his techniques, has the mark of a *hungry tiger*. The dedication and work required to stay a cut above the average results in a winner who can be depended upon in any type of a flap.

The first item to be addressed in the following chapters, and one that constitutes about a third of the fighter pilot's mission, is the air-to-ground role. In a conventional war, this consists of two major areas: *close air support* and *interdiction*. Both of these involve a variety of weapons, and numerous delivery techniques for each. Included here are high and low-angle dive bombing, strafing, high-altitude level bombing, and gunship escort. The problems and techniques associated with each of these will be discussed in detail in Part I.

The other area that requires a large percentage of a fighter pilot's time to learn and perfect is air-to-air combat tactics. The close-in dogfights of World War I have evolved into far-ranging aerial battles, covering many cubic miles of airspace and fought with electronic wizardry and sophisticated missiles. The tactics discussed in Part II will not be the basic fighter maneuvers utilized in one-on-one engagements. Rather, they will focus on the broader picture of how fighters are employed on a larger scale. The techniques used to escort and defend large raids of fighter-bombers in and out of hostile territory, as well as the methods of conducting a Barrier Combat Air Patrol, will be covered completely.

The complexity and broad scope of air operations in modern warfare necessitated the development of specialized air defense tactics. The details of when and how these are employed are also contained in this section. Interwoven with the descriptions of these missions, which make up the fighter pilot's stock in trade, will be a look at what must be done before and after these flights to ensure their success. Good mission planning and a thorough debriefing, or the lack of it, can make or break the hungriest of tigers. The weapons and delivery systems in use today demand careful pre- and post-mission analysis to be employed effectively. A good portion of this requirement is devoted to planning the necessary coordination of the various agencies involved in any strike, and the essential feedback of intelligence information into the system. Also touched on throughout the book will be the various administrative functions that are required of every aircrew member, even in a combat zone. The paper war goes on, regardless of the level of actual hostilities.

The best way to study a tiger is to view him in his natural habitat; in the following pages this line of reasoning is extended to his aerial counterpart. Since all of a fighter pilot's training points toward the combat situation, this is the ideal place to take a close look at just what is involved in being a hungry tiger. The constantly changing requirements of a war keep a pilot's skills sharp in all areas. One day he may be doing high-angle dive bombing, the next might be fighter escort. That night he may be bombing under flares, and, of course, there is the ever-present threat of being bounced by enemy fighters.

Naturally, interspersed among all these activities are those skills which, by this stage of the game, must be refined to the point of being second nature. A high level of proficiency in night flying, instrument flying, formation techniques, and midair refueling procedures is expected of every fighter jock entering a combat zone. These are the givens, since no time can be spent on training or refresher flights in these areas. A new pilot's first mission in combat may very well require all of these skills, with the possible exception of refueling.

Thus, as we take an in-depth look at how the hungry tigers go about their business, the wars of recent years will serve as a convenient backdrop. The post-Korean era, the Mideast, the Falklands, and (especially) Vietnam, all had particular aspects that can best tell the story of the fighter pilot in his element.

The majority of the book will deal with air operations in Vietnam, since during the many years of our involvement in that conflict, just about every type of mission in the fighter jock's repertoire came into play. And, to further set the stage, the many other activities that surrounded, or were a part of, the world's most exciting job will be interwoven with the descriptions of the missions. These are the preliminaries and peripherals to the actual flying game that are either an integral part of it or play an essential supporting role. They will also help to point out that there is a lot more to flying fighters than jumping in, cranking up, and leaping off.

The close air support missions flown in 'Nam will be the setting for the air-to-ground activity described below. More specifically, the story will focus on the operations of the 12th Tactical

Fighter Wing (TFW), located at Phu Cat Air Base in central South Vietnam. Although we were only one of many operational bases in the theater, the details of the sorties are fairly representative of how the war was fought in the 1970-1971 time period.

During these years, there were a few givens through which the conduct of the war at that time must be viewed. Between 1968 and 1972 there was a halt in the bombing missions against targets in North Vietnam. This halt put an end to the large-scale raids on the airfield, industrial, and port facilities in the Hanoi/Haiphong area, which characterized the earlier days of the war. For the most part, the only targets in North Vietnam that were hit during this period were SAM (surface-to-air missile) sites along the border in the extreme southern portion of the country. Raids against these sites were very infrequent, and occurred only as a defensive reaction. This happened when a SAM site fired missiles at the good guys who were working a target just across the border in South Vietnam or Laos.

However, the fact that we were not going North by no means meant that we were idle. The bombing halt merely changed the emphasis of the mission from a modified strategic role to that of close air support and interdiction. A great majority of those missions were flown at the request of our ground forces located throughout the region. They were designed to help out troops actually engaged with the enemy, or soon about to be. The purpose of these sorties was to nullify a numerical or positional advantage held by the enemy, or to generally soften up an area prior to its being attacked by ground elements. Airpower's inherent flexibility in weapons and delivery methods made these close support missions very popular with the grunts (infantry), since their job was correspondingly made easier and quicker.

The other predominant effort of the 12th TFW was that of interdicting the enemy's supply, communications, and support functions. These missions involved knocking out truck traffic on the Ho Chi Minh Trail, mining and cratering choke points in their transportation system, and attacking base camps and supply caches. Although these different missions are essentially the same as those flown against the Hanoi/Haiphong area earlier in the war, we enjoyed two very significant advantages that contributed to both longevity and operational effectiveness. The first of these was our complete air superiority over the entire area where we worked. There was never a problem with enemy fighters, since they lacked the range to counter our efforts in Laos and South Vietnam, and opposition by SAMs was relatively infrequent. The other plus on our side was a lower density of flak, as compared with that found around Hanoi and Haiphong.

There is one other phase of the air-to-ground role that was not utilized in Vietnam—the special procedures and techniques required for the delivery of tactical nuclear weapons. The employment of such devices would most likely occur if a major war broke out in Europe. The destructive power and aftereffects of these weapons require that very precise delivery parameters be met. And since the area in question is crisscrossed by radars and other detection apparatus, the routes to and from the target require detailed planning and execution. A brief look at this facet of the air-to-ground mission will wrap up Part I.

Vietnam shares the stage with the Mideast and the Falklands in Part II, as our discussion shifts to the techniques used in modern aerial combat. The latter two wars seemed to feature a back-to-the-basics movement in neo-classical dogfighting. The engagements of large numbers of opposing fighters (particularly in the Mideast) is reminiscent of the titanic fighter battles waged over Germany toward the end of World War II, as the Allies asserted their supremacy in the air.

The F-4 Phantom II was the real workhorse of the Vietnam war in both the counter-air and the air-to-ground roles. In this light, all of the discussions on tactics and procedures used in this war will be based on the F-4 and its employment. The later wars introduced fighters of the next generation, whose potential was an order of magnitude above that of the Phantom. Their capabilities will be touched upon as they relate to the conflict they were engaged in.

Finally, in Part III we take a look in our crystal ball to see what the tigers of tomorrow will be doing: What type of birds will they be flying, and will they be doing anything different than their progenitors of today?

Now that the scenery is all in place and our course is set, let's see where the hungry tigers plied their trade, and what it takes to "fling your frail pink body at the ground," as dive bombing is so often described.

Part I

Air-to-Ground

Chapter 2

Where We Worked

Any description of the close air support mission in Vietnam must take into consideration the physical and military attributes of the area. The maps on the following pages show how the country was divided into regions of military activity, the location of the major cities and air bases, distances to the most popular target areas, and some of the more prominent physical features of Southeast Asia.

The primary significance of the four Corps areas was to organize and define the responsibilities of the ground forces in South Vietnam. These divisions had no impact on the close air support mission in the theater, since orders for all strikes flown anywhere in the area came from 7th Air Force Headquarters in Saigon. The airbases shown in Figure 2-1 are only the major operational fields that were active in the 1970-1971 time frame. There were numerous other facilities with paved runways available, particularly along the coast. Nearly all of these were large enough and maintained in such condition that they could be used as emergency recovery bases for just about any bird flying in Vietnam. The shorter strips used by the Forward Air Controllers (FACs) and liaison aircraft were literally all over the place, since they were built when and where the ground situation demanded. The usability of these small fields at any given time was dependent on a number of factors: how much the jungle had reclaimed,the extent of the monsoon floodwaters, and—most important of all—who owned it at the time, the good guys or the bad guys.

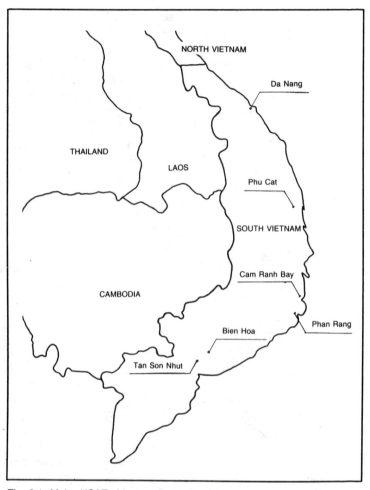

Fig. 2-1. Major USAF airbases, South Vietnam, 1970-71.

The physical location of the bases suitable for jet traffic did present a problem on a good number of our missions. A glance at the map will show that there are no jet facilities in western South Vietnam, southern Laos, or northeastern Cambodia. A large percentage of our strikes were flown in these areas, and if you took a hit over the target, you had quite a distance to go before finding some friendly concrete. "Friendly" is the key word here, because most of this region was crawling with people bent on doing you bodily harm. This was particularly true if you had to punch out anywhere near the target, since you could hardly expect much hospitality from people you had just napalmed.

Figure 2-2 shows the flying distance from Phu Cat to the various target locations hit most frequently by the 12th TFW. Any that were more than 200 miles from the home drome did require some special planning in the area of fuel management. Working time on these targets was usually very restricted, especially if the weather at the recovery base was a problem. This normally meant a maximum of two passes per aircraft, followed by an enroute joinup while on a vector for home plate. On some missions, where we were stretched out to the limit of our range, everything had to be dropped on the first pass.

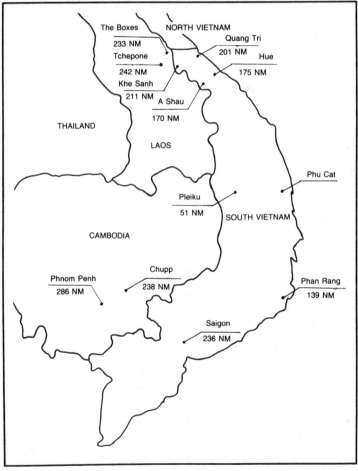

Fig. 2-2. Flying distances from Phu Cat.

There was one other factor that always had to be considered, even though it did not happen too frequently. Bingo fuel on all missions was computed on the assumption that no bombs would be brought home from the target area. Thus, if there were delays in getting on the target, or a sudden change in the ground situation precluded a drop, some fast recalculations had to be made if you wanted to recover at Phu Cat. The weight and added drag of a full load of bombs decreased the range of an F-4 by about 20 percent. Therefore, a new Bingo fuel had to be figured to take this into account. If a lot of things went wrong on the mission up to this decision point, the delays in getting on the target might result in a computed Bingo fuel greater than what you actually had left—just the type of news you need to cap an already frustrating day. Even though Bingo fuel is normally figured a little on the fat side, this cushion is only enough to allow a go-around and closed traffic in the event of a landing emergency. Obviously, in this case you have to get rid of the bombs. If the FAC can't put you on the target for one reason or another, he will direct you to an area clear of friendlies where the bombs can be pickled off in level flight. This was not a very satisfying way to complete a mission. Nonetheless, except for an emergency jettison situation, bombs were always dropped in an armed condition. This was to ensure that they exploded on impact, thus preventing the enemy from recovering a dud, extracting the explosives, and using them against our forces.

Geography and Weather

A very generalized picture of the major geographical characteristics of the theater is shown in Fig. 2-3. The Annam mountain range is perhaps the most prominent feature of the area, and is an interesting study of contrasts. In South Vietnam and Laos, the highest point in this chain is less than 9,000 feet above sea level—not unlike the Appalachians in the eastern United States. However, in the Annams, the ridgelines are sharp and pronounced, and the valleys are quite deep with steeply inclined sides—much like the higher levels of the Rockies. Another somewhat unusual topographical feature found in the Annams is *karst* areas. These are regions where the rock formations, because or erosion, have developed into numerous flat-topped precipices with nearly vertical sides. Individual formations in a karst area are separated by deep, trenchlike valleys that provide antiaircraft batteries with an excellent hiding place that is well protected from air attack.

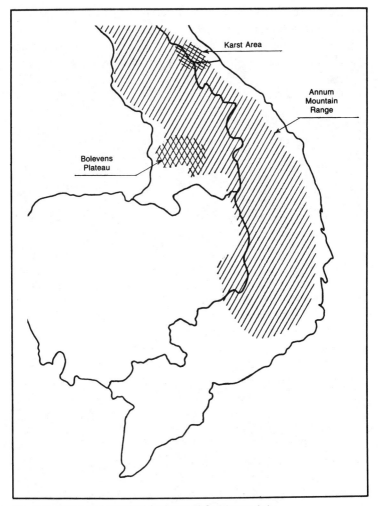

Fig. 2-3. Major geographical features of Southeast Asia.

Another distinctive landmark for the troops operating out of Phu Cat was the Bolevens Plateau. The eastern edge of this 50-mile-wide tableland was particularly striking, as the elevation dropped over 4,000 feet in a very short horizontal distance. The top of the Bolevens was sprinkled with small landing strips, base camps, and helicopter landing areas. The ground war in this region was unique in that our forces were airlifted in at first light, and controlled these facilities and the immediately surrounding area during the day. When our people were on the ground, the 12th TFW

Fig. 2-4. South Vietnamese landscape looking toward the Chu Lai area from 25,000 feet. This base was between Phu Cat and Danang, and the rugged terrain with few distinguishable landmarks was typical of that along the Annam Mountain range.

supported their operations on a regular basis. At twilight, the good guys would be picked up by choppers and returned to their main base, while the enemy moved back into the areas we just left.

Perhaps the most striking impression of Vietnam, as seen from

Fig. 2-5. A plant typical of those found in the jungle in Vietnam. The sawtooth edges on the leaves would make running through a clump of these a painful experience while trying to escape and evade the enemy after being shot down.

14

the air, is the lush greenness that covers just about every bit of the land. It almost looks like someone had draped the entire country in deep green velvet. This effect is created by the triple canopy jungle that flourishes with abandon just about everywhere. It is so named because of the three distinct layers of vegetation that make up the total ground cover: the low shrubs, bushes, and small trees; larger trees and vines reaching up to 30 to 50 feet; and the taller trees that can grow to a height of well over 100 feet. In the southern area around the Mekong delta, the jungle gives way somewhat to innumerable waterways, canals, marsh areas, and backwaters. The totality of this green cover obscures nearly all roads, trails, and small rivers. The only area where these transportation networks are visible is along the coast, where most of the larger bases and population centers are located.

The weather in Vietnam can best be described as hot and sticky most of the time. The normally high humidity made even fairly warm days somewhat uncomfortable. This situation was not helped by the preferred uniform of the day for most aircrews, a Nomex flying suit. Since this cloth has good fire-retardant properties, it was required wear on all flights. However, its texture and weave do not lend themselves to tropical use. They were hot and itchy, and definitely not conducive to comfortable living in this type of

Fig. 2-6. City of Danang from 25,000 feet. The air base is in the center of the town, and the radar site called "Panama" was located on the peninsula at the top of the picture, on a hill named Monkey Mountain.

climate. After donning all the gear required for a mission, crewmembers were completely soaked with sweat by the time they had finished their preflight inspections and strap-in.

Air conditioners ran constantly in both living quarters and work areas, but they could only do so much to counter the excessive humidity. This created a problem of almost instant mildew, and infrequently used clothes—especially shoes—would be completely covered in a very short time. A partial solution to this was to keep a light bulb burning in the bottom of your closet to generate a little heat where it was most needed.

The monsoons dominated the weather for a good portion of the year in one area or the other in Southeast Asia. During the winter the northeast monsoon held sway, and everything east of the Annums had continuous rains. Before they started, it was hard to visualize such an extended period of wet weather, but after the first week or so, you became a believer. Except for brief interludes during which it always looked threatening, it rained day and night. This was usually a steady, moderate rain, interspersed with numerous showers that were *real* gullywashers. It seemed as if the whole world could be measured in degrees of wetness ranging from damp to soaked. Just about everyone used the standard GI pup tent half as a poncho to help stay a little less wet. The standing water and the red soil peculiar to the Phu Cat area combined to make a gelatinous mud that clung to everything with unbelievable tenacity-wet or dry.

Operationally, the northeast monsoon had little impact on our day-to-day routine. Ceilings and visibilities were rarely poor enough to cancel a mission or cause a divert to an alternate. However, wet runways did pose something of a problem during this period, especially if a heavyweight landing had to be made. The wet surface reduced braking action a little, but the main danger was that of hydroplaning in large areas of standing water. The F-4 had a design peculiarity that made hydroplaning a particularly hairy situation. All three gear on this airplane are just about equidistant from each other. Because the supporting points of the airplane form an equalateral triangle, there is no inherent castoring action to help straighten out the bird once she started to slide. This "free skating" tendency could put the airplane in some very awkward positions, which invited serious damage if the hydroplaning stopped while the bird still had a good bit of momentum. Although it didn't happen too frequently, once in a while a mission would be canceled soon after takeoff, and the Wing command post wanted the aircraft back on the ground right away. If there was standing water on the runway, and a landing had to be made under full fuel and bomb load conditions, an approach-end engagement was the best plan of action. (This procedure, which almost replicates a Navy-style carrier landing, will be described in greater detail later on.)

Although the cloud cover generated by the monsoons was widespread, it lacked the extensive vertical development usually associated with tropical weather. Thunderstorms during this time were rare, and the general tops were usually around 20,000 feet.

The extensive weather brought close air support missions east of the Annums virtually to a standstill. The only missions flown in this area during the rainy season were interdiction sorties. However, west of the mountains the weather was great, with only the usual fair weather cumulus to contend with. This allowed us to conduct business as usual in the "Steel Tiger" area of Laos during the northeast monsoon.

The southwest monsoon influenced the theater during the summer months, and the weather patterns were reversed. Now everything west of the Annams was clobbered in, and to the east it was wide open. In line with the weather, our missions also changed directions. Close air support was the order of the day in the east, and interdiction was the name of the game in the west. When the weather finally broke after either monsoon season, the rivers and streams throughout the affected area were well beyond their normal banks,and were, of course, very muddy. This enlargement and marked color contrast with the freshly greened vegetation made for easy recognition of key landmarks. The use and importance of these signposts will be described in succeeding chapters.

Base Facilities

As bases went in South Vietnam, Phu Cat could be considered fairly typical. Facilities-wise, it was neither the best nor the worst of the major operational fields. The level and degree of the amenities at any in-country base was in direct relation to its importance to the overall conduct of the war, and the length of time it had enjoyed this prominence. Da Nang and Cam Ranh Bay had things just a little better than Phu Cat, while we seemed to have a slight edge over Bien Hoa and other fields of that size. These differences were by no means great, since by 1970 all the large active bases were equipped with the extras that made life bearable.

The living quarters for all officers were very adequate, with

Fig. 2-7. Your first look at Phu Cat upon arrival. The building is Base Operations, where the weather station was located, along with flight planning facilities for transient aircraft. The ramp in front of the building is made from steel planking topped with an antiskid compound.

each person having his own room. They were a tad small however, measuring only about eight by twelve feet. There were no windows, in order to avoid the danger of flying glass fragments during a rocket attack. Every room had an air conditioner to provide both cooling and ventilation. Furnishings were somewhat sparse, consisting of a standard GI bed, dresser, chair, and night table. A refrigerator was also shared between adjoining rooms. Over the years, each succeeding occupant added a few touches to make the quarters more livable and functional. Desks and shelving built from scrounged materials and cabinets made from ammunition cases were the most popular improvements. All BOQ buildings had 24 rooms, with shower, latrine, and laundry facilities located centrally in each. Enlisted personnel lived in two-story barracks with four or six guys to a room. The furnishings and air conditioning were the same as the officers'.

Keeping the rooms clean and getting laundry done was somewhat of a problem due to our round-the-clock operations. However, Vietnamese women were hired by the base from the surrounding villages to take care of these chores. The fee was minimal, and your room got straightened up and swept each weekday; laundry was done as required, usually once a week.

All living quarters had a double brick wall around the outside, about three feet from the building. It was about four feet high, and the space between the two walls was filled with sand. Its purpose was to provide protection from fragments of exploding rockets when we were under attack, and hopefully absorb most of the damage in case of a near direct hit.

The work areas on the base followed the same lines as the living quarters—spartan but functional. Each of the two fighter squadrons at Phu Cat had its own Operations building, as did the FAC unit and the troops who flew the "Electric Goons." A good portion of the squadron ops building was devoted to the storage and maintenance of each crewmember's flying and survival gear. Included here was a walk-in vault for the safekeeping of sidearms, ammunition, and classified documents that were carried on each flight. The rest of the building consisted of briefing rooms, offices for the operational and administrative staff, a Squadron Duty Desk to coordinate and post the daily mission schedule, and a recreation room. The latter had the usual ping-pong and pool tables, and was decorated with numerous Viet Cong souvenirs and mementos that were acquired over the years.

The operational status of the aircrews and equipment assigned to both fighter squadrons was maintained on an up-to-the-minute

Fig. 2-8. Operations building for the 480th Tactical Fighter Squadron, where just about all daily activity took place. The "bread trucks" parked in front were used to take crews to and from their aircraft.

Fig. 2-9. A typical flight briefing room with maps, airfield, and munitions data on the walls.

basis by the 12th TFW Combat Operations Center. Here, on large plotting boards, was shown the actual combat readiness of the Wing as a complete unit. Each pilot and GIB were listed by name, and whether they were available, sick, or on leave, TDY, or R&R. The maintenance status of every aircraft assigned to the Wing was shown, and if a bird was not in commission, the estimated time and date it would be back in service was noted. All support equipment—refueling vehicles, auxiliary power units, aircraft tugs, munitions handling trucks, and general purpose vehicles—were also shown in a similar manner. Scheduled flying activity for the day was indicated by aircraft tail number, crew, target, and the times involved. The manning of the alert force was also posted; if they got scrambled, their mission particulars were reflected on the board immediately. Current and forecast weather was also depicted for all primary bases in the theater. All of the information on these boards was updated continuously so that the Wing Commander or duty officer had a complete picture of how the Wing was functioning at any given moment. All data relating to the combat readiness of the Wing was always forwarded to 7th Air Force Headquarters.

The flight lines of major fighter bases in Southeast Asia were much the same as their stateside counterparts. There were, however, two marked differences. The first was the constant activity, nearly always conducted at a hectic pace, that was necessary to

Fig. 2-10. F-4s being refueled after a mission.

sustain 24-hour operations. Sorties launched and recovered at all hours, and the maintenance and support effort needed to "keep 'em flying" seemed to never end. The other was the individual, hardened shelters for each aircraft and its auxiliary equipment. These shelters were large, open-ended Quonset huts made of corrugated steel sections. In order to make them impervious to all but large-bore weapons, about 24 inches of concrete was poured over the steel arches. Of course, with the open ends, it was possible for a lucky shot or a ricochet to hit the aircraft in the shelter. And since all of the birds were kept fully fueled, and a good number of them were loaded with bombs, the potential for a fire and explosion was in-

Fig. 2-11. Fuel bladders enclosed by dikes, which were used in place of storage tanks for aircraft refueling.

21

Fig. 2-12. Reinforced concrete shelters used for all aircraft of the 12th Tactical Fighter Wing. The eagle's head insignia denotes the 480th Fighter Squadron's area.

deed great in case of a hit. In this light, the shelters served a dual purpose: Not only did they protect the bird from all but a chance shot, they also helped to contain fire and minimize explosion damage to adjacent aircraft. During the monsoon season, they also provided a temporary respite from the weather for the crew chiefs, armorers, and maintenance specialists working on the airplanes.

This type of hardened shelter was only used to protect the F-4s at Phu Cat. Other aircraft based here—mostly EC-47s and O-2s—

Fig. 2-13. View from the control tower of the entire flight line at Phu Cat. Note that all aircraft are protected by revetments or shelters in case of rocket attacks.

22

Fig. 2-14. EC-47 "Electric Goons" in revetments. These aircraft were used for electronic surveillance of enemy ground activity.

were shielded somewhat by steel revetments about ten feet high.

Along one side of the flight line in the fighter area were all the maintenance shops needed to support our operations. These consisted of machine shops, electronics test and repair areas, engine maintenance shops, and sheet metal fabrication shops, as well as shops for specialized work in the areas of hydraulics, pneumatics, instruments, electrical systems, drag chute repacking and repair, and aircraft tire and wheel buildup. Overall, these shops were capable of performing what is known as "field level maintenance." A good portion of the remainder of the base was devoted to offices and facilities necessary for coordinating and expediting the primary mission of the Wing. Among these would be the supply, personnel, finance, medical, transportation, and food service functions.

As was true of just about any large installation in Southeast Asia, the longer it was in operation, the more of the amenities of military life it acquired. Phu Cat was no exception, and with an eye toward the correct order of priorities, it provided clubs for of-

Fig. 2-15. O-2s in their revetments, with the control tower in the background. These aircraft were flown by the "Tum" FACs stationed at Phu Cat.

Fig. 2-16. The officer's club at Phu Cat. The trees are all banana palms, but the fruit is not palatable and was known as "monkey bananas."

ficers, NCOs, and airmen. The O Club was fairly well appointed, considering we were in the middle of a combat area, and it did provide an alternative to the mess hall for meals. The menu was pretty restricted and the steaks were of mediocre quality, but it was handy and its hours of operation were more convenient. Occasionally the club offered entertainment in the form of USO shows; however, these were always Japanese or Korean hard rock ensembles, who appealed mostly to the younger troops. Every couple of months, each squadron held a big party at the club to honor the guys going

Fig. 2-17. The Base Exchange at Phu Cat. The two small buildings to the right sold specialty items, such as cameras, kitchenware, and leather goods.

24

home, and to welcome the newcomers with appropriate initiations to the war zone.

For some of the more mundane necessities of life, the base also had a small Base Exchange (BX) and Commissary. The selection of wares at the former was pretty much limited to toilet articles, detergent, military items, and small household paraphernalia. The commissary offered only nonperishable canned or dried foods, most of which were used for snacks or cooking one's own meals on the squadron patio. Frozen steaks could be special-ordered in bulk quantity, and these were quite a popular item.

The base Chapel at Phu Cat was very complete and well-furnished, offering services for all major denominations. Attendance at these services seemed to be good despite the odd working hours and the expected laxity usually associated with this type of situation. Perhaps the occasional rocket attacks had a bearing on this.

Although most aircrews preferred to wear flying suits on and off duty, civilian clothes were used by some for lounging around the BOQ area and going to the club. Since most people did not want to risk these items to the tender mercies of the GI laundry, or to the *mamasans* who cleaned the rooms, the laundry and dry cleaning shop did a brisk business. They also provided a sewing service, which was quite popular for putting rank, insignia and unit patches on uniforms and party suits.

Fig. 2-18. Aerial view of Phu Cat looking east toward the Phu Cat Mountains. Just beyond the hills is the South China Sea.

Fig. 2-19. A closeup of the Phu Cat Mountains. A VC base camp was located on the promontory on the left, therefore, this area received regular attention by the sorties fragged for the 12th Tactical Fighter Wing.

There was one facility on the base that did not quite measure up to the standards of the rest, and this was the theater. It showed fairly recent movies three or four times every day to accommodate the various work schedules. However, it was too small for the demand, and long lines and crowded conditions were the norm, unless the picture was a real loser. In addition, things were not too rosy once you got inside and found a seat. The air conditioning was not up to the task, and the wooden folding chairs were about as comfortable as a granite block.

Even though the base did not have all the facilities and extras of a stateside operation, it was surprising how much had been done to make a year at war a lot easier to bear. The name Phu Cat means Beautiful Mountain in Vietnamese, and our surroundings were just that. To the east, a small mountain range about 1,500 to 2,000 feet high paralleled the coastline, which was only 12 miles from the base. These hills lacked the rugged features of the Annams, and their more smoothly finished contours provided an aesthetically pleasant background to the harsher realities of the military enclave where we lived and worked.

The terrain west of the base was relatively level for about five to seven miles, where it again gave way to some low foothills of the Annams. None of the high ground that more or less surrounded

Phu Cat presented a problem for approaches to the field during instrument conditions. Part of the GCA pattern was flown over open water, and when inland, it was well above and clear of all terrain obstacles. The approaches to our one north-south runway were over pretty flat ground for quite a few miles off either end. This also facilitated straight-in letdowns and approaches to the field for birds returning with minimum fuel.

Chapter 3

Daily Operations and Routine

The life of a fighter pilot is a busy one, even under normal peacetime conditions. Long hours and continual practice are required just to stay abreast of the constantly changing world of fighter tactics and techniques. This means that even a fully qualified pilot or GIB must fly at least 20 to 25 hours each month to stay sharp in all areas. Once a tiger starts getting hungry, the amount of time he must devote to his craft just to maintain the competitive edge is correspondingly larger.

In a combat zone, the total number of hours worked each day is probably not very different. However, the big change occurs in the hours of the day during which you earn your keep. The eight-to-five routine of peacetime operations gives way to the necessity of maintaining constant pressure on the bad guys. This requires people from many skill areas to be on tap around the clock to carry the war to the enemy. The crews flying the mission are actually only the tip of the iceberg. The support effort needed to get each plane on target at the proper time with the correct armament is enormous, yet the people involved, for the most part, go unheralded.

Modern war by its very nature is continuous and intense. Winning the day for queen and country, as it were, no longer suffices, and in order to ensure complete victory, the contest of the wills must also be won. The enemy's spirit and will to resist must be broken, and broken entirely. The methods necessary to accomplish this feat are not pretty, nor do they rest easy on the mind. But then again, none of the aspects of war are really palatable in any sense. What must be done to win, must be done. Therefore, continuous attacks to destroy the enemy physically and mentally and constant pressure to wear down his resolve are the proven basic keys to success.

This was the rationale for spending an incalculable number of man-hours in the dead of night and in all kinds of weather in order to impose our will on the Viet Cong (VC) and the North Vietnamese. Fighting a guerrilla force on the ground, as we did in Southeast Asia, was slow, expensive, frustrating, and yielded only marginal results. Airpower was the only way to keep hitting this highly mobile foe wherever he went, keeping him constantly on guard for a sudden attack from the sky. Nor did he gain any respite from darkness or bad weather; our precision bombing systems allowed us to keep the pressure on under all conditions.

Daily Frag Orders

Flying operations for each 24-hour period originated with the fragmentary order, or "frag" as it was commonly called. The frag was made up at 7th Air Force Headquarters, and was teletyped to each operational base in the theater. It listed the sorties to be flown by each unit the next day, giving such particulars as the number of aircraft, their call signs, the armament to be carried, the call sign, frequency, and location of the FAC who would work the mission, and the times involved.

Once this information was received by the Wing Command Post, the total sorties for the day were divided between the fighter squadrons, and the aircraft were assigned by tail number for every mission. The scheduling officer from each squadron would pick up his portion of the frag and go back to his unit to assign the aircrews for each flight. This is when the real cat-and-dog fight began, and the scheduling officer needed the patience of Job and the wisdom of Solomon to face this aggravation every day.

The reason for this daily flap was the intense competition by every pilot and GIB to get on the flying schedule as often as he could, by hook or by crook. The type of mission didn't matter, nor did the target or its defenses. Everyone wanted to accumulate as many missions as he could. Naturally, the scheduling officers kept an exact record of the sorties flown by every crewmember, and used this religiously to keep things in balance. By the time the frag arrived at the squadron, quite a few people would be gathered to "oversee" the posting of the names. When the decision factors were close as to who got the nod, the schedulers frequently had to listen to long and loud arguments for each side. Usually, neither had a convincing story, other than the fact that they wanted to fly. Often things got so hectic that the scheduling officers simply picked up their charts and locked themselves in a room, where they could work alone and in peace.

All their efforts did pay off, however, since everybody went home with about the same number of missions. Toward the end of 1971, pilots usually ended up with about 160, while the GIBs normally had around 200. A year earlier, these figures were about 12 percent higher due to the war's increased level of activity at that time.

The sorties ordered by the frag were missions that were known about in advance, and thus could be planned. These requests for air strikes usually originated with the ground forces operating throughout the theater, and were not of an immediately urgent nature. Such requests for routine missions would normally come in one day and be filled on the following day's frag. They included close air support sorties that were designed to soften up or nullify enemy positions that were objectives of planned ground operations. A variant of this mission would be a Landing Zone (LZ) preparation, where a selected area of the jungle would be cleared instantly by specially fused bombs so that assault helicopters could land with their troops as soon as the strike was over.

Other types of fragged sorties included interdiction missions, where transportation chokepoints such as passes through the karst areas, river fords, and major roads were rendered unusable by cratering and/or mining. A mission closely related to interdiction was that of harassment. This consisted of strikes against established enemy concentrations such as base camps, truck parks, training areas, and bunker complexes. A final type of mission that regularly appeared on the frag was the Stinger escort. This was a specialized form of interdiction the main purpose of which was to stop the night-time truck traffic on the Ho Chi Minh Trail. The particulars of how all these various sorties were flown will be detailed in the following chapters.

From the above description of how the fragmentary order was constructed and implemented, one key point is apparent. Fragged missions were not time-critical. Those that did appear on the flying schedule were the result of an overall analysis of the many daily requests for air support throughout the theater balanced against the available resources. These were the targets that needed hitting most. As you might guess, the highly fluid conditions in any war—particularly a guerrilla war—do not lend themselves to a totally preplanned schedule. Our ground troops might suddenly come across an enemy force, have a fire fight develop, and need an air strike immediately; a FAC on routine patrol might spot a truck convoy that moved into his area during the night and would escape if not hit at once; an already fragged mission might uncover a larger target than previously thought to exist, due to the number and size of secondary explosions and fires caused by their bombs, and this opportunity must be quickly exploited or lost. These are but a few of the many situations in a war that require an immediate response in order to capitalize on newly found but fleeting circumstances.

Pulling Alert

To meet this need, another facet of the Wing's 24-hour operation comes into play, the Alert Force. At Phu Cat this was made up of four aircraft, fully fueled, loaded, preflighted, and set up so that they could become airborne in five minutes or less after the scramble order was given. These birds were loaded with a mix of weapons that were commonly used for close air support. Numbers one and two had napalm and 500-pound high-drag bombs; the lead bird also carried a 20mm Gatling gun, or "Pistol" as it was called, for strafing. The other two alert aircraft each carried a full load of 500-pound conventional bombs.

Crews were assigned to alert duty for a 24-hour period, which began at midnight. In order to ensure proper crew rest after a tour of alert, which often resulted in very little sleep, these people would not be put on the flying schedule until the morning after they came off this duty.

As indicated above, the mission of the alert force was to provide an immediate response to unplanned requests for air support. These might be generated by ground troops in contact with the enemy who were pinned down or otherwise stymied by some unexpected turn of events. Targets of opportunity might present themselves when no other aircraft or crew was available except those on alert. Also, during lulls in the ground war—especially at night during the monsoons—alert birds were used for harassment on Combat Sky Spot missions. (This unique type of bombing will be discussed in detail later on.)

Some tours on alert were the epitome of boredom—no

Fig. 3-1. A view of the alert building—and the long distance to the first four shelters, where the alert aircraft were parked.

scrambles and nothing to do but reread (for the umpteenth time) the dog-eared paperbacks and magazines that had found their way to the alert facility. Others were just the opposite, with scrambles, aircraft changes (which necessitated another preflight and setup), and false starts filling the entire 24-hour period. The latter were particularly aggravating, since the crew quarters were located about 75 yards from the shelters where the aircraft were parked. This distance had to be covered at a dead run in order to meet the five-minute maximum allowable time from scramble order to being airborne. After such a wind sprint, it was quite exasperating to call the tower for instructions between gasps for breath, only to be told the mission was cancelled.

However, if you *did* get airborne, there was a limit to the number of times a crew could fly during an alert period. Three was the magic number, since it was felt that after this many flights, crew rest became a factor. Although it caused a lot of grumbling, it was a wise policy because the lack of adequate rest could impair a pilot's judgement and efficiency on additional flights, especially at night. A majority of this grumbling came from the backup crews, who had to be rousted out in the middle of the night and told to suit up and report to the alert hangar.

Alert duty was not all than onerous, however, since the facility had its own kitchen, staffed by Vietnamese, to prepare and serve three meals each day. The food was the same as that offered in the mess hall, and there was usually peanut-butter-and-jelly available for snacks around the clock.

Off one side of the main room in the alert shack was a bed-room that could accommodate about eight people. Sleeping on alert was fitful at best since you had to stay fully clothed at all times in order to meet the five-minute requirement. Many crewmembers also kept on their G-suits and web belt with pistol and hunting knife—all of which further reduced the probability of getting comfortable enough to catch a few winks. The older troops seemed more inclined to put up with this extra paraphernalia than the younger guys. The probable reason for this was it saved them the few seconds it took to don this gear in the event of a scramble—time that was better spent in running to the bird.

Even those who did doze off slept very lightly, since they were subconsciously listening for the phone to ring with their scramble order. And ring it did—seemingly a thousand times a night when you were trying hard to get some shut-eye. There were calls about the weather, changes of aircraft or alert status, was so-and-so at the alert hangar?, what movie was being shown?, and so forth and so on. Yet, like Pavlov's dogs, everyone on the alert force had an ear cocked each time it rang, listening for his number to be called for a scramble.

Other things that helped pass the time while on alert were a pool table and a different—although slightly dated—movie almost every night. Anytime a film was not being shown, the pool table was in constant use, and there was a standing list of challengers ready to play the winner of each game.

Anytime a large scale operation was being conducted, where

Fig. 3-2. Crewmembers waiting for a scramble in the alert facility. In the background is a small food preparation area, where meals delivered from the main mess hall were served to both aircrews and ground crews.

the situation changed too fast for air strikes to be planned, a Quick Reaction Force (QRF) was set up. This force usually consisted of four to eight aircraft and crews, who were on five-minute status identical to the alert force. The birds assigned to the QRF were loaded with munitions that the special operation called for. More often than not these configurations were not compatible with alert requirements, and so each was considered a separate entity. Scrambles would come in for one group or the other, causing pandemonium every time the phone rang, with all crews rushing for the door in hopes that their flight had been tapped.

The QRF did cause one problem at the alert hangar because of the lack of adequate space. The facility was designed for about eight to ten people, and when two or three times that many were on duty, there were simply not enough chairs and beds to go around. Every available flat surface including the floor was used during periods of maximum manning, and while the movie was on, even the pool table served as a row of seats.

Regardless of which squadron was pulling alert, there was one almost-permanent resident of the alert facility. This was Sabre, the mascot of the 12th TFW. Sabre was an uppity dog of nondescript and ignoble lineage who had been adopted by the fighter jocks at Phu Cat while he was a pup. The base was equipped with F-100s during those days, and rumor had it that Sabre was actually taken along on a few bombing missions while he was still small enough to fit comfortably atop the instrument shroud. The problem of oxygen was neatly solved by fitting him with a cut-out tennis ball that served as a mask. Attached to this was a bailout bottle that would be actuated when the cockpit altitude became critical.

Sabre was not the friendliest of animals, and it is still a mystery why just about everyone liked him so much. Unless bribed by a scrap of meat or some other goodie, Sabre heeled to no man—except the Wing Commander (a very political dog). He considered the base his empire and roamed it at will, hitting the chow hall at mealtimes for a handout, and the squadron patios whenever a cookout was in progress, returning to the alert hangar for a snooze in air-conditioned comfort. There, even under the crowded conditions of a QRF, he would take his ease in the most comfortable lounge chair while crewmembers stood or sat on the floor.

In all his wanderings about the base, Sabre rarely walked. He knew where to board the shuttle bus, and the drivers invariably stopped anytime they saw him waiting. Upon seeing his destination come up, he would let the driver know he wanted off by standing in the stairwell by the door. History does not record what happened to this "legend in his own time" once the base was turned over to the Vietnamese in early 1972. However, it's a good bet that he became a featured entree on the menu of the first Vietnamese family that found him.

When it was required, another facet of our round-the-clock operations was the Search and Rescue (SAR) Alert. This occurred anytime an aircraft went down anywhere in the theater. For all intents and purposes the air war in Vietnam stopped cold whenever a bird was shot down or a crew had to bail out for any reason. All resources of every base were immediately put at the disposal of the rescue commander, and everything else went on hold until he made an on-site inspection of the situation and determined what forces were needed for the rescue. Once the requirements were laid out, those based nearest the scene would normally be tasked to provide crews and aircraft loaded with the specified weapons for as long as the rescue effort was in progress. The SAR force was set up in the alert facility exactly the same as a QRF. However, due to the changing ground conditions at the rescue site, there was a lot more switching of munitions loads to counter each new threat to the pickup. The urgency and personalized nature of the mission—whether you knew the downed guys or not—brought everyone to the fore, ready to do any job needed. The long hours and crowded conditions of a SAR Alert never generated a complaint for the same reasons. Everyone could readily envision that tomorrow it could be him out in the jungle, hiding from the VC and depending on just such a rescue effort.

There were four other functions directly connected with the Wing mission that also operated on a 24-hour schedule. The first and most important of these was the aircraft maintenance section. These troops put in long and hard hours—many of which were out in the heat or the rain—to get our birds ready to fill the Wing's commitment. Aborting a sortie for maintenance problems was a rare occurrence at Phu Cat, whereas at a stateside base it was a fairly common event. This was true even during the surge periods of a QRF or SAR alert. Considering the working conditions and the number of sorties generated, the dedication, innovation, and perseverance of the maintenance complex at Phu Cat was truly outstanding.

Working alongside the maintenance folks was another group who put in just as much time and effort to ensure that the Wing met its mission. These were the armorers and munitions handlers—

the guys who put the bite behind our bark. There's a lot more to arming an airplane than just hanging bombs on the racks. Electrical circuitry had to be checked, fuses set and installed on each bomb, arming wires attached to ensure that the fuses did not arm before the bomb was released, and the cartridges installed in the shackle mechanism that attached each bomb to the aircraft. These latter devices were similar to shotgun shells, and were electrically detonated at the instant of bomb release. The expanding gases from the cartridge opened the jaws of the bomb shackle while simultaneously actuating an ejector piston to physically push the bomb away from its attaching points. This action assured a clean separation of the bomb from the airplane and minimized the danger of the weapon striking any aircraft structure.

The other two sections that worked day and night to support the flying effort were the troops from intelligence and weather. Every flight that took off from Phu Cat, no matter what the hour, was thoroughly briefed on all aspects of the weather affecting the mission, as well as the latest information about what to expect from the bad guys in the target area. Also, after each flight, the intelligence people met and debriefed the aircrews on the results of the mission.

Other Routine Duties

Up till now we've only talked about those activities in a fighter pilot's daily routine in a combat area that are directly mission-oriented. However, during the normal duty day there were numerous other functions that had to be addressed by those not on the flying schedule for the day. New aircrews arrived just about every week or so, and someone from the squadron would be assigned to take these new guys under his wing and help them get settled into the unit. This involved selecting and moving into a room, processing through the usual offices on the base (personnel, supply, medical, chapel, etc.), and attending a few required in-theater briefings.

When the level of flying activity permitted a few airplanes to be freed up, newly arrived front-seaters would be given a "dollar ride." This was strictly a local area orientation flight, and the aircraft carried no bomb load. It was designed to acquaint the newcomer with the more commonly used landmarks and checkpoints in the area, and enable him to take a look at some of our primary alternates and perhaps shoot a practice approach at each.

The back seat on these rides was always occupied by one of the "old heads" in the squadron. "Old" here strictly referred to someone who had been in-country for a considerable time and pretty well knew the ropes. After familiarizing the new guy with the local geography, he would select one of the numerous small islands just off the coast and ask the front-seater to make a practice dive bombing pass on it. Almost invariably it would be a classic textbook pass—standard roll-in, 45-degree dive, with ample tracking time and a straight-ahead pullout. Although great for the bombing range back home, this technique would obviously not do in Vietnam, as we shall see in Chapter 9. The *proper* method of attacking a hostile target would then be demonstrated, with a heavy accent on the jinking required to confuse enemy gunners. The "dollar ride" was undoubtedly the best way to introduce a new pilot to the real world of combat. However, when the availability of aircraft or low ceilings and visibilities precluded this luxury, a newcomer's first sortie would normally be as a wingman on a level precision bombing mission at night.

Another type of non-combat flying that took place on a regular basis during the day was test hops. When certain types of maintenance are performed on a plane, an airborne check of the repaired system must be accomplished. These flights were normally made by a pilot in the maintenance organization, or, if he was tied up, one of the more experienced pilots in the squadron who was specifically designated as a Functional Check Pilot.

The daily grind also included a number of administrative functions which, although sometimes irksome, had to be attended to in a regular fashion. These jobs were assigned as additional duties to aircrews, and dealt with such things as squadron administration, billeting, awards and decorations, aircraft and aircrew publications; if a special event was coming up, an *ad hoc* social officer might even be appointed. Most of these tasks required only a few hours each week to stay on top of, with the notable exceptions of administration and awards and decorations. The former was normally a full-time job for a non-rated officer. Thus, trying to keep up with the mountains of reports and correspondence that had to be answered, in addition to flying his normal share of combat missions, meant that the admin officer had to burn a lot of midnight oil. Since this was not one of the most sought-after jobs in the squadron, the one who did fall on the grenade was usually given special consideration on the flying schedule as to the timing of his flights.

Awards and decorations was another seemingly endless chore,

and one that also required a flair for writing military prose. Some of the very few tangible rewards for serving a tour in Southeast Asia were the medals presented for various actions against the enemy. The citations that accompanied these medals required a great deal of effort to research and write up in acceptable form for submission to higher headquarters. The primary source of the requisite information for these awards was a logbook that was filled out by each crew after landing. Entered here would be the names, date, and time of the flight, along with such particulars as the call sign of the FAC, type of target, munitions dropped, and the results of the strike. Given a fighter pilot's normal disdain for writing reports of any kind, however necessary, these mission descriptions tended at times to be a trifle laconic. Comments such as "All bombs hit the ground" or "Lousy weather; great mission" gave the awards and decs guys precious little to go on. In cases like this, the intelligence debriefing form had to be dug out and the crew questioned in order to pin down some of the details. Sometimes it was necessary to call the FAC who ran the mission to see if he could add any particulars.

Over and above the additional duties assigned to all aircrews were the routine operational tasks that are common to any fighter outfit. These jobs are closely related to the flying schedule, and, with one exception, had to be filled any time fighters were airborne. The one exception was the Supervisor of Flying (SOF), whose tour of duty ran from four in the afternoon until eight the next morning, regardless of the flying activity. The requirement for an SOF was levied by Wing Headquarters, and his job was to oversee all operational factors that affected the Wing's mission while he was on duty. This included handling the routine problems associated with the nighttime flying, keeping an eye on existing and forecast weather so that airborne crews could be advised, checking the runway and taxiways for debris, and monitoring the general security of the flight line and shelter area. Should an urgent matter arise, such as the loss of an aircraft, or one returning from a mission with battle damage that could result in a serious emergency, the Wing Director of Operations would be notified. Only rated pilots with field grade rank (major or above) who had been on the base at least two to three months were eligible for SOF duty. Although the SOF was allowed to sleep during the night, he usually didn't get too much. The runway and ramp checks had to be made every four hours, and in between there were always numerous phone calls from the Command Post, advisories from weather or maintenance, or a problem to be solved. In addition, the SOF had to read all incoming classified messages and notify the appropriate people if any immediate action was required.

One of the other jobs required during all flying operations involving fighter aircraft was mobile control. This safety-oriented function is an Air Force institution that probably dates back to around the mid 1930s, when the first retractable landing gear was introduced. The mobile unit is a small aircraft control tower mounted on a trailer and positioned just off to one side of the runway about 700 feet from the approach end. It is equipped with radios, binoculars, signal lamp, flare gun, and emergency procedure checklists. The primary responsibility of the mobile control officer, who must be a pilot current in the unit's aircraft, is to observe each takeoff and landing with an eye toward safety. Landings are the most critical, and each bird on final approach is viewed through the binoculars to ensure that the gear is down and locked. If mobile sees anything amiss on the landing aircraft, he calls them on the radio and advises that the approach be abandoned until the problem can be checked out further. If the radio call is not heard, and the mobile officer believes that a go-around is advisable, he then fires a red flare across the path of the landing aircraft. Birds lining up for takeoff are also given the once-over through the glasses to check for loose or missing panels, obvious leaks, extended steps, or any other item that might be a hazard to flight. Additionally, the mobile officer logs the exact takeoff and landing time of each fighter, and calls these in to the Wing Command Post.

Another very important function of mobile control is to monitor the approach visibility during periods of deteriorating weather conditions. The base weather guessers only report prevailing

Fig. 3-3. Mobile control and its power unit surrounded by sandbags, as seen from the taxiway. The small building to the left is for the weapons arming crews.

visibility, which is the average of all quadrants around the field. Deciding to make an approach based on this information could be hazardous to your health because while the visibility might be good around most of the base, it could be zilch off the approach end— the only place where it really counts. Therefore, when the mobile officer sees an aircraft breaking out of the murk less than a mile from the end of the runway, the command post is notified immediately. They in turn pass this information along to the various agencies who control returning aircraft, or, if things have really turned to worms, make the decision to recover the birds elsewhere.

If an aircraft had an emergency and was in VFR conditions, the usual procedure was to contact mobile control on a discreet frequency and discuss the situation, particularly if it would affect the landing. Expert advise from specialists in maintenance could be relayed to the crew, and the appropriate emergency procedure could be jointly reviewed for complete compliance. In many cases the crew would make a low pass over mobile so that a visual inspection could be made of the underside of their bird. This was necessary to determine the exact status of a hung bomb, a stuck gear, or a blown tire.

At night, the mobile officer's safety observations of departing and arriving aircraft were fairly limited. About all he could do in this area was to ensure that the airplane on the approach had its landing lights turned on. This was a pretty reliable check, though, since the lights would not come on until all gears were down and locked. At Phu Cat, however, there existed a situation that precluded making this check until it was almost too late. The VC, who were living in great numbers in the many villages surrounding the base, occasionally would run off a clip from an AK-47 at our birds in the GCA pattern. In order not to make themselves an easy target at night, most crews waited until they were definitely inside the base perimeter before switching on the landing light.

The last of the jobs required anytime flying was going on was Squadron Duty Officer. Since both mobile control and SOF were always pulled by pilots, this latter task was normally given to GIBs in order to even things out. "Spreading the wealth" in this way was pretty much of a necessity in order to keep peace in the family. All of these jobs were looked upon with jaundiced eye by anybody flying fighters. It was not a case of the hours involved nor the perceived pettiness of some of the tasks each job required. The main reason these duties were anathema to aircrews was that they kept them off the flying schedule.

The primary responsibility of the Squadron Duty Officer was to coordinate the daily flying activities of the unit, and, in essence, act as the last link in the chain of command that began at 7th AF. This consisted of keeping the operations board posted with the names, aircraft numbers and parking spots, call signs, and times for each scheduled mission. Other functions included rounding up additional aircrews in the event of a QRF or SAR alert, fielding what seemed like a thousand phone calls, and ensuring that crews filled out all the post mission forms and logs. The squadron duty desk served as the focal point of all activity in the unit. It kept the commander and ops officer advised of what was going on at any given moment, acted as a centralized information point for anything dealing with the squadron, and got the word out to all troops by displaying notices whose importance ranged from profound to trivial. A UHF radio was also available so that airborne emergencies could be monitored without adding to the crowd or confusion at mobile control or the Wing Command Post.

It might seem from the above descriptions of all the flying and ground functions needed to fight a war around the clock that there would be very little time for anything else. This is not entirely the case, because as we shall see in the next chapter, there were many other activities going on—of both semiofficial and personal natures.

Chapter 4

Between Missions

"War is Hell!" declared Sherman, and Vietnam was no exception. However, despite the hectic schedule, there was enough time available to individuals between extra duties and missions to make this "hell" somewhat bearable.

There were a few things of an official nature that did dictate how a person's time off was spent. Most important among these was crew rest. Anyone who was scheduled to fly at some oddball hour (between 10:00 P.M. and 6:00 A.M.) was expected to get the proper sack time so as to be adequately rested for the mission. Briefing times between ten in the evening and three in the morning were the toughest, since these meant that you should be in bed right after the evening meal. It was almost impossible to go to sleep this early, and crew rest consisted mainly of a lot of tossing and turning while trying to doze off. However, this rest was better than nothing, and if you were lucky you might be able to catch a few Zs before heading for the flight line. Missions during this time frame often fell to people filling squadron or Wing staff positions, since the demands of their jobs frequently prevented them from flying during the duty day. Nor did the staff types who flew in the middle of the night enjoy the luxury of sleeping in the next morning. They were required to be at their desks at the regular time, ready for a full day's work.

Another required item that had to be attended to on one's own time was the bimonthly reading of the Rules of Engagement (ROE).

These were top secret documents that spelled out in great detail just how and where we could prosecute the war. The ROE were policies, directives, and regulations that set the parameters for our operations; they were updated constantly, thus the bimonthly requirement. Because of the classification of this material it was kept in the intelligence building, where security was maintained at a high level. This meant that when it was time to review the ROE, it required a trip down to intelligence, gaining admission, signing out the file, and, after it was read, signing it back in again. Once accomplished, it had to be certified that the ROEs had been read on a given date by initialing a roster kept for this purpose. The powers that be really meant business when it came to the ROE, and had an effective means of enforcing it. Anyone not up to date in this area stayed off the flying schedule until they were.

The troops stationed at Phu Cat had to put up with a problem that was most likely unique to that base. Had it been more widespread, the hue and cry would have been heard all the way back to the Pentagon. The difficulty centered around the base finance section, and since it dealt with pay, it was indeed a very touchy item. It also took a considerable amount of a person's off-duty time to make repeated trips down to finance to get things straightened out. The result of these trips in nearly all cases was increased frustration and confusion. They did, however, give you a chance to socialize a bit, since most of your friends would also be there with similar problems.

Unlike stateside bases, just about everybody's pay was completely fouled up, and to make things even more infuriating, the personnel at finance were entirely disinterested in solving the problem. Some even had the gall to suggest that you go without a portion of your pay for the entire tour because it was easier to do this than to correct the records. During the 1970-1971 time period, finance was the only section at Phu Cat that was not 100 percent mission-oriented.

Pleasurable Pastimes

Occasionally, VIPs from 7th Air Force or higher headquarters would visit the base, and before their arrival all hands were expected to pitch in and help get things ready. In the main, this amounted to arranging tours through each unit, parties, cookouts, skits, and anything else appropriate for the visit. These informal gatherings gave people an opportunity to meet and talk with the commanders who were calling the shots for our day-to-day operations. The tasks involved in the preparations were not difficult, and, in large measure, the driving force was unit pride. Squadrons would unofficially compete with one another in their efforts to show the visitors each unit to its best advantage.

There was one semiofficial function that was just about a command performance for all off-duty people—and any of those *on* duty who could possibly make it. This was the Last Flight Ceremony, whose purpose was to honor each crewmember as he completed his tour of duty in Southeast Asia.

The ceremony started on the taxiway at the turnoff end of the runway, where the birds dropped their drag chutes and went through dearming procedures. Here the aircraft would be met by three or four pickup trucks and/or crew vans loaded with as many squadron mates as they could hold. After dearming, the vehicles would lead the planes in a parade down the taxiway to the parking area at the fuel pits. During the parade, colored smoke grenades would be ignited in the trucks and placed in cans attached to the vehicle. These grenades produced huge clouds of dense smoke, whose color would usually be that of the unit celebrating the event. Taxiing behind all these trucks billowing thick smoke could be a little tricky, since at times the visibility would momentarily drop to zero.

By the time the birds were parked at the refueling area, a large crowd had gathered, which included the Wing Commander, who manned a hose from a small fire truck used for these occasions. As soon as the honored guest had unstrapped and was climbing out of the cockpit, the hosedown began. A wild melee followed in

Fig. 4-1. "Parade" for aircrews taxiing in from their last flight before returning home.

Fig. 4-2. Obligatory "hosedown" of last flighters in the refueling area.

which those getting soaked tried to wrestle the hose away from
the Wing Commander. The former always won, and they in turn
would try to spray everyone gathered around for the occasion.
Sanity returned when the crowd had retreated beyond the range
of the hose and the fireman turned off the pressure. The group

Fig. 4-3. The author (L) and Major Dick Slowey pose for last flight pictures behind
the sign, after being hosed down.

45

reassembled and the guys going home got congratulatory hand-shakes from everybody. Champagne was opened, and while the bubbly was being sampled by all, pictures were taken behind a sign listing the last-flighters and their total number of missions. These final missions were usually scheduled a week or so before a person left for the States so that ample time would be available for packing and out-processing.

Planning for leaves and R&R trips was another area that took up a good portion of off-duty time as these events drew near. R&R was a one-week respite from the war at some well-known vacation spot. The most popular ones seemed to be Honolulu, Hong Kong, and Sydney, and the best part of all was the free transportation to and from each R&R site. No one was eligible for these trips until they had been in-country for about nine months, and, since they were available to everyone, the system had become quite routinized. A few weeks before your departure, reservations had to be made with the base R&R center, and, once confirmed, everything else was taken care of. This included quarters at the departure base, all the required briefings, and bus transportation from the destination airport to the various hotels.

In spite of standing in the inevitable lines while being processed, the entire R&R operation was very well run. Mapping out your shopping strategy in every detail was an absolute must for one of these trips, particularly if you were going to Hong Kong. The wide variety of luxury items you always wanted but couldn't afford, coupled with once-in-a-lifetime prices, had just about everybody going broke trying to save money. One week was hardly enough time to get to all the specialty stores and see the myriad of items they offered, in addition to taking tours to the various places of interest.

Along with your own shopping list, just about everyone going on R&R had a list from two or three other people of things they would like picked up or ordered. Since baggage was limited to one suitcase on R&R flights, nearly all the goodies purchased had to be shipped back to your home base in Vietnam. This required that crates be custom-made for all packages and then taken to the post office for mailing.

Given all these constraints of time on an R&R, shopping lists had to be *very* detailed, specifying the *exact* item, since browsing time was fairly limited. This necessitated a lot of catalog research before the trip, as well as quite a few letters back home to coordinate the selections with the better half.

Late in the war, two-week leaves were authorized in addition to the R&R trip. The big difference between these two was that you could go to the States while on leave, and you also had to pay the air fare. Because of special arrangements made with the airlines who conducted the leave flights, the cost was very minimal. Leaves were granted at the mid-tour point, and the reservation arrangements were handled much the same as R&Rs.

Life in the High-Rent District

Another activity that many people engaged in (when they were not tied up with official duties) was improving their living quarters or the squadron patio area. The former involved rounding up scrap lumber, plywood, and nails, and then sweet-talking supply out of some stain or paint. These would be mainly used for modifying rooms to each individual's taste with respect to shelves, lighting, installing stereo systems, adding small cabinets, and just about anything else that suited one's fancy.

The squadron patio area was another place where capital improvements could be made to occupy idle hours. Each fighter squadron had all its aircrews living in three BOQs that were located next to each other. Part of the space between the buildings was devoted to a patio, which was a slab of concrete about 20 feet square against the end of one of the BOQs. The patio had a large barbecue grill made from two halved oil drums, picnic tables and benches, a storage cabinet for utensils and supplies, ample lighting, and a phone.

In good weather the patio was in use almost nightly with about

Fig. 4-4. Squadron patio with aircrew quarters in the background. A crewmember is taking the sun in a one-man life raft filled with water, with a lawn sprinkler at his feet in an effort to keep cool.

Fig. 4-5. The "pool" set up by the 480th TFS near their patio.

a dozen or so guys trying their hands at cooking up something different. Constant use required almost constant refurbishing and repair to keep the place looking respectable, and, of course, there was the never-ending search to come up with some innovative idea to make your patio better than the other outfit's. The troops in the 480th Tactical Fighter Squadron (TFS) scored a real coup in this area when they installed a swimming pool. The "pool" was actually a 20-man rubber life raft that was part of the normal survival gear carried by large transport aircraft. Word had it that the supply people said the raft was surplus; however, beyond that, details of its acquisition are fairly sketchy and best forgotten. Once inflated and filled with about two feet of water, the raft was ideal for basking in the sun on hot afternoons, and was thoroughly enjoyed by one and all.

Regular runs also had to be made to the commissary and base exchange (BX) in order to keep your refrigerator stocked with beer and snacks. All booze and a large number of other goods in these stores were rationed. Some of the items that were controlled included beer, liquor, cigarettes, cameras, and other luxury items. One day at Phu Cat some perverted mind started the rumor that the beer resupply ship had not made it to our port facility at nearby Qui Nhon. The rumormonger had done his work well, since the story was swallowed hook, line, and sinker by everyone. The BX was quickly swamped by long lines of people not wanting to be caught short, and the scene was reminiscent of the run on the banks during the Depression. However, as the Bard said: "Much ado about nothing," and "The Great Beer Scare" came and went with nobody going without suds. And, in retrospect, the suds in question were hardly worth all the commotion, since we only had four brands to choose from, two of which were nondescript, and all of which were 3.2.

Each of the fighter squadrons at Phu Cat had one officer from the Royal Australian Air Force assigned to fly with them. These guys were true professionals who really knew their business, both in the air and on the ground; in addition, they were great individuals personally. The main contingent of Australians were located at Phan Rang and flew B-57 Canberras. The Aussies definitely had their act together when it came to keeping their people who were TDY to the various fighter units supplied with beer. Every few weeks a B-57 would make the rounds of the bases with its bomb bay loaded with Australian beer. A couple of cases would be dropped off for each officer, and in most instances it was already chilled from being at high altitude. Some service! On these occasions it was a great treat to be invited to the Aussies' room to sample their excellent brews, which made ours seem like dishwater by comparison.

None of the BXs in-country offered a selection of the items that the Orient was most famous for, such as cameras, jewelry, brassware, and china. However, all of these exchanges were controlled by the Pacific Exchange (PACEX) located in Tokyo. For the benefit of people in Vietnam or other remote bases in the Pacific, PACEX published a catalog from which all the goodies of the Far East could be ordered. The order was filled in Tokyo and the merchandise mailed either to your base or back home to the States. PACEX did a brisk mail-order business, and catalog shopping took up a lot of off-duty time.

Every once in a while, when the right connections could be made for the supplies, the squadron would have a unit cookout on the patio. These were usually steak fries or Mexican parties, and the change of menu was welcomed by all. Costs were shared by those attending as was any work that needed to be done, and every one of these affairs was a roaring success.

Parties were also held at the O Club for special occasions, and often included all flying units on the base. The proper dress for these shindigs was a "party suit." These were custom-made replicas of our normal flying suits, complete with all the pockets and zippers. The individual's name and wings were embroidered on, but no rank. Here the similarity ended, as party suits were the same shade as the primary color in the squadron insignia. Crews in the 480th TFS wore Kelly green, those in our sister squadron, a bright red, and the Wing weenies wore jet black.

The front and back and upper sleeves of the typical party suit had numerous patches and unit insignia sewn on, most of which poked fun at the war and our status. All of these were embroidered in a variety of colors, and were relatively inexpensive to order in quantity. Some typical examples were a map of all the countries in the theater circled by the phrase "Participant—Southeast Asian War Games;" a Jolly Roger flag lettered with the enemy's favorite epithet for us—"Yankee Air Pirate;" or an enlarged policeman's badge with the inscription "Laotian Highway Patrol," which referred to our activities on the Ho Chi Minh Trail.

The relatively easy access via the PACEX catalog to very high quality cameras and hi-fi equipment—at prices you couldn't afford to turn down—soon proved to be more than most people could resist. Stereo systems that would vibrate the very walls became standard equipment in quite a few rooms, much to the dismay of troops trying to catch some crew rest before a late evening mission. Camera buffs were in pig heaven, and took advantage of it to the fullest. Every conceivable gadget and attachment known to the photographer's art, along with special lenses of every size and description, were scooped up like they were going out of style tomorrow. Many were designed for only unique photographic situations, yet the prevailing rationale was "Buy it now and be prepared for anything!" Once all these photographic goodies were acquired they had to be tried out, at least till the novelty wore off, and picture-taking of every variety was a very popular pastime.

For the affluent, one item that attracted quite a lot of attention, because of its rarity during that time period, was a portable video recorder system. One bachelor couldn't resist the temptation, and it wasn't long before we had miles of tape showing people walking across the lawn or milling around the patio. Considerable footage was shot from mobile control of F-4s taking off and landing, and a few last flight ceremonies were also recorded for posterity.

Pets and Pranks

One night while preparing for a mission, a crew was walking from the operations building to intelligence for the preflight briefing. The distance between the two buildings was only about 40 yards, all of which was a neatly mowed lawn. This area was crossed regularly at all hours by crews from both squadrons going to and from intelligence for briefing. The night was quite dark and the one light over the door to intelligence illuminated the area just well enough to let you see where you were going. This crew's pre-

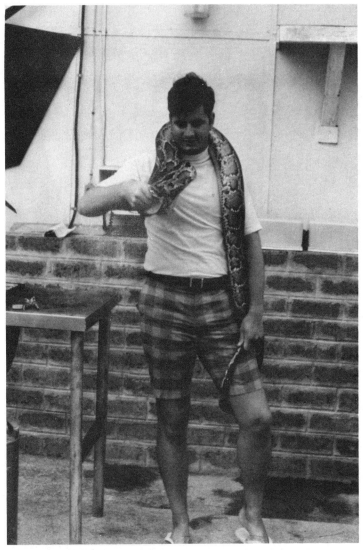

Fig. 4-6. Skip Sutton with his pet python "Fresco."

mission reverie was suddenly shattered when they came upon a 15 foot python stretched across the path in front of them. While everybody else headed for the "high ground," Lt. Skip Sutton decided to capture the snake, for reasons best known to himself. This he did, and "Fresco," as it was subsequently named, was given one of the spare rooms in the squadron BOQ and unanimously proclaimed as the unit mascot—another first for the 480th!

Fresco did not require much care other than an occasional feeding, although his room had to be cleaned up regularly to keep the smell to a minimum. The squadron got a lot of mileage from Fresco, PR-wise. Just about everybody on the base and most visiting firemen got a chance to see the snake. Even Miss America and her court posed for pictures with Fresco during their tour of Phu Cat.

Feeding time for the snake became a major event on the base, and the time and place were always posted on the squadron operations board. Fresco ate about once a week, and his diet consisted of either a live chicken or a duck, which would be purchased from one of the Vietnamese working on the base. Once placed in proximity to the snake, the bird didn't last long, and was consumed in typical snake fashion—headfirst and whole.

Watching Fresco eat became such a popular pastime that his BOQ room was soon too small to accommodate the crowd. Therefore, he was taken out on the lawn for his repast, but this didn't work out too well because the heat and bright sun apparently caused him to lose his appetite. This difficulty was solved by moving him into the large shower room in the middle of the BOQ building. Here the cool dampness was more to his liking, and the duck disappeared in a trice.

When Phu Cat closed in early 1972, Skip Sutton was transferred to a base in Thailand to finish out his tour—and Fresco went with him. This was done by putting the snake in a large bag just after he had eaten, when he was the most lethargic. The bag was then stuffed into an empty napalm can that had been converted to a baggage carrier by the addition of a door on the side. The flight to Thailand was made at a relatively low altitude so that the lack of oxygen would not be a problem. In order to prevent heart failure when the crew chief at the new base helped Skip unload the bird, the contents of the nape can were appropriately marked on the door.

Although otherwise a very normal and likeable guy, Skip Sutton's hobbies did tend to be a trifle bizarre. Along with keeping

Fig. 4-7. Skip Sutton's cornfield.

the snake, he developed a yen for corn on the cob soon after arriving at Phu Cat. This was not served in the mess hall, so Skip sent home for some seeds and planted his own cornfield right next to the BOQ, complete even to the white picket fence.

The traditions of Easter time brought out the artistic talent in the crew chiefs of the birds standing alert. In keeping with the season, "eggs" were appropriately "dyed" before being delivered

Fig. 4-8. Alert aircraft with their "eggs" decorated for Easter.

Fig. 4-9. A load of high-drags in Easter finery.

to the VC. The eggs in this case were 500-pound bombs and cans of napalm decorated in a dazzling variety of colors and patterns with spray paint. Suitable Easter greetings were also included.

Idle time was also known to generate quite a few pranks, usually aimed at the other squadron or the Wing. The 480th took quite a bit of heat from the base commander as a result of one such jest pulled by the other fighter squadron on the base. Our unit emblem was an eagle, and, as mentioned before, the squadron color was a bright green. Some industrious troops from the 379th painted giant eagle tracks, about three feet across and naturally in a bright green color, all along the sidewalks in the BOQ area. The base was understandably perturbed at this defacement of the facilities, and, as intended, the blame fell on us.

The Director of Operations (DO) for the Wing was also the butt of considerable mischief from both squadrons. Always considered great fun and worth a million laughs was the trick of lighting off a smoke grenade and rolling it into his room in the middle of the night. The smell and the grimy residue left from the great clouds of smoke (before the grenade could be kicked out the door) made this a hanging offense, and thus undertaken by only the very foolish or the very brave. Again, the color of the smoke used would be instrumental in shifting the blame on one squadron or the other.

The DO also carried a small portable radio so that he could be contacted instantly anywhere on the base. The network was so designed that you could reach the DO on his radio by calling a special number on the phone. Although restricted, this number soon became common knowledge, and anonymous calls were far from infrequent. The DO did get his revenge on one, however. Hearing music in the background, he quickly got up and went over to the squadron area, all the time keeping the conversation going on the radio. After checking a few locations, he found the culprit, still chatting away on the phone while the stereo in his room blared away. The caller was so engrossed in his task that he was completely unaware of the DO's approach until the latter was just a few feet behind him. The DO then played his trump card by telling the caller, over the radio, to turn around.

Sometimes these pranks assumed a grand scale, as was the case at the Da Nang O Club. A large party was being thrown by all three fighter squadrons for their DO, who was going home shortly. It was a swank affair with a rock band, and extra large steaks grilled on the club patio, which was formed by three cinderblock walls about 10 feet high. When the after-dinner speeches were over, the band started to play and everyone was settling down for a full night of partying. Unbeknownst to the crowd, a couple of base fire trucks had pulled up outside the patio wall during the speeches and farewells. Then, as the party was gathering steam, they raised the remotely controlled nozzles on top of the trucks above the wall and instantly hosed down the entire crowd. Thinking that this was a great send-off for the DO, everyone cheered loudly and stood on the chairs as the patio became awash in a few inches of water—everyone, that is, except the musicians, who had to be quite nimble to keep from being electrocuted by their own instruments in the deluge.

A good percentage of the shenanigans described above were perpetrated by pilots or GIBs who had completed their tours and only had a few days left before returning to the States. Since these stunts were not court-martial offenses—and the individual's personnel records had already been closed out—there was very little that could be done in the way of disciplinary action. A severe chewing out and threats of follow-up reprimands were the usual consequences if anyone got caught. For the most part, however, they were all taken good-naturedly, and, if at all possible, overlooked.

In spite of all the fun and games, the serious business of war continued uninterrupted. This was true for us and the enemy, and the latter always made sure we were constantly aware of his presence by sending us a few calling cards now and then.

Chapter 5

The Enemy Around Us

Phu Cat is located in the southeast corner of Binh Dinh province, which is about the size of Connecticut. During the time when the communists controlled all of South Vietnam, this province was a primary recruiting ground and training area for the VC. "Recruiting" is perhaps an overly kind word to use here, since the Viet Cong's techniques more closely resembled impressment—it was a case of sign up or else!

Because just about every able-bodied male in the area was forced into service of some kind, and a good portion of their military training was conducted in the province, the VC maintained a strong hold over the population. This was due to the fact that nearly every family had a husband, father, son, or close relative serving with the guerrillas. Thus, through fear of reprisals, the VC had a virtual army of sympathizers to exploit in any way that furthered their cause. And this they did assiduously, forcing the people to provide them with supplies, shelter, intelligence, and concealment whenever required. Their effectiveness in this area is attested to by the continual frustration of our troops in their efforts to seek out and destroy local VC units.

Rocket Attacks

The Viet Cong were not the only bad guys operating in the hills surrounding Phu Cat. The 12th North Vietnamese Army Artillery

Fig. 5-1. Damage done by one 122mm rocket after an attack on February 1, 1971. Note the thickness of the brick wall erected for blast protection, and how completely it was demolished by the rocket. At the left is the wing commander and the infamous mutt Sabre.

Regiment occupied more or less permanent positions just to the west of the base in the foothills. Repeated ground sweeps against this force were not too successful since they quickly moved out as our forces approached, and their whereabouts would not be revealed by the villagers in the area. Pursuit beyond known enemy locations was pretty futile, as the terrain was very rugged and offered innumerable hiding places and ambush spots.

The communists claim to be a classless society where everyone is considered equal, and the 12th Regiment was a good example of this dogma. Intelligence reports had it that the unit was commanded by Major Lom, who was a woman. Despite the rigors of directing combat operations in the field under fairly primitive conditions, the good Major apparently knew her onions. She conducted several rocket attacks against the base, and was most likely responsible for getting sappers inside the ammunition dump at Qui Nhon and blowing it up. The latter provided a spectacular display of fireworks while the facility burned all night, but the attacks on the base fortunately resulted in only minor damage and no casualties. These attacks did, however, serve to keep everybody on edge, and any sudden loud noise usually had people diving for cover. Whenever the base was struck, it was usually by three or four 122mm

57

rockets fired in quick succession. In most cases, by the time you realized what was happening, the attack was over.

Our intelligence sources both on and around the base did attempt to provide us with some indication of the probability of an attack. When conditions or information suggested that one might be forthcoming, the entire base was put on a "Yellow Alert" for the time period involved. This required that all personnel have a flak vest and helmet immediately available while the alert was on. Given the usual rapidity of the strike, it is doubtful that this protective gear could be donned in time to do much good. However, if intelligence had information that an attack was imminent, a "Red Alert" would be declared and everyone had to wear the flak vest and helmet until the alert condition was downgraded. A good percentage of these alerts would be called during the nighttime hours, and the vest and helmet would have to be kept at your bedside. Most people felt that their immediate reaction to an attack in the middle of the night would be to get under the bed as quickly as possible. This would allow the GI mattress to act as a full-length protection against rocket fragments.

During Major Lom's tenure, the base was usually rocketed in the early hours of the morning, when nearly everybody would be asleep. Thus, in case of a hit in a vital area, more damage would be done before our reaction forces could be mobilized. Her superiors must have been impressed with her work, because early in the spring of 1971 she was promoted and moved on to bigger things. Her new assignment was to harass the base at Da Nang in the same fashion as she had worked over Phu Cat. Her replacement was not made of such stern stuff, as we were only attacked once after he took over, and this was in the late afternoon—definitely not promotion material!

The 122mm rockets used in these strikes were quite an effective weapon if they hit anything. They caused considerable blast damage, and usually started fires if the target was flammable. Their biggest drawback was the archaic method used for launching. The forward end of the rocket was elevated by a tripod made of sticks lashed together, while the tail end rested on a mat of woven twigs. Although this setup could be locally manufactured and would normally be left at the launch site, it certainly did not lend itself to precision aiming of the weapon.

Another factor that was in our favor concerning these munitions was that they were in short supply in the Phu Cat area. This is not surprising since, being Russian-made, they had to be brought down from North Vietnam, which was at least 225 miles away as the crow flies. Given the tortuous wanderings of the Ho Chi Minh Trail, this journey was quite a bit longer for the trucks (and, at times, individuals) bringing these rockets to Phu Cat. It must have really been discouraging for the guy who just carried one of these weapons on his shoulder all the way from North Vietnam to be told on arrival: "Thanks; go back and get another one!"

Although their method of launching left quite a bit to be desired as far as accuracy went, the bad guys did not lack the necessary information as to the exact location of the target. As mentioned before, the base employed many of the local Vietnamese to work as BOQ maids, grass cutters, kitchen help, and general cleanup. These people, in their travels from place to place on the base, never took shortcuts. They would shuffle down one street to the actual intersection before turning and going up another, regardless of the well-worn path across the empty lot they were circumventing. However, there was method to their supposed madness. In reality, they were pacing off the length of all streets on the base so that these figures could be used in plotting the coordinates of the target. After leaving the base to go home in the evening, they would pass these numbers along to the VC. Such activity by these sympathizers was difficult to prove and nearly impossible to stop. They were always

Fig. 5-2. Captured VC weapons. The 122mm rocket in the foreground is shown on the lashed stick and woven mat support, typical of those used during attacks on Phu Cat.

women or old men with little or no knowledge of English, and any questions by our intelligence people were met with a shrug and the "no understand" look.

These mamasans and papasans working on the base also had a tendency to be light-fingered, particularly where items that could be used by the guerrillas were concerned. Pocket-sized transistor radios were almost guaranteed to disappear if they were not locked up. Apparently the electronic components of these radios could be put to a variety of uses by the VC, none of which were for our good.

Infiltrators and Base Defenses

Another danger faced by all bases in South Vietnam to one degree or another was that of infiltrators. These people would sneak inside a base at night to plant explosives in a precise location, or to do other damage of a specific nature. To help guard against such intrusions, or an overt attack in force, the base employed passive and active defense systems. The former consisted of an antipersonnel minefield completely encircling the base, along with a formidable array of triple concertina barbed wire. The area on either side of the wire was flat, and kept clear of any vegetation that would provide cover and concealment in the event of a firefight. An armored guard tower was erected at each corner of the base perimeter, and was equipped with a .50-caliber machine gun. These towers were manned continuously, and during the night the crews would fire a few bursts at random intervals into the edge of the jungle bordering the outer cleared area. This harassment fire had no specific target, since it was intended mainly to keep the bad guys honest by discouraging any attempts to infiltrate the base.

The guard towers also controlled another system designed to uncover any nighttime probing of our defenses. This was a string of remotely operated flare guns positioned near the edge of the base which paralleled the runway, and was also adjacent to a wooded area. Flares would be fired at random times and from random spots along this two-mile stretch, and would illuminate the entire area for about two or three minutes.

The combination of the flare shots and the stream of tracers suddenly coming from the guard tower certainly helped to keep the mobile control officer alert during the wee small hours of the morning. The mobile units were located quite close to the runway, and thus were not all that far from the woods bordering our defensive area. Because of this, it was a little eerie pulling night mobile at Phu Cat, particularly for those with a vivid imagination. It was easy to visualize a group of fanatics, armed to the teeth, sneaking under the barbed wire with only mobile control between them and an airplane-packed flight line. You also were convinced that on a dark night they would be on top of you before you knew it because of the five-foot wall of sandbags around the mobile unit, which kept you from seeing anything closer than 15 feet from your position inside. Every mobile officer wore his .38 while on duty, but this would be of little value against a grenade that came rolling in the door.

While you were mulling over thoughts such as these as you sat there in the inky darkness, a flare would go off and tracers would begin arcing from the guard tower into the nearby woods. "Oh, no! Here they come!" was the all-pervading thought instantly shattering your reveries. The combination of these pyrotechnics always had a startling effect, regardless of how long you had been in-country.

The active base defense force had a twofold mission: to engage and repel an enemy force attempting to penetrate the base, and to conduct intelligence/reprisal sweeps in the area surrounding Phu Cat. The Air Police assigned to the base were responsible for defending one quarter of the perimeter, while the Korean army took care of the remainder. The ROK army had an encampment immediately adjacent to the eastern half of the airbase, which was part of their commitment to the Vietnam conflict.

The ROKs were a very tough and efficient bunch of fighters who did not take too kindly to surprises from the VC. One night Major Lom made the serious mistake of having one of her rockets aimed a little long. Instead of landing on the base, it flew completely across and landed in the ROK camp. Although it caused little damage, it was tantamount to poking a hornet's nest with a stick. The next morning the ROKs swarmed out of their camp and into the foothills to the west, ready and eager to kick tail and take names. Their sweep lasted for a few days, after which things were quiet around Phu Cat for a long while.

The ROKs were particularly effective on these missions—much more so than the Americans, since they understood and knew how to deal with the oriental mind. When our troops entered a village suspected of harboring Viet Cong and asked the head man where they were, we got the "I don't know" shrug. Since everyone in the village was dressed in black pajamas and a coolie hat, there was no way of telling the good guys from the bad, so our people moved on to the next town. The Koreans, however, were not so easily convinced. If the ROK commander got the same answer the first time the question was asked, he would throw a grenade into the village food storehouse and a year's supply of rice vanished in a flash. The head man would be asked the question again, and if the response did not change, another grenade came out. This time it went into the corral holding the village's water buffalo, and presto, no animals left to plow with next year. By this time the head man and the other villagers were getting the drift of things, and suddenly the entire assemblage became a veritable fountain of intelligence information. Once this meeting of the inscrutable oriental minds was accomplished, the basic plan of action moved ahead swiftly.

This and the foregoing chapters have described the framework and the "givens" against which the war was fought by the troops at Phu Cat. Although a lot of the factors discussed so far are not the essence of what makes a hungry tiger, they typify the environment in which all tigers must operate. The problems and procedures that surfaced in Vietnam are much the same as those that would be found in any operational theater in the world. Different climate and locations may require different adaptations than those talked about here, but the basis of what it takes to make a good fighter pilot are universally applicable, regardless of the background or the setting.

With this in mind, let's now take a look at some of the weapons used in Vietnam, and the bird that delivered them.

Chapter 6

The Tools of the Trade

Regardless of how hungry the tiger is, before he can carry the war to the enemy, he needs a mount worthy of the task.

There were many, many types of aircraft that took part in the Vietnam conflict over the 11 or so years of our active involvement. Each served its purpose and served it well; however, none left a mark so indelible as the McDonnell F-4 Phantom II. It was the workhorse of the close air support mission because it could carry a large amount of just about anything you could hang on an airplane, and it could take it a long distance. In the air-to-air phase of the war, it was the only bird we had that could take on the MiG-21 and come out a winner. the F-4's capability, versatility, and reliability were just what the doctor ordered when it came to supporting the many and varied requirements posed by the type of war we fought in 'Nam.

All things considered, the Phantom was truly the bird for all seasons.

The Airplane

As one approaches an F-4 for the first time, its lines and size immediately cause a single word to leap into the mind—*ugly*! In this case, first impressions are the truest, because the Phantom was definitely behind the door when looks were passed out. On the ground it is angular, squared-off and brutish looking, with none of

Fig. 6-1. McDonnell Douglas F-4D. (courtesy National Air and Space Museum, Smithsonian Institution)

the graceful lines that suggest swiftness or eagerness for flight that characterize the more aesthetic birds. In the air, where others epitomize the ability to vault effortlessly through space, the F-4 only confirms the old saw that *anything* will fly if you hang a big enough engine on it.

However, despite its not being in the glamour girl category, the Phantom was the ideal machine for the job at hand in Southeast Asia. As mentioned earlier, the F-4 is a big bird, with a wingspan of a little more than 38 feet and a length of just over 58 feet; it stands about 16 and a half feet high. It is also heavy, tipping the scales at 47,000 pounds, which includes full internal fuel, two 370-gallon drop tanks, plus engine oil and the crew. These figures, which do not consider armament of any kind, are for the D model as set up in the usual configuration for missions flown out of Phu Cat. The E model, used by the "Gunfighters" at Da Nang, was five feet longer and 1,900 pounds heavier.

The F-4 was powered by two General Electric J79-15 engines, each of which is rated at 10,900 pounds of thrust at military power. When the engines are running at 100 percent rpm, afterburner operation is achieved by simply moving the throttles outboard and pushing them to the full-forward position. A/B lightoff and acceleration is smooth and continuous, bringing the rated thrust of each engine almost instantly to 17,000 pounds.

With all this push, it is possible to take a clean F-4 on out to better than Mach 2. However, reaching this speed is a mission in itself, requiring just about the entire fuel load, and allowing for very little maneuvering. The ability to reach Mach 2 does not have much tactical significance, since air-to-air engagements are usually fought near or below Mach 1. Nevertheless, it does serve to demonstrate the airplane's great potential for acceleration and energy maneuverability.

From the pilot's point of view, the Phantom is a fairly easy airplane to fly—not too heavy on the controls, and quite responsive in pitch and roll. The latter is achieved by a unique combination of ailerons and spoilers, in which ailerons are used only to raise a wing, and spoilers just to lower it. Instead of the usual stabilizer-elevator arrangement, the Phantom uses a full-flying tail called a stabilator. The entire surface moves, and since it has an area about one quarter that of the wing, it is like sticking a barn door out in the wind. As you might guess, it is very effective in bending the bird around. All the flight controls are hydraulically actuated, and moving the stick merely repositions valves to meter the correct amount of fluid to the desired surface. This necessitated an artificial "feel" system being built into the flight control mechanism to simulate the correct air loads on each surface as it moves. Trim is available on all three axes, as is stability augmentation, which automatically counteracts any tendency for the aircraft to oscillate in pitch, roll, or yaw.

The Phantom's cockpit visibility is very good except for two areas: directly to the rear, which is blocked by the ejection seat structure, and downward on either side, because of the large intake ducts. The GIB has a slightly better view out the back and he can twist around a little more since he isn't involved with flying the aircraft. To help keep an eye on this vital "deep six" position, rear view mirrors are installed on the canopy bow in each cockpit.

The F-4 has an anti-skid wheel brake system that is a definite asset whenever a heavy weight landing must be made, and whenever the runway is wet. This device allows the pilot to apply maximum braking pressure as soon as the nosewheel is on the ground after touchdown. It detects the start of a skid at the wheel and automatically reduces the brake pressure according to the severity of the skid. This permits the wheel to keep turning while maintaining the maximum safe braking action on that wheel.

One of the annoying features of the F-4 is the need to wear "garters" in order for the ejection seat to function properly. The garters are two-inch wide nylon belts that are buckled around each leg just above the knee, and around the ankles. Through D-rings attached to each garter ran a heavy nylon lanyard, one end of which is attached to the seat. The other end goes through the front of the seat to breakaway fittings in the floor beneath the seat. The whole idea of this rig is to keep your legs from flailing about during an ejection sequence. The way it works is that when the seat starts to rise up the rails and out of the cockpit, the end of the lanyard attached to the floor pulls your legs up tight against the front of the seat and holds them there. This is done by the use of a snubber in the hole where the lanyard passes through the seat front. It permits the lanyard to travel in only one direction, and locks instantly when any opposing force is applied. As the seat continues to rise, the lanyard is pulled taut and locks the legs in place, then the floor anchors break as the seat clears the aircraft. The Martin-Baker ejection system (about which more will be said later) never had a failure, so rather than argue with a record like that, everyone used the garters despite the inconvenience.

The Phantom has another system that really came in handy when there were lots of things that needed grabbing in the cockpit and not enough hands to do the job. This is the Automatic Flight Control System (AFCS), which amounts to an autopilot—of sorts. In reality it is nothing more than an attitude hold, which means that it will maintain whatever attitude the aircraft was in when the system was engaged. For example, if you are in a climbing right turn when the AFCS is turned on, it will keep the bird climbing to the right until you run out of airspeed.

The original F-4s were built for the Navy, and when the Air Force adopted this design in 1962, some of the heretofore strictly Navy features were retained. One of these was the Angle of Attack (AOA) system, which allows a pilot to fly final approach at the slowest speed possible while still keeping things controllable. The neat part of this gadget is that from base leg to touchdown, you never have to look in the cockpit at any instrument, including the airspeed. To get the most out of flying AOA, you have to have reference to an outside source of glidepath information, such as a VASI or a mirror system. If none is available, you just select a touchdown spot on the runway and sight over the nose of the bird at this aiming point. The thing that makes it possible to fly the approach without looking at the airspeed is the AOA Indexer. This is a small rectangular box containing three lights; it is mounted on both sides of the windshield bow. A probe on the side of the nose senses the aircraft's angle of attack and sends this information to the indexer. If the center light is on, the bird is right in the groove with the proper 19 units AOA. If the top light is on, your angle is too high and a stall is imminent, while the lower light indicates too shallow an angle. These are the extremes, and the lights can come on in combinations that indicate smaller variances from the norm. Thus, when looking through the windshield at the glideslope reference, the indexer is in your line of vision, and cross-referencing these two is all that you need. If either is off, corrections can be made in pitch and/or power to bring the bird back to where it belongs. After being schooled in the Air Force way of doing things, the AOA system took a little getting used to, because the proper corrective action was just the opposite of what you were accustomed to.

For a fighter that was designed in the mid 1950s, the load of external stores that can be carried by the F-4 is truly impressive. Five "hardpoints" or stations are available on which to hang armament or fuel tanks: two on each wing and one in the center of the fuselage. Normally, each of the outer wing stations carried a drop tank, and the other three positions were used for bombs of one variety or another, or a gun pod containing a 20mm cannon. Bomb loads for just about all missions flown out of Phu Cat fell into one of the following categories: twelve 500-pound "slicks" (conventional bombs); six 500-pound high-drag bombs and three cans of napalm; or six 500-pounders with fuse extenders, plus two 2,000-pound bombs, also with fuse extenders. (Descriptions of these and other munitions will be found later.)

In addition to the hardpoints designated for bombs or fuel tanks,

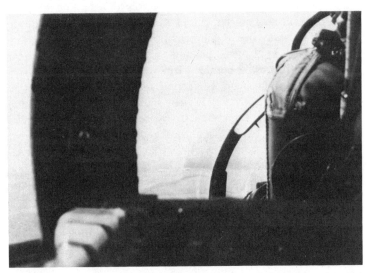

Fig. 6-2. Looking over the pilot's left shoulder from the back seat of an F-4 on final approach. The striped handle at the bottom left is the emergency canopy jettison control. Just above that can be seen the angle of attack indexer with the lower pair of lights illuminated.

the F-4 also has four stations on the fuselage designed specifically for AIM-7 Sparrow missiles. This is an air-to-air weapon; however, in 1970-71, the Wing at Phu Cat was not charged with the counter-air mission. In addition, on the two or three occasions the Wing went into North Vietnam, it was in the extreme southern portion, where enemy fighters were not a threat. For this reason, the F-4s at Phu Cat were only loaded with two Sparrows—and on a good percentage of the flights, these would not pass the operational checks made by the GIB when taxiing out.

Adding up everything that was hung on the bird for a normal close air support mission, the total weight of bombs, fuel tanks, suspension gear and missiles was 14,000 pounds or better—not too shabby for a fighter, considering that in WWII, the normal load for a B-17G was around 10,000 pounds.

Avionics

The radar installed in the Phantom was designed to complement the three major missions of the aircraft. It can provide range information to the gunsight in an air-to-air engagement, locate and track targets while supplying missile guidance information during an intercept mission, and provide target data for a variety of computerized bombing modes. All of the controls for operating the radar are in the rear cockpit, but the pilot does have a duplicate scope up front to display steering information while he is running an intercept. The GIB also has the only controls for setting up a radar and computer-assisted bombing run.

While the radar is quite adequate for the air-to-air and air-to-ground missions, it certainly leaves something to be desired in the area of air defense interception. Compared with systems designed for other fighters of the same vintage, the F-4 radar is almost primitive. Against targets in a heavy jamming and chaff environment, it was almost useless since it had no special circuitry to cope with these countermeasures. A good bit of communication between the two cockpits was necessary in order to realize the full potential of the radar when engaging another fighter or intercepting an unknown force. Both crewmembers had to think as one in the area of target selection, timely lock-on, and scope monitoring. Any misunderstanding between the pilot and the GIB as to the plan of attack could blow the whole mission, since things happen too fast and opportunities are too fleeting for second guessing once you are committed to a target.

A rather handy piece of equipment installed in both cockpits of the F-4 was the Radar Homing and Warning (RHAW) gear. This detected enemy radars directed at the aircraft and alerted the crew to their presence. Because of the swiftness and accuracy of modern weapons, this system was a proven lifesaver, particularly at night or in the weather. (A more detailed description of how the RHAW gear worked will be given in Chapter 8.)

The radio equipment in our Phantoms was the standard UHF set with the capability of dialing in any frequency in that spectrum. These radios were relatively troublefree and were normally operated by the GIB, although control could be switched back and forth between the cockpits. One of the best features of the F-4 was the inertial navigation system. This was a fully automatic unit that used a gyro-stabilized platform, controlled by three very sensitive accelerometers. Once aligned properly, the inertial system provided information to the navigation computer, radar, automatic bombing system, and the gunsight. After all the years of having to rely on fickle TACANs, fading VORs, and erratic ADFs, the inertial navigator was really a Godsend for getting from A to B. Instead of doglegging around to stay in range of the available TACANs, you simply set the GEOREF coordinates of your present position and destination into the computer and fired 'er up. As soon as the platform was aligned and the system turned to "operate," the needle would instantly swing to the proper bearing to the target, and the distance readout would indicate how far you had to go—all this before you even left the chocks!

As you followed these directions on your way to the target, the navigation computer also provided the aircraft's present position in longitude and latitude, ground speed, magnetic ground track, and drift angle. If the winds were anywhere near right, the system was very, very accurate. Just before taking off from Phu Cat for Guam, the GIB dialed in the coordinates of our destination, Anderson AFB. The needle swung over and didn't move more than a degree or so for the nearly five hours of flying time into Guam. Upon arrival it was right on the money, despite the fact that it had not been updated anytime during the flight. This may sound like old hat when compared to modern sophisticated and miniaturized navigation gear, which can do all this and probably more. However, it was indeed heady wine to those who were weaned on the vagaries of VOR and the trials of TACAN.

The Phantom was also equipped with the usual things found on fighters of that era, such as TACAN, SIF, an arresting hook, and provisions for midair refueling. In addition, it had a few items that were traceable to its Navy lineage. These were a radar altimeter and a UHF direction finder, both of which were welcomed by Air Force pilots not accustomed to such luxuries.

General-Purpose Bombs

The bombs carried by the F-4s flying out of Phu Cat were just about always one of the following types: high-explosive, antipersonnel, or fire bombs, more commonly referred to as napalm.

The 500-pound general purpose bomb was the most popular weapon for close air support work. It actually weighed 531 pounds, was 7 feet 3 inches long, and had a diameter of 10.8 inches. For high-angle missions, the bomb was fitted with a conventional fin assembly and was then known as a "slick" (as opposed to the "high-drag" version, which will be described later). These weapons normally had fuses in both the nose and the tail to ensure that there would be no duds. Whenever the mission was to mine an area, a time delay fuse or a pressure-sensitive fuse would be employed. In this case, the bomb would burrow under the ground and explode at some set time after impact, or when disturbed by passing vehicles.

Should the target be troops who were not too well dug in, or

Fig. 6-3. Three 500-pound bombs with fuse extenders mounted on a wing pylon. Just behind the bombs is a 600-gallon fuel tank installed on the centerline station.

if an LZ prep was on agenda, a fuse extender would be used with this bomb. This device was a 36-inch-long metal pipe filled with explosives that was screwed into the nose of the bomb in place of the fuse. On the other end of the pipe, the regular bomb fuse was installed. The extender caused the bomb to detonate three feet above the ground and not waste any of its energy in cratering. The effect was devastating, and the shower of metal fragments blasted outward wreaked havoc over quite a large area. Bombs with this configuration were aptly named "daisy cutters."

Slicks were never used if the target required low-angle bombing techniques. The reason for this was that the shallow delivery angle might cause the bomb to skip after impact, just like a flat stone across a pond. Even worse, it might ricochet at such an angle to endanger the aircraft on its pullout. A more serious problem existed even if the bomb impacted correctly and did not bounce. After release at a relatively flat angle, the bomb would fly along beneath the airplane at roughly the same speed until it hit. This would put the bird well within the fragmentation envelope at detonation, which could spoil your whole day.

All of these unpleasant problems were solved by installing a modified tail assembly on a regular 500-pound bomb. The new assembly consisted of four flat plates hinged together at the rear and folded forward along the sides of the bomb. The fins were held against the bomb with a metal band which had a quick-release that opened when the weapon was dropped. This allowed the fins to spring to the full open position, forming a cross over five feet wide that was attached to the rear of the bomb. With the flat side into the wind, this device acted as an effective brake on the forward trajectory of the weapon. It virtually stopped the bomb in its tracks, and caused it to impact fairly close to the point where it was released. By this time the bird would be well out of harm's way.

Of course, if the fins failed to open, or came off the bomb when they did deploy, you were back to square one as far as the problems listed above. Here again you would have a slick riding along a little below the bird—and nothing in the cockpit to indicate that anything was amiss. This larger tailfin assembly increased the weight of the bomb by about 30 pounds, and in this configuration, they were appropriately named "high-drags."

The only other size bomb normally carried at Phu Cat was the 2,000-pounder that was used for LZ prep missions. This thing was a real giant, measuring over 12 1/2 feet in length, and 1 1/2 feet in diameter. Its total weight was 1970 pounds, and for these mis-

Fig. 6-4. A 2,000-pound bomb on its trailer illustrates the relative size of this weapon. The reinforced concrete and steel arch structure of the aircraft shelter can also be seen in this view.

sions it was always fitted with a fuse extender. These weapons were always dropped by high-angle delivery methods, and they were never modified to the high drag configuration.

Fig. 6-5. A 2,000-pound bomb with a fuse extender installed hung on the outboard wing station. The steel arches behind the airplane deflect exhaust gases upward during runup to prevent any damage to people, vehicles, and airplanes using the taxiway behind the shelter.

Antipersonnel Bombs

Certain missions were designed primarily to kill people. These would be those flown against flak batteries, enemy base camps, or the favorite target of all, "troops in the open." Anytime intelligence reported that the bad guys were not dug in, and were not under thick jungle growth, antipersonnel bombs were called for. The actual bomb is spherical, about the size of a tennis ball, and contains the fusing mechanism surrounded by the explosive, which is impregnated with numerous steel balls. Upon detonation, these balls are propelled outward at high velocity, and are especially effective against people.

For the type targets mentioned above, these munitions were delivered by high-angle bombing methods. Slightly more than 660 of these small weapons were carried in a large, bomb-shaped canister about 7 1/2 feet long. The canister was made in two halves, with the split running the length of either side. This unit was equipped with a self-contained radar-activated fuse that would detonate at a preset altitude above the ground. When this occurred, it separated the two halves of the container, which dispersed the smaller bombs over an oval-shaped impact pattern. They exploded upon hitting the ground, and the hundreds of silver flashes occurring almost simultaneously provided a graphic picture of the wide coverage realized by this weapon. This was particularly vivid at night, and it was hard to imagine that anything could survive the hailstorm of steel pellets produced when all these small bombs went off as they hit.

If the purpose of the mission was to mine a certain area and deny its use to enemy troops, a different type of dispenser and

Fig. 6-6. Close formation with an F-4 on a J mission. The light colored rectangles just below the external wing tank are the packets of bomblets in their dispensing canister.

73

Fig. 6-7. Seeding an area around the DMZ with Cluster Bomb Units. Each of the packets being dispensed contains numerous bomblets, which will fall out as the packet tumbles during its descent.

delivery method were used. In this case, the dispenser remained attached to the bomb racks, and the smaller bombs were ejected in packets out through the open bottom. This dispenser was about 9 1/2 feet long and resembled a finned bomb with a squarish cross section. Six of them were carried on each bird in the flight, and the small bombs they contained had a different fuse mechanism than those delivered in the clamshell canister. These did not explode on impact; rather, they would lie on the ground until disturbed by someone, and then would go off—not as spectacular a nighttime display, but certainly more effective.

The only problem with these bombs, or "Js" as they were called from their code letter on the frag, was the method of handing them out to the bad guys. In order to get the dispersion pattern for mining roads, which was the usual target, the bird had to be flown straight and level at a very low altitude. Flying over hostile territory at 300 to 500 feet with no jinking was not anyone's idea of a fun afternoon. Luckily, there was no limitation on *speed* for dispensing these munitions. Throttles were wide open as the bird swung down and leveled out on the attack heading. Most people felt that flying at 550 knots or better at that altitude was thrill enough for one day's work. Once the bird settled into the groove on a J run, the bomb release button had to be held for what seemed like an eternity before the dispensers were completely empty. Speed, and the short time you were in the enemy's field of view, were the only defenses on these sorties.

Another good weapon that was quite effective against troops—even those fairly well dug in—was napalm. This versatile munition could also be used with equally good results on targets such as light trucks and structures. Napalm, or partially jellied gasoline, was carried in bomb-shaped cans about 11 feet long; each weighed 850 pounds when filled. "Nape" was always delivered by low-angle methods, and since the cans were not finned, they tumbled freely as they fell toward the target. The absence of fins also caused an occasional bump on the aft fuselage when the can did not release true and twisted before it had cleared the bird.

The lack of a precise trajectory was not too critical with napalm because the splashed mixture covered such a large area after impact. Fire bombs were fused to detonate as they struck the ground, and instantly a sea of flames was created that covered an elongated oval area. Of course, this coverage was reduced quite a bit when the bomb was dropped into thick jungle. More often than not, the can would disappear into the top of the trees, and you would be off target and in your climb to orbit before the thick cloud of oily black smoke would seep up through the foliage.

Napalm got a lot of bad press during the war due to the peaceniks decrying it as a cruel and inhuman weapon. Their ill-founded cries were backed by posters showing a Viet Cong covered with flaming napalm, running through the jungle screaming. As with most of their other tenets, this is pure, unadulterated garbage! Anyone caught in the napalm attack isn't running anywhere, because he is dead, and dead almost instantly. The flames, the intense heat, and the complete lack of oxygen cause a quick (although probably a somewhat painful) demise. Comparing this with the excruciating death by impalement caused by many VC booby traps makes napalm seem quite humane.

The Pistol

The Gatling gun was the last of the weapons carried by the 12th TFW's F-4s. This modern-day version of a principle developed just before the Civil War was a 20mm cannon with six rotating barrels. These six barrels were mounted around a central axle running their entire length and extending into the breech mechanism of the gun. The complete assembly was spun at 1,000 rpm by the combination of an electrical motor and gun discharge gases. As each

Fig. 6-8. The Gatling gun in its pod hung on the centerline station. The six muzzles are just behind the disk on the front of the pod. The hose leading into the belly of the airplane conducts high-velocity air from an external cart to the starter for one engine. After the first engine has been started, the hose is switched to the other side to crank the second engine.

barrel passed the lowest point of its rotation, its shell was fired electrically, which resulted in a rate of fire of 6,000 rounds per minute. The gun, the machinery to drive it, and its ammunition and feed belts were all contained in a pod a little over 17 feet long and 22 inches in diameter. This gun pod, which weighed 1,739 pounds, was mounted on the centerline station of the fuselage and held 1,150 usable rounds of ammunition.

Firing the "pistol" was a unique experience. When the trigger was pressed, there was none of the rat-a-tat-tat or chug-chug that you normally expect to hear when a machine gun or cannon is fired. Instead, the Gatling gun produced a continuous roaring sound as the target was fire-hosed with lead. Because of the extremely high rate of fire, the trigger only had to be pressed for the briefest of instants to inflict a considerable amount of damage on another airplane during a hassle. However, for our purposes at Phu Cat, strafing was the name of the game, and a description of a typical mission will be given in Chapter 9. The ammunition used for this weapon was a mixture of armor-piercing incendiary and high-explosive incendiary cartridges. Such a combination gave us the capability of attacking almost any kind of target and damaging it severely.

Much to the disappointment of all the jocks in the 12th TFW, strafing missions were rarely encountered, since they were never fragged. The only chance you had of shooting the "pistol" was to be scrambled off alert in the number one bird, which was the only one equipped with a gun. The number three and four birds on alert usually got scrambled more frequently, since their two dozen 500-pounders could be used on just about any target. But the napalm, high-drags, and gun on numbers one and two could only be employed on low-angle missions during the daytime. Thus, if you had your 'druthers, the big decision was whether you wanted to strafe or get more missions. The latter usually won out.

As with most everything else in life, the tools of the trade are only as good as the tradesman that uses them. Tiger land is no different. Putting all this machinery and destructive power in the right place at the right time does not happen automatically. Effective fighter-bomber sorties, even those flown by hungry tigers, require planning to the nth degree, as we shall see next.

Chapter 7

Mission Preparation

Now that we've got a handle on the tools of the tiger's trade, it's time to take a look at what's involved in getting all of them from A to B.

There are no "standard" missions in a combat situation; each target has its own peculiarities and defenses to be dealt with specifically. Even repeated strikes on the same target do not become routine because of changing defenses and friendlies moving in and out of the area. Although close air support missions have a lot of similarities, the differences are significant enough to affect the ultimate success or failure of the flight if they are not properly addressed.

Planning is the name of the game, and giving detailed attention to this vital aspect of any combat mission is the hallmark of the hungry tiger. Sluffing off in this area shows a definite lack of professionalism, and brands one as either a fledgling or a fool—maybe both!

Mission Planning and Briefings

In getting ready for any mission, the first order of business is to do a little preliminary flight planning. The intelligence building at Phu Cat provided large tables, aeronautical charts, and technical manuals containing all the required data for the airplane and the weapons. Also posted were the particulars of each mission, giving the call sign of the FAC, the rendezvous point, the type of weapons to be carried, and the altitude of the target above sea level. Take-off times were set by 7th AF to put us over the rendezvous point at the desired time. Therefore, navigational planning was fairly minimal. The only thing required was to determine the course and distance to the rendezvous. Once corrected for winds, the time enroute and fuel required would be calculated.

The bottom line here was fuel, and all the figuring was done to establish a "Bingo" fuel for the flight. Bingo fuel is the amount with which you must leave the target area in order to get home safely. In poor weather this would include the climbout from the target, enroute cruise to the approach fix, a weather penetration and GCA, plus the absolute minimum needed for a missed approach and closed traffic. Each base had regulations establishing the amount of fuel required over the letdown fix, and these varied depending on the local geography and approach pattern. If the weather was good, the flight always planned for an enroute VFR descent, which allowed a lower Bingo over the target.

Knowing the amount of fuel it would take to get to the target, and the Bingo fuel, the flight leader could then estimate how much working time they would have over the target. This in turn would pretty well decide how many passes each bird would be able to make—*if* everything went according to plan. It could result in dropping the whole load on the first run, which was the least desirable situation since aiming corrections could not be made to ensure maximum target coverage. On the other hand, if the target wasn't too far and was lightly defended, the bombs could be dropped one at a time.

Weapons planning came next. The target altitude was compared with high terrain obstacles in the area so that a release altitude could be determined that would provide adequate clearance as you bottomed out of the dive. High ground was not the only factor entering into the selection of a pickle altitude. If the locality was usually defended by the heavier weapons (37mm and 57mm), a higher altitude might be chosen to minimize exposure to these guns.

Once the release altitude had been set, the bombing pattern altitude around the target was also established. The rules for determining pattern altitude depended on whether it was a high-angle or a low-angle mission, and these will be covered as each type of sortie is discussed in the following chapters.

Of course, none of these altitudes is set in concrete at this time. Often, conditions in the target area are different than expected and a modification must be made, or the target itself might be changed from the floor of a valley to the top of a hill. In either case, all new figures must be calculated on the spot.

With all this information in hand, the only remaining data to be looked up were the mil settings for each type of armament carried. These values were obtained from bombing tables calculated for each kind of weapon, and varied according to release speed and release altitude. The mils for the different types of bombs carried would just be copied down on the mission card at this time, along with the other flight information. Once airborne, these values would be set in the gunsight, and a description of how they affect the sight picture will be included in Chapter 9.

Although it didn't happen too frequently, there were occasions when no FAC was assigned to control the mission. If this were the case, all the information concerning the target would have to be obtained from aerial photographs and large-scale maps provided for this purpose. Each member of the flight would have to study these pictures in order to become familiar with the target and the surrounding area. If hills and valleys were a factor, preferred run-in headings would have to be selected that allowed the most bombs to be placed on the target. Naturally, all of the other data relating to navigation and ordnance delivery parameters would also have to be calculated for self-FAC missions.

The next step in preparing for any mission would be the briefings conducted by intelligence and weather personnel. These briefings—particularly the former—were tailor-made for each mission, and concentrated mainly on the specifics affecting that flight. Generalities such as the overall intelligence picture for the day were covered; however, the substance of the briefing was devoted to the following topics:

The probability of receiving hostile fire during takeoff and landing would be gone over if intelligence reports showed this to be a threat. If such activity was at a high level, modifications would have to be made to departure and approach procedures. All of the available information describing the target would be passed along, but in most cases this tended to be a little sparse. "A bunker complex on the side of a hill," "a truck park in a grove of trees," or "a VC base camp" are typical examples of how targets would be described. These details, however terse, came from ground troops requesting the air strike, and were completely adequate for our needs.

The briefing then proceeded to an item that had *everybody's* attention each time it came up. This dealt with the amount and the type of defenses in the target area. The latest intelligence reports would be used to pinpoint the location of each flak position, and the size of the gun installed. In many cases these reports would be fairly old, especially if the target had not been hit for a while. Also, the bad guys had a penchant for moving gun positions around, just to confuse the issue. But hearing a report of "three 37mm guns on the ridgeline north of the target, a 57mm site 200 meters to the west, and a ZPU to the south" *definitely* made you sit up and take notice, regardless of its age.

Along with pointing out where all the guns were positioned, the intelligence officer would also give the recommended attack heading that would cut down the time you were exposed to their fire. In hilly areas, these headings might or might not correspond to those that would best assure target destruction. Thus, if the target was on the floor of a valley, the communists would always try to place guns parallel to the long axis of the valley on either side of the target. This would give them maximum shooting time, since they knew our attacks would normally follow the orientation of the valley.

Target defenses were the bad news in the briefing. The "good news" was where you could go if you took a hit. This was known as the preferred bailout area, and was based on the latest information on the amount of enemy activity in the locality immediately surrounding the target. Due to the mobility of the VC, these reports were only the best guesses available at that time, and if the bad guys were all over the place, the preferred bailout area only represented the area where they were the *least* dense.

The recommended bailout data was very general in nature, and usually consisted of a heading and a distance, such as: "Go northeast for ten miles." The purpose of these directions was to provide a single heading to which you should immediately turn if you received a damaging hit over the target and the aircraft was still controllable. If the bird could be flown for even a short time, it would allow you to put some distance between you and the target before punching out. Every mile gained here would improve your chances of avoiding capture and being rescued once you got on the ground. If the hit was not too severe, but bailout was still a good possibility, you followed the best bailout heading until you were well clear of the target area, then you headed for what were labeled as "safe areas." These were fairly large sectors, normally in extremely rugged terrain that had no military value and consequently were not inhabited by the bad guys.

Naturally, some safe areas were safer than others, and none provided an absolute haven from the Viet Cong. Around some targets the enemy owned practically all the real estate, and in these instances there really was no preferred bailout area. If this were the situation, the intelligence types would usually brief us to "Go feet wet" if we took a hit. This meant that we should head for the nearest coastline and try to get over open water before ejecting. The chances of getting picked up in the ocean were infinitely better than being yanked out of the jungle when surrounded by the VC. Unfortunately, a large percentage of our targets were located a good distance inland, and "going feet wet" meant nursing a crippled bird along for quite a few miles before it was safe to leap out.

Hearing all this cheery news about targets bristling with gun emplacements—and good places to bail out—did not tend to improve your pre-mission frame of mind. Sitting in the briefing room, each man with his thoughts, is probably the time when just about every tiger has a case of the butterflies. Intelligence usually briefed the worst possible situation, which rarely materialized. However, in the back of your mind there was always that lingering doubt: "Maybe today all those guns will be up."

Everyone's attack of the jitters, be it large or small, disappeared or diminished markedly with the end of the briefing. New topics came up that demanded your attention, and the pace was too brisk to allow any time for nerves to play on the mind. Once the mission was airborne, no more thought was given to any nervousness that may have cropped up during briefing. The job to be done was at hand, and the overriding objective was to put the bombs on the target. Doing this job right in a minimum amount of time required the full concentration of both the pilot and the GIB in each bird.

After the intelligence types finished their spiel, it was the weather guessers' turn. Theirs was a very standard briefing, covering the general weather patterns over the entire theater and the specifics on all the major recovery bases we might be using. If it was monsoon season, any impact that these might have on the mission would also be included. This occurred mainly during the northeast monsoon, when all of the bases along the South Vietnam coast would have relatively low ceilings and rain.

Once in a while a particular weather system would come through that would generate fairly strong winds below 10,000 feet. Naturally, the speed and direction of these winds would have a direct effect on the trajectory of a bomb. Therefore, these values were noted on the mission card so that aiming corrections could be computed and applied on the bombing run.

Expected ceilings and visibilities in the target area would also be briefed so that flight leaders could plan their tactics accordingly. On high-angle missions, an 8,000-foot broken cloud deck moving in and out of the area could cause considerable problems in identifying the target and getting clearance from the FAC. It might also force attacks at less desirable dive angles in order to maintain an eyeball on the mark through a hole in the clouds.

There were many times when the weather briefing did nothing to offset the gloomy news handed out by intelligence. It was bad enough to learn that the target would be heavily defended, but then to be told that the weather would require you to work it lower than you wanted was indeed the last straw. However, once in a *great* while things would go the other way, with CAVU weather and the bad guys out to lunch—a piece of cake mission!

After the intelligence and weather people had their say, the crews would go back to the squadron building to hold individual flight briefings. These would follow standardized guides to make sure all pertinent items were covered. Although procedures were fairly stereotyped at Phu Cat by 1970, the particulars of each phase of the flight had to be mentioned so that the mission plan was very clear in everyone's mind. Such variables as: Do we join up below the clouds or on top; close formation after level-off or spread; and post-attack joinup over the target or enroute home were spelled out as much as possible. The major portion of the flight briefing dealt with how the leader wanted things done over the target. Included here was the approximate position he would put the flight into trail formation to orbit the target, the FAC identification procedures, sequence on the target, codes to be used on roll-in (these will be explained in Chapter 9), and fuel management procedures. Although there was no question in anyone's mind as to what would be done in an emergency situation, these procedures were covered anyway, just to make sure that nothing slipped through the cracks.

If all of the people on the mission were old heads, the normal items in the briefing would be gone over somewhat quickly. Everyone had been there before, and the routine procedures were firmly set in their minds. But if anyone was on his first half-dozen or so missions—especially the front-seater flying the wing position—the leader would spend more time on the details. The main items that were stressed with newcomers were proper spacing in the dive bombing pattern, the need for a lot of jinking, and the necessity of keeping your speed up and using the proper dive angle. Of course, the GIB riding with the new front-seater would always be one of the more experienced troops, and would constantly remind him of what to do, when.

Regardless of the experience of the crews involved, the mission briefings had to be of a fairly generalized nature. Too many variables could—and usually did—occur on every combat sortie to precisely nail things down beforehand. Sometimes the entire strike was changed to another area after the flight became airborne. This resulted in a lot of last-minute calculations just before starting the attack—and playing the rest by ear. Despite the fluid situation found over just about any target, these eleventh-hour changes rarely caused a mission cancellation. The experience level of the flight leaders allowed a great deal of flexibility with a minimum amount of sweat. This just about guaranteed the bombs being put to some good use, rather than carrying them home.

Suiting Up

All the aforementioned briefings prepared the mind for the mission; now came time to prepare the body. Suiting up in all the required gear was the last thing on the agenda before going out to the birds. The Nomex flying suits referred to earlier were mandatory on all flights, and although uncomfortable, were a necessary evil to counter the risk of fire if you took a hit. Also required for the same reason were Nomex flying gloves. These had a soft leather facing sewn on the palm and the inside of the fingers to ensure a positive grip on controls and switches.

Jungle boots completed the first layer of essential flying gear. These were worn by everybody in 'Nam, and were an excellent and long-overdue piece of equipment for summertime flying. The uppers were made of a synthetic fabric about the heaviness of canvas, which made them very light and comfortable in hot weather compared to leather flying boots. The thick soles had a heavy tread, almost resembling cleats, to facilitate walking through marshy jungle areas. These boots also incorporated a flexible metal innersole as protection against punji stakes, a favorite VC booby trap. These were sharpened bamboo stakes set in the bottom of a shallow hole with their points up. The hole would be located in a well-traveled path and would be camouflaged by a thin layer of grass and twigs. An unwary GI stepping in this trap with regular combat boots would be impaled on the stakes, and since the sticks were usually smeared with feces, the resulting infection put the guy out of action as effectively as would a bullet.

G suits, or Go Fast Pants as they were sometimes called, were the first things to be donned in preparation for the mission. The G suit was a tight-fitting garment covering the abdomen and legs whose purpose was to keep the wearer from blacking out during high-G maneuvers. This was done by a system of interconnected bladders inside the suit that were automatically inflated with air anytime the bird was pulling Gs. The bladders were across the stomach and the outside of each thigh and calf. They were connected by a hose to a valve that metered air to the suit in proportion to the number of Gs on the aircraft. The inflating action tightened the suit considerably, and thus helped to prevent blood from pooling in the lower extremities. The suit was a pretty effective piece of gear, since it increased a person's G tolerance by at least two or three. The Go Fast Pants' only drawback was that they were fairly uncomfortable in hot weather because of the tight fit needed to make them work properly.

Next came a functional check of your oxygen mask, microphone, and headset. This consisted of plugging the mask into a replica of the aircraft system and making sure the exhalation valve was not stuck, since this would effectively prevent any breathing at all. At the same time the communications gear could be checked for proper operation. If you could hear yourself breathing in the mask, everything was okay.

Over the G suit went a standard GI web belt to which was attached a hunting knife and a holster for a short-barreled .38 revolver. These guns and their ammunition were always kept in a walk-in vault except when being carried on a mission or while pulling mobile control.

Another required item was the survival vest, which had numerous small pockets attached to it for carrying a variety of goodies. One pocket contained a locator beacon which, when activated, would transmit a warbling tone on Guard channel. In case you had to bail out, this signal would allow rescue aircraft to home in on your position on the ground, thereby facilitating a quick pickup. Another pocket held a survival radio which, unlike the locator beacon, had the capability of both transmitting and receiving. This enabled a downed airman to talk directly to the rescue forces and give them precise directions as to his location—or to advise them of a possible flak trap being set up by the VC. Both these radios were checked for proper operation before each flight, and spare batteries for the survival radio were also carried in the vest. The rest of the pockets were used for a number of other survival items including water purification tablets, compass, water bag, maps, extra ammunition, matches, flint-and-steel set, flexible saw, candle, and so forth.

Additional survival gear of a more bulky nature was stored in a fiberglass case located in the bottom of the ejection seat in the airplane. Along with a one-man life raft, this case contained such things as a raft repair kit, spare radio, desalter kit for making sea water drinkable, survival book, sea dye marker for coloring the water so that your position would be more visible from the air, shark repellent, and cans of water. This kit was attached to the crewmember's parachute harness and stayed with him after separation from the seat during an ejection.

While in the vault picking up his gun and ammunition, each man had to place all personal items in one of the small boxes provided for that purpose. Wallets, money, wedding rings, and anything else that might be in your pockets was left behind. This was to prevent these things from being used by the enemy for intelligence or psychological purposes in the event you were shot down and captured.

There were, however, certain items that had to be carried on each flight in order to conform to international law. Everyone had to wear a set of dog tags and carry a Geneva Convention Card, which identified the person as a member of the United States armed forces. No one had any illusions that this card would make any impression on a Viet Cong guerilla, who most likely had never heard of Switzerland, much less Geneva or its convention. Another required item to be carried by each crewmember was a blood chit. This was a piece of cloth printed with an American flag and a reward offer spelled out in all the indigenous languages in the theater. This offer promised the equivalent of $10,000 to anyone helping the downed crewmember get back to the safety of the American lines.

If you took a hit and had to bail out, and were able to avoid being captured after landing, escape and evasion (E&E) was the next order of business. The aeronautical charts that everyone carried were not exactly the type of map you needed for finding your way about on the ground. For this reason, everybody was issued E&E maps that contained more detailed information on trails, roads, villages, and rivers to help you find your way to safe areas, the coast, or known friendly positions. These maps were printed on silk, which allowed them to be used for extended periods under rugged jungle conditions, even when wet. It also enabled large maps to be folded into relatively small packets that were easy to carry in the survival vest.

Even after getting all this stuff checked out and stowed in the right place, you still weren't through. On the outside of each calf of the G suit were large pockets that were used to carry just about anything else you thought you might need—in the air or on the ground. A fairly standard item that would be kept here was an emergency water container. This was a plastic baby's bottle, and although it held only eight ounces or so, it was enough for a quick swig while you gathered your wits after hitting the ground. A small pocket flashlight was another item that had to be kept readily available before and during the flight. This was needed for checking details during the preflight inspection of the aircraft (even during the daytime, since the shelters kept everything pretty well shaded around the birds). It also came in handy for looking up information on the mission card or letdown plates on night missions. Aeronautical charts covering the entire theater and marked with headings and distances to all alternates were also carried in the G suit pockets. Cigarettes, a lighter, pencils, and a handkerchief took up any room left over.

Some pilots preferred to use a kneeboard strapped to their thigh for the mission data card. However, this tended to be a little bulky and interfered with a comfortable grip on the stick. A simple paper clamp that clipped the data card to the G suit was the best solution to this problem.

On top of all this went the final piece of personal equipment, the parachute harness. This was just the webbing, straps, and buckles that attached the chute to the man. The parachute itself always stayed in the aircraft except for periodic inspections and repacking. This unique feature of the Martin-Baker ejection system as used in the F-4 was really appreciated by all crewmembers, since another 30 or so pounds of gear did not have to be lugged to and from the bird. The chute was packed in a horseshoe-shaped container above the headrest on the seat, and only required attaching the two buckles that connected the risers to the harness.

The entire ejection system, designed by the British, was extremely reliable, and was one of the first to provide a "zero-zero" capability. This meant that a person could eject from an aircraft at zero altitude and zero airspeed and still be guaranteed at least two seconds under a fully deployed canopy before hitting the ground. Such a capability provided the only way out if an airplane caught fire on the ground and was immediately engulfed in flames from ruptured fuel tanks. Before the development of the Martin-Baker seat, few escape systems promised even a small chance of survival unless the aircraft was going at least 120 knots and had attained a minimum altitude of 125 feet.

The only drawback of the F-4 seat was the extreme firmness of its so-called cushion. Sitting in a Martin-Baker seat was like sitting on granite; however, this hardness was designed in to prevent spinal compression fractures during the ejection sequence.

After suiting up, the only thing that remained to be done before going out to the bird was to grab your helmet and mask and a small canvas bag containing two sets of checklists and a "goodie book." The latter comprised about two dozen clear plastic envelopes, held together with a pair of ring binders, loose-leaf style. In these envelopes were mimeographed cards containing a variety of data that would change from time to time—frequencies for just about every base and radar site in the theater, coordinates of refueling tracks, safe areas, selected data from the bombing tables to make last-minute changes, and armament jettison areas, for example. Although it wasn't used too frequently in the air, it had to be taken on each flight because it was a case of when you needed it, you needed it *bad*—and in a hurry.

The checklists carried were the standard ones issued for the operation of the F-4. The front-seater's contained aircraft preflight, normal operating procedures, and emergency procedures, while the GIB's covered the same areas in relation to the weapons delivery/navigation system. The latter also had a section on preflighting the various weapons carried. Each crewmember took both along, since some emergency procedures could be done from either cockpit, and, in a situation where the front seater's attention was entirely devoted to flying the airplane, the GIB could read him each step of the applicable procedure. Having two sets of checklists to back up one another was also handy in case someone dropped his book under the seat, where it couldn't be reached because of all the survival gear that was worn. The bag containing the goodie book and the checklists was normally stowed on the right rear console in each cockpit, where it could be reached without too much difficulty.

When you had reached the point where there was no room left to put anything else on, all pockets were stuffed, and both hands were full, it was time to head for the flight line. Given the hot, sticky

Fig. 7-1. Author in full flight gear just before a mission.

weather and the load of gear each person carried, it was a little much to ask him to walk 500 yards to the aircraft shelters. Munificent to a fault, the United States Air Force provided crew vans to take the troops to their individual airplanes—and, if things weren't too busy, to pick them up after landing.

With everyone all dressed up and definitely having someplace to go, the next phase of the mission was to get things cranked up and leap off into the blue.

Chapter 8

Mission Common Denominators

Every combat sortie, regardless of the type of target, the kind of weapons carried, or the time of day or night it was flown, had certain aspects that never changed. Yet, although they were routine, they were not treated lightly, because when you're going out to be shot at, every facet of the mission is vital to its overall success—and your personal longevity. At Stateside bases, aircraft preflight is an area that sometimes gets less than the required amount of attention, more so from the turkeys than the eagles. Their casual approach to preflight inspection at times amounts to little more than kicking the tires. These are also the ones who usually have a lot of airborne problems, most of which could have been discovered and corrected on the ground. In Vietnam, a thorough and complete preflight was the normal order of business, and the crew's attention to detail would have gladdened the heart of the most hard-bitten safety officer.

Preflight, Start, and Taxi

Life in the aircraft shelters just before a mission was a world dominated by earsplitting sound. The auxiliary power unit (APU), which was an engine-driven generator, was running wide open to supply current to the bird's electrical systems. Right next to it was the aircraft starting cart, which was a small jet engine whose exhaust was ducted to a turbine-driven starter attached to each engine in the airplane. When this baby really wound up just before cranking the engine, it felt like a red-hot nail being driven into each ear. In addition, the parabolic walls inside the shelter seemed to reflect the noise back downward with a cruel intensity. Conversation was all but impossible, and ear plugs had to be worn to prevent hearing damage. Crewmembers who had been flying other airplanes with less noisy ground support equipment disdained the use of ear plugs as not befitting their fighter pilot image. They soon became believers, however, after working around an F-4 for a few days— using ear plugs was a lot better than flunking the audiometer test on their next annual physical.

The front-seater's task during the preflight was to check over the entire airplane for the usual items such as leaks, loose panels, charged accumulators, popped rivets, and other dings or bruises. While the bird was being given the once-over, the GIB had two jobs to take care of. The first of these was to align the inertial platform in the aircraft's navigation system. This involved setting the coordinates of the base into the control box, turning the power on, and then waiting about five minutes while the lubricants warmed to operation temperatures and the gyros came up to speed.

After being turned on, the inertial system needed no further attention until after engine start, so the GIB proceeded to his second job—preflighting the weapons. This was mainly a check to ensure that the bombs were securely attached to the mounting shackles and the fin assemblies on each were not loose or bent. Each weapon was also checked for the proper fuses being installed and set according to the mission requirements. Clipped to each fuse was an arming wire that prevented activation of the fuse mechanism until the bomb left the aircraft. The other end of this heavy wire was secured to the bomb rack, and stayed with the bird after the weapon was dropped. The security of these wires and their clips was another checklist item, along with ascertaining that each ejector mechanism had cartridges installed.

By 1970, operations in Vietnam had acquired quite a few of the policies usually associated with peacetime flying back in the States. These were promulgated in the name of Flying Safety, and thus took on the aura of Motherhood and Apple Pie. One such directive issued by the Wing at Phu Cat was that checklists would be carried and used by each crewmember during preflight inspections. This was a little farfetched considering the high level of professionalism shown by just about every pilot and GIB assigned to the base. Also, any fighter pilot worth his salt should know the preflight checklist like the back of his hand. If he doesn't, he hasn't been doing his homework, and should not be considered as fully checked out.

Strapping in the airplane was an arduous task that was definitely made easier with the assistance of a crew chief. After settling in the seat, the main survival kit had to be attached to the parachute harness by a pair of buckles. Quite a bit of squirming around was needed to find these buckles down between the kit and the seat, and to lengthen their straps enough to clip them on. Retightening these straps was just about always good for a banged elbow when they slipped out of your grip and your arm flew up and hit the underside of the canopy rail. The chute buckles were a little easier, since the crew chief handed them to you and made sure they were locked in place.

When everything was battened down, the prestart checklists were accomplished quickly, and the crew chief plugged himself into the intercom system. Every detail was gone over carefully in the cockpit, and after engine start, power-on checks were made of each system that could be worked on the ground. The F-4 was a pioneer among fighters in this concept of bringing the crew chief into the pre-taxi checks as an active participant. No longer was it necessary to try to catch his eye with a hand signal to warn of speed brakes coming open or flaps going down. As each item in the checklist came up, the crew chief was there to call for the appropriate action and check for proper operation.

While the pilot was seeing if all the primary aircraft systems were working properly, the GIB would run BIT checks on the radar to determine that it was performing up to specs. BIT stands for "Built In Test," and all it required was entering certain values into the set and looking for programmed responses that indicated all systems were okay. If everything was "Go," the gear-down lock pins were pulled by the crew chief , shown to the crew, and it was time to taxi out.

The shelters did not provide an awful lot of wingtip clearance on either side of the bird, and the taxiways between the shelters were also quite narrow. Therefore, once the airplane got rolling, a great deal of care had to be exercised to keep the nosewheel right on the centerline painted on the taxiways. An unloaded F-4 is fairly easy to steer, and the throttles only have to be a tad above idle to move it along at a brisk pace. Sometimes it even requires a touch of brakes to keep the speed down to where it is easily controllable. But load a Phantom with 6,000 pounds of bombs and their suspension gear and it's an entirely different matter. Taxiing becomes a very sluggish operation, and once you get it moving, the beast seems to have a mind of its own. Power changes and braking actions become more frequent, greater in magnitude, and have to be anticipated well in advance to keep things going as desired.

While taxiing out, the usual calls for takeoff information were made to ground control. Before taking the active, each bird had to pull into a specially designated area near the runway for the "Last Chance" inspection and final arming procedures. In Last Chance, the airplane was given a quick going-over for leaks of any kind, tire cuts, forgotten safety pins, or anything else that would interfere with accomplishing the mission. While the Last Chance crew was inspecting the bird, armorers would pull the ground safety pins from all weapons.

Takeoff and Climbout

When cleared, the aircraft would take the active as a flight and line up as if it would be a formation takeoff. However, all departures were "in-trail," which meant that the wingman rolled five seconds after the leader released his brakes. Safety was the overriding reason for in-trial departures. First of all, the bomb load increased the takeoff roll to about 5,000 feet, which would require quite a bit of deft handling to stay on the wing before leaving the ground. Instinctive steering and braking actions by the wingman would put undue stress on the gear—particularly the tires—at these gross weights. Also, formation takeoff procedures dictated that the leader use a little less than maximum power so that the wingman would have something to play with to stay in position. This, in turn, would lengthen the takeoff roll for both aircraft and compound the above problem by setting up ideal conditions for a blowout. Another reason was that if the leader had to abort during a formation takeoff, there was a good probability that both birds would go off the runway and be destroyed. If this happened, there would be six tons of bombs rolling around in the flames to add to the risk.

Even if everything went according to the book during a formation takeoff, and the birds got airborne, there was a third reason for avoiding this type of departure. A bad guy hiding in the bushes off the end of the runway, waiting to hose off a clip at the birds taking off, might miss a single aircraft that could do even a little jinking. However, he would have to be a really lousy shot to miss *two* airplanes close to one another whose freedom to maneuver would be so restricted.

The five-second delay on brake release between the wingman and the flight leader resulted in the former being about three miles behind once the two fighters got into the air. If the ceiling was high enough to permit a joinup in close formation, this was usually done to keep the flight more intact. Once number two was on the wing, the pair would then penetrate the weather and continue their climb to level-off altitude. When the ceiling was 5,000 feet or less, the leader would normally elect to keep the flight in trail until they broke out on top. This was easily done by the GIB in the second bird, who locked his radar on the leader as soon as he could after getting airborne. Once "tied on," the front-seater would adjust his power to maintain zero overtake on the radar display, and thus keep the three-mile interval all the way through the clouds.

Just about the time you were joining up, or hitting the clouds and going on instruments, one of the problems of flying in a hot, humid climate such as Vietnam came into play. As mentioned earlier, both crewmembers would be soaked with sweat before the engines were started. Taxiing out and sitting in the arming area—most likely with the hot exhaust blowing back over the cockpit—didn't do much to ease the situation. Finally, when you were ready to go, the canopies would be shut and the air conditioning system turned on—full cold! With the engines at 100 percent power, the system was running at full blower and welcome relief poured into the cockpit. However, it wasn't long before the cooled air and the high humidity combined to form instant fog. The air vents streamed a thick vapor into the cockpit, which quickly obscured everything, including the instruments. This necessitated a mad scramble to switch hands on the stick, fumble around for the air conditioning control knob and turn it to the normal range while trying to slide smartly into position on the leader's wing. By this time the flight was high enough to be picked up by "Panama," which was the call sign of the GCI site located near Da Nang. Standard procedure was to give these folks a call and check the flight in so that it could be identified on their radar.

The climbout continued until the flight reached 25,000 feet, which was the normal altitude for traffic outbound to the target. Trying to get much higher than this wasn't too practical, because the weight and the drag of the bombs would result in less than optimum airspeed and fuel consumption. It was a rare day in Vietnam when the tops of solid cloud decks were above 20,000 feet. Therefore, as soon as a flight penetrating the overcast in close formation broke out on top, the leader would immediately fishtail his aircraft as a signal to move out in spread formation. This was a lot easier than flying on the wing, and increased the visual coverage of the flight, particularly in the rear hemisphere. Flight maneuverability—especially for SAM avoidance—was another advantage of this formation.

Enroute to the target, Panama would monitor the flight continuously and provide any traffic advisories that were appropriate. It was very similar to being under positive radar control back in the States. Any updated information affecting the mission would be passed along through the GCI site. This might be a new FAC call sign, or a different frequency to contact him on. Changing conditions on the ground might require that the rendezvous point be moved, or the sortie could be canceled entirely. Updates like these from the radar controllers gave the close air support mission the ultimate in flexibility to meet new situations as they developed.

During the enroute phase, the lead GIB handled just about all the radio calls for the flight. He also had the primary responsibility of navigating the flight to the rendezvous point. Naturally, the GIB in the bird flying wing also kept track of the situation so that he would be immediately available as a backup. Rendezvous fixes were always given in terms of a radial and a distance from the TACAN station closest to the target. Fortunately, there were ample TACANs in South Vietnam and Thailand to provide all the coverage needed for targets just about anywhere in the theater. The frag would normally designate the fix in a standard format, such as: 240/25/69. This meant the FAC would be met 25 miles out on the 240 degree radial of TACAN channel 69, which was located at Hue. Changes or confirmation of the fix would use the same phraseology when broadcast from a GCI site. If a number of flights were scheduled to work the same target at approximately the same time, each would have a separate fix. These would be far enough apart to provide plenty of clearance between each pair of fighters as they orbited while awaiting their turn on target.

Target Defenses

One thing that really kept you on your toes during the more or less routine enroute phase of the mission was the frequent activation of the RHAW gear. The Radar Homing And Warning system consisted of a series of red lights mounted above the instrument panel and a small round TV screen about two inches in diameter. The purpose of the system was to let the crew know that a hostile radar was locked-on to their aircraft. The frequency of the incoming signal would be analyzed to determine what kind of weapons system it was coming from—gun-ranging radar from another fighter, search and track radar from an interceptor, or, most important of all, the radar used for the control and guidance of SAMs? Each weapons system operated on a specific frequency band, and once this was known, the appropriate light identifying the threat would be illuminated.

Different defensive reactions were required in each case, therefore the proper information had to be available instantly. The counter to all these threats was always an immediate turn in one direction or the other, including down, and going the wrong way would almost certainly prove fatal. To solve this problem, the RHAW scope displayed a strobe to indicate the direction from which the hostile signal was coming. Thus, if the strobe ran from the center of the scope to where the four would be on the face of a clock, the crew would know that the threat was in their four o'clock position. (The "clock code system" is a universally used method for describing the position of an object in relation to an object in relation to an aircraft, and is fully described in the Glossary.)

Enemy fighters were usually not a problem anywhere in the theater except arround Hanoi and Haiphong. This left SAMs as the major source of worry on all flights that went near the North Vietnamese border, or were over Laos. SAM firings were not a common occurrence on the missions flown in '70-'71; however, the few that *were* launched served to keep all of us respectively honest in this area.

There was a very large number of friendly radars of every type and description operating in South Vietnam and Thailand. The air was so crisscrossed with their beams that it was like flying through a microwave oven. Undoubtedly, the RHAW gear was activated by harmonics created by all these conflicting radiations, which for an instant resembled an enemy radar. But every time the buzzer sounded when the strobe appeared, it brought you up with a start, and all eyes immediately began searching for the telltale line of smoke from a rising SAM. Although everyone knew of this anomaly, and it was a frequent distraction during the flight, you could not afford to be complacent and ignore it.

The more conventional types of flak were a definite problem over every target, and they had to be taken into consideration regardless of the activity level reported by intelligence. Nearly all the major targets (key transportation chokepoints, large truck

Fig. 8-1. The "H"—a landmark where the village of Tchepone was located, and since this was a key terminal of the Ho Chi Minh Trail, flak was usually guaranteed.

parks, troop concentrations, etc.) were defended by 57mm and 37mm antiaircraft guns. Although they were frequently reported in a target area, it was rare that the 57mm guns actually fired on a flight. However, if these weapons were up, they posed a very real threat anywhere in the bombing pattern, even while orbiting the target at altitude. The 37mm guns were encountered more often, and every now and then the bad guys would hose off a clip or two at an attacking fighter. Most of these retaliatory efforts came at night, which made the orange goof balls arcing up through the darkness that much more impressive—and scary. Fortunately, their aim was bad since all fighters worked blacked-out at night, and the gunners were sighted mostly on sound. This usually resulted in the rounds going behind us, but it still served to keep everyone alert.

A situation like this occurred most often during attacks on the "Boxes." These four areas just southwest of the DMZ that contained the major roads leading through the karst formations so prevalent in that region. These roads were vital to the resupply efforts of the communists for all their activity in South Vietnam, since they were the shortest routes from North Vietnam to the Ho Chi Minh Trail. The Boxes were hammered incessantly, by both visual and radar bombing techniques, in an effort to slow the truck traffic as much as possible. These areas soon became a stark contrast to the lush, green jungle surrounding them. Their appearance reminded one of the surface of the moon—pockmarked by innumerable craters and devoid of all vegetation.

Conventionally fused bombs were used to render the dirt roads impassable by cratering, and some with delayed fusing were mixed in to mine the entire area. These latter bombs would burrow into the ground and explode later at a preset time, or when triggered by the pressure of a passing truck. It must have been a thrill a minute for the drivers of these trucks as they approached the Boxes after a raid. How many "sleepers" were buried out there, and how many would go off in the next hour or so, or when the truck rolled over them? Even though they pressed on, these guys weren't the gutsy bunch of individuals that such heroics might suggest. In order to preclude the fainthearted from abandoning their trucks under these conditions, the communists would chain the driver to his cab. The key that would release him could only be obtained at the destination of the supplies he carried. Reliable sources had it that these drivers even had a song to describe their plight as they sat around the campfire at the rest stops along the Ho Chi Minh Trail. Reportedly, each chorus ended with the refrain: "Sittin' in my truck, filin' my chain!"

Targets that were not of a high enough priority to warrant the

Fig. 8-2. "Charlie" Box, located a few miles southwest of the DMZ. The lighter areas just to the right side of the river show how continual bombing had cleared this part of the Ho Chi Minh Trail of vegetation, as compared with the heavy foilage to the left of the river.

Fig. 8-3. The innumerable pockmarks on either side of a river south of the Boxes show the effect of saturation bombing by B-52s, known as Arc Light missions.

larger guns were usually defended by a ZPU. There were Russian-built .50-caliber machine guns that were highly mobile and quite effective. For this reason they were encountered frequently, and always commanded healthy respect. There are, however, exceptions to this latter generality. One day four Army helicopter gunships were trying to pinpoint the location of a ZPU site. They had nailed down the general area to a heavily foliaged section of the jungle, but needed to know its exact position in order to make a strafing run. They had made numerous passes over the area in an attempt to get an eyeball on it, but all they got for their pains was an occasional hosing down by the well-hidden gun. We were monitoring all this on the radio at the squadron duty officer's desk when the flight leader came out with this classic: "Tango flight, this is lead: You guys stay out of sight to the west there, while I go trollin' across that clump of trees where we think he's at. As soon as he starts shootin' at me, get a fix on his position and come on in to take him out!" We all marveled at this fearless—or brainless—chopper jock, but the ploy worked and as soon as the ZPU rose to the bait, the other three swooped in and did a number on it.

Anytime a fighter was within 4,500 feet of the ground, it was within the effective range of small arms fire. Just about every one of the bad guys carried an AK-47, and they were all prone to taking a few shots at the "Yankee Air Pirates" trying to drop napalm on them. They knew that in just about every instance we would be using a standardized bombing speed of 450 knots. Therefore, after a few calculations, they came up with a simple but effective device for figuring the correct lead when shooting at a moving target. They attached a stick to the muzzle end of their rifles that had a nail driven in it at the correct spot for properly leading a 450-knot target. All they had to do was keep the nail on the target and pull the trigger.

Small arms fire was a given on just about all missions, and what it lacked in accuracy, it made up for in volume. The complexity of modern jet aircraft made a hit from even rifle-caliber weapons potentially disastrous. A jacketed slug from an AK-47 going through the compressor section of a jet engine would cause an immediate explosion and disintegration of the aircraft.

FACs and Their Birds

The resident experts on flak and all its varieties in Southeast Asia were the Forward Air Controllers (FACs). Nearly all of the FACs were ex-fighter pilots who, because of the "exigencies of the service," were assigned to this vital mission. Experience gained during the Korean War proved that fighter pilots made the best FACs, since they knew what it took to dive-bomb a target and all the other factors associated with this type of mission. They talked the fighter jock's language and were aware of the problems he faced in attacking a ground target.

A FAC's mission was twofold: To patrol a given area of responsibility and become intimately familiar with all enemy activity occurring within it, and to direct air strikes on targets in this area. Accomplishing the former required many hours on patrol over the same terrain to learn how it looked under all conditions. Knowing the normal state of things on the ground, he would be able to recognize anything out of the ordinary on the roads, trails, villages, and waterways. This usually signified enemy activity, and that particular locality would get an extra dose of surveillance for the next few hours or days to see what was developing. Naturally, intelligence reports from all sources concerning goings-on in his area would be checked out completely.

If, while tooling along, a FAC would unexpectedly come upon a lucrative target, this information would be radioed to the nearest control center immediately. This would normally result in a pair of alert birds being scrambled from the nearest base to capitalize on such an opportunity.

Keeping a proper eye on things in his sector required a FAC to routinely fly quite low, so that he was able to look under the highest layer of trees to spot any suspicious activity. These low altitudes, and lots of circling at slow speeds, made them a very inviting target for enemy gunners. At times they were so low that a VC with a good arm could have brought them down with a coconut. The bad guys, however, were faced with a dilemma while eyeballing such an easy shot: should they open up and hope to bring him down on the first volley, and thus become heros? If they missed and he got away, they would have now revealed their positions and most certainly an air strike would be on top of them in less than half an hour. The would-be heros are now the goats—and most likely dead ones at that. Perhaps discretion is the better course of action— do nothing and stay hidden, since chances are he didn't spot you, and will go away shortly. But then again, his circling may be to line up for a smoke rocket pass that will mark your position for a pair of fighters ready to roll in. Decisions! Decisions!

Apparently the VC usually opted for discretion, since FACs weren't bothered too much by flak while on patrol. However, once

Fig. 8-4. Cessna O-1 (L-19) Bird Dog. (courtesy National Air and Space Museum, Smithsonian Institution)

Fig. 8-5. Cessna O-2 Skymaster. (courtesy National Air and Space Museum, Smithsonian Institution)

the enemy knew an airstrike was on the agenda, the FAC took his lumps along with the fighters. Thus, after putting in his mark, the FAC usually moved out of the immediate target area to a position where he could observe both the fighters and the target. In this way he could clear each pass, adjust the aim point if required, and avoid the majority of the defensive fire. The particulars of how a FAC controls an air strike will be covered in later chapters, as we discuss each type of bombing mission.

Two of the aircraft used by FACs in Vietnam were the Cessna O-1 (L-19) Bird Dog and the O-2A/B Skymaster built by the same firm. These were militarized versions of civilian aircraft that were already in production when the need arose. It was inefficient to use jet fighters to seek out and mark targets, since they didn't have the endurance or the slow flying characteristics needed for the job. Although these lightplanes filled the bill as far as economics and loiter time were concerned, the extra gear needed for FACing seriously hampered their performance. To allow the controller to talk to both ground and air elements and navigate around the countryside, a large variety of avionics were stuffed into the aircraft, including UHF, VHF, and FM radios, TACAN, ADF, and a radar transponder as navigation equipment.

On top of this was the beefed-up electrical system required to run the additional electronic gear. As you can imagine, all this added a considerable amount of weight to the bird, and yet provisions still had to be made for a second occupant in the aircraft. This was necessary for the many occasions when a Vietnamese interpreter had to go along when the FAC was working with their army units. Also hung on these airplanes were smoke rockets and their launching tubes, along with the gunsight and all the associated armament system circuitry.

There was, of course, a penalty paid for adding this extra equipment. The bottom line was less performance—to the point where a very hairy situation could develop quickly, if everything was not just right. The word from the O-2 drivers was that if you lost an engine on takeoff before the gear was up, that was all she wrote. One engine was simply not enough to accelerate the bird to a safe flying speed before you hit the ground. If one mill quit after the gear was retracted, things were still very dicey unless you had a good head of speed built up.

Faced with the shortcomings in existing birds, the Air Force contracted for the development of an airplane specifically designed

Fig. 8-6. North American OV-10 Bronco. The .30-caliber machine guns can be seen protruding from an armament pylon just below the rear edge of the cockpit. (courtesy National Air and Space Museum, Smithsonian Institution)

for the FAC mission. The North American OV-10 Bronco was the result, and it was an order of magnitude improvement over the previous equipment. It had two-engine reliability, was more rugged, and had greatly improved visibility for both the pilot and the observer. It was also armed with four .30-caliber machine guns in addition to the usual smoke rockets. These guns helped keep the enemy's heads down while the FAC was looking over a target or getting ready for a marking run. However, in spite of all the improvements, pilots still reported that it was underpowered for the gross weights that were required for their mission. Again, the loss of one engine on takeoff was extremely critical unless sufficient altitude had been gained to affect a recovery.

This overall lack of get-up-and-go was also a consideration if the FAC had to work a target shortly after takeoff, while the bird was still heavy. Before he had fired a few smoke rockets and burned off some of the fuel, the high gross weight limited the sharpness of any jinking he might attempt, as well as his ability to accelerate quickly for any maneuvering. In nearly all cases, the FACs did a marvelous job in Southeast Asia, in spite of the less than optimum performance of their aircraft. They epitomized the hungry tigers who always get the job done regardless of the obstacles and the hazards involved.

Up to this point we have planned, briefed, pre-flighted, leaped off, and—with the able assistance of GCI—found our way to the target. Now it's time to put it all together and go to work. Although things start happening pretty fast, and both crewmembers are quite busy with last minute checklist items, the pucker factor definitely tends to rise once you're over the target. Idle conversation stops, and everything between the two cockpits and the two aircraft is strictly concentrated on the business at hand.

Chapter 9

Types of Missions Flown

Now that all the actors in the drama have been identified and their jobs outlined, it's time to take a look at what it's like to work a target on a close air support mission. This is where it all must come together properly, since the chips for both sides are on the table. Mistakes here on anyone's part usually prove to be costly.

The first type of mission we'll discuss is high-angle dive bombing, which accounted for a majority of the strikes flown by the jocks at Phu Cat. As the name suggests, high-angle dive bombing consists of dropping ordnance on a target while in a relatively steep dive—normally at a 45 to 60-degree angle from the ground. While things do happen fairly fast in a high-angle weapons delivery, the technique allows a good degree of accuracy while minimizing the aircrew's exposure to defensive fire.

In the textbook, or on the practice range, high-angle dive bombing (or any other type of weapons delivery, for that matter) does not appear too complicated. You simply circle the target until you hit the desired run-in heading, dive the aircraft at the proper angle and speed, put the pipper on the target, and hit the pickle button at the right altitude. A piece of cake, right? Well like almost everything else in life, achieving any measure of success in dive-bombing demands the ultimate in concentration by the aircrews in order that the exact parameters of the drop can be realized. To get a hit, the pickle button must be pressed when the pipper is right on the target and the airspeed, dive angle, and altitude are all *precisely* what are called for in the bombing tables for the ordnance carried. If the pipper is off target, a miss is obvious. Releasing too high will cause the bomb to hit short of the target; too low, and it will impact beyond the target. If your airspeed is too low or too high, the results are the same as above—you'll hit short and long respectively. A dive angle that is too shallow will result in a short round, while diving too steeply will cause the bomb to hit long. Also, your wings must be level at the instant of release to preclude other errors from entering the equation. If the bomb is dropped when the bird is in a slight bank to the right, it will hit to the right of the target.

An easy way to remember most of this is by the rule of thumb: "Tigers hit long, pussycats are short." This means that the jock who flies his bird like a tiger—that is, with a tendency to dive too steeply, at too high an airspeed, and pickles below the desired altitude—will get a long bomb. Those who approach the problem less vigorously, with a proclivity for shallow dives, low airspeeds, and higher-than-programmed releases, will hit short of the target.

Dive-Bombing Techniques

Even in the controlled environment of the practice bombing range, it is tough to get all these variables to come together just when the pickle button is pressed. When setting up a bombing pattern to work any kind of target, probably two of the most important factors to consider are establishing the proper base leg from which to dive on the target, and achieving the correct dive angle on the roll-in.

Let's elaborate on the first consideration for the moment. The base leg—or, if you are circling the target, the radius you maintain around the target—really sets the stage for the entire bombing run. If the base is established correctly, you should be able to roll out on the attack heading with the pipper just a little short of the target. Then, as the dive progresses, the pipper will move across the ground toward the target, and hopefully will be right on it when the drop altitude is reached. Setting the base leg in too close necessitates a steeper dive angle to get the desired pipper placement in relation to the target. This in turn causes your speed to build up more rapidly, which, if not corrected for, will most likely put you over the proper airspeed at the release point. Throttle movements to counter the excessive airspeed buildup during the run are not too effective because of the inherent deceleration lag in jet engines as compared with the few seconds spent in the dive.

If you have the correct dive angle when you start the run, but find that the initial pipper placement is on or beyond the target because of an improper base leg, the pass may be salvaged by "bunting." A "bunt" is accomplished by momentarily pushing forward on the stick to bring the pipper back to where you want it—a little short of the target. However, by doing so you increase your dive angle beyond the optimum, and airspeed control again becomes difficult. Another instance where the "bunt" is resorted to is when the pipper reaches the target before you hit the release altitude. Here, just a tad of forward stick keeps the pipper on the mark; however, the same angle and airspeed errors are once again brought into play. Along with these problems, releasing a bomb while in a bunt introduces inaccuracies of a more serious nature. These are caused by different-than-programmed G forces acting on the bomb at its release, which have a definite influence on its trajectory. Probably the best course of action to follow if a situation develops that necessitates a moderate-to-large bunt is to go through dry and make the proper base leg adjustments on the next pass.

Getting and holding the correct dive angle brings us to the second important consideration—a proper roll-in technique. The roll-in is a smartly executed, hard, diving turn to the attack heading, utilizing a little bottom rudder to keep the nose from rising. If the run is to be made in a specific direction, this heading must be led by about 95 to 100 degrees to ensure rolling out with the proper lineup.

When the roll-in is completed, you should be pointing at the target with the correct dive angle, the pipper a little short of the mark, and the airspeed starting to build. This increase in airspeed is a designed part of the run, and normally amounts to about 100 knots in the F-4. Most bombing runs in this bird are calculated for a release speed of 450 knots. Therefore, the pattern must be flown at a minimum of 350 knots so that the airspeed buildup in the dive will bring you to the correct drop speed.

The distance it takes a diving F-4 to increase its speed by 100 knots determines how high above release altitude the pattern will be flown. This distance was usually about 6,000 feet. Thus, if defensive fire or terrain clearance on the pullout dictates a release altitude of 6,500 feet, you orbit the target at 12,500 feet and maintain at least 350 knots so that the release parameters will be met exactly when you hit the pickle button.

Naturally, no matter how much you practice, every dive-bombing run does not end up with the exact dive angle, airspeed, altitude, and wings-level attitude called for in the bombing tables. Also, initial pipper placement may not be right on the money. Therefore, if any of these problems arise during the run, the pilot has some fast calculations and decisions to make if he wants to improve his chances of getting a hit.

First off, if he's way out of the ballpark with respect to any of the numbers, it's probably best to abort the run and try again with a better setup. Being just a *little* off in any *one* of the desired parameters may be compensated for if the combined errors in the problem will tend to cancel each other out. To illustrate, if your dive angle is correct but your airspeed is a tad low, the bomb will hit short of the target, as pointed out above. The corrective action called for in this situation is to hit the pickle button late, or just a little below the desired altitude. Normally, releasing too low will result in a long round; however, in this case, the lower airspeed will hopefully correct for this and move the impact point back toward the target.

Again, if your dive angle is too steep but your airspeed is okay (normally resulting in a long round), you can correct by releasing the bomb early, or a little above the planned altitude. Once more, the errors will approximately cancel each other out and result in a more respectable CEP.

As you might guess, when applying these corrections, things are really not that clean-cut. The fly in the ointment is that delivery errors resulting in long bombs are not exactly compensated for by corrections in the opposite direction. As an example, if being ten knots faster than your planned release speed will cause the bomb to hit 30 feet beyond the target, being ten knots too slow will result in an error of quite a bit *more* than 30 feet on the short side.

Of all the corrective actions a pilot can take during a dive-bombing run, releasing low—or "pressing," as it is called—is probably the least desirable. The reasons for this are that it may result in your going below the minimum safe altitude specified for the ordnance you are dropping. Should this happen, you stand a good chance of being hit by the exploding bomb fragments of your own munitions. In combat, "pressing" also increases your exposure to small arms fire. Also, "pressing" too long makes for a very nervous GIB.

Compound delivery variances that are additive, such as a shallow dive angle and a low airspeed (each resulting in a short bomb), introduce such a large impact error that corrective actions are pretty much reduced to a wild guess. As mentioned before, your best bet here is to go through dry and try it again.

So far in this *very* generalized overview of dive-bombing we have only considered pilot-induced errors and corrections. However, as every throttle-bender knows, there is an external aspect that influences nearly every phase of flying, and dive-bombing is no exception. This is the wind, and it introduces a drift problem both on the aircraft on its run and the bomb while it's in flight. Exact correction factors are available for each type of ordnance and for all wind speeds and directions, but applying an 80 or 100-foot correction from 11,000 or 12,000 feet is a different matter. In addition, both the wind speed and direction will undoubtedly vary from pattern altitude to the ground. Therefore, about all the pilot can do is to take whatever wind information is available and calculate the correction necessary to compensate for the wind speed. Then, after rolling out on the attack heading, he guesstimates this distance into the wind in order to determine how much to offset the initial pipper placement from the ideal (no-wind) position.

High-Angle Missions

Now that we're all qualified as entry-level dive-bombers, let's see how these techniques are applied in a combat situation.

First, let's briefly consider the kinds of targets that are normally attacked by high-angle dive bombing. Just about anything worth bombing falls into this category, although pinpoint targets such as a truck, a tank, or a rocket launching position are usually handled better by low-angle attacks (the procedures for which will be discussed later). Some targets that are commonly worked by high-angle dive-bombing are large area targets such as bunker complexes, storage areas, truck parks, base camps, or other personnel concentrations. Although these usually occupied considerable space, only a small portion was normally visible since the VC were very good at camouflage and practiced it religiously. In most cases, targets such as these were effectively hidden from the fighters at bombing pattern altitude, and only the FAC's knowledge of the terrain and lower vantage point permitted an accurate placement of the mark. In nearly all cases, his smoke rocket was the only clue as to the location of the target in the rugged, jungle-covered landscape that is typical of Southeast Asia.

Flak positions are another type of target best attacked by high-angle bombing. This is because it is more difficult for the defending gunners to accurately track a steeply diving airplane than one that is approaching at a flatter angle. Also, the high elevation of the gun barrel necessitates the operator working almost directly beneath the gun—and, if the attacker has planned things right, the gunner is also forced to look right up into the sun.

The preparation of a specific area as a landing zone for helicopters is another mission that lends itself well to high-angle dive-bombing, and again, the detailed particulars of an LZ Prep mission will be covered later on. This type of attack can also be used for cutting roads, where the main idea is to run a string of bombs across a road at a shallow angle and thus render it unusable to vehicular traffic due to cratering.

Often a target such as a key road intersection or a flak position is physically located where high-angle bombing is the only way to get at it. Targets in karst areas or on the floors of steep valleys are examples of this situation. Two problems arise here, the first of which is the selection of a release altitude that is low enough to ensure good accuracy while still affording minimum terrain clearance on the pullout. The other problem when bombing in deep valleys or karst areas is the requirement for your run-in heading to follow (or cross at a very slight angle) the long axis of the valley. Attacks that go directly across the valley or karst formation allow too many bombs in the string to hit on the sides, rather than on the floor of the area where the target is located. Both of these problems tend to tip the scales a little in favor of the defending gunners. They know that you must come in fairly low and along a definite line to be successful. Thus their gun placement and target tracking problems are greatly reduced.

The bombs carried on nearly all high-angle missions flown out of Phu Cat were 500 or 2,000-pound "slicks." These bombs were fused according to the type of target being attacked: normal impact fusing for general demolition and cratering work, delayed fusing for mining operations, and fuse extenders for antipersonnel or LZ Prep missions. Another type of ordnance delivered by this method was the radar-fused canister bomb containing antipersonnel bomblets. These were most effective against enemy troops in a relatively clear area such as open fields or other terrain with no profusion of trees.

Up till now we've been talking in a very generalized way about the techniques and problems of dive-bombing, the kinds of targets attacked, and the weapons used. With these thoughts in mind, let's consider a combat situation where the bad guys are shooting back, and what additions and/or modifications must be made to the basic dive bombing procedures as a result.

Fig. 9-1. A standard load for high-angle bombing, consisting of six 500-pound "slicks" on the centerline rack and three on each wing pylon.

We'll pick up the action on a typical mission at the point where the fighters rendezvous with the FAC. As mentioned before, the flight approaches the fix in spread formation; as the leader nears the point, he turns to set up an orbit around it. At this time he also directs the wingman to take up an in-trail position. Number two just eases off a tad of power, or flies the orbit a little wide, until the desired separation is achieved between his bird and the leader's. The ideal situation here is to have both aircraft orbiting the target on opposite sides of the circle.

While getting settled in the orbit, the flight lead checks in with the FAC, giving him the flight call sign, ordnance carried, and, if fuel is becoming a problem, their estimated working time before reaching Bingo fuel. The next item on the agenda is to locate the FAC visually and positively identify him as the one you're supposed to be working with. More often than not, there are quite a few low-flying aircraft in the vicinity of the target—choppers of every description, Army liaison birds, and other FACs. The guy you're looking for will normally tell you his general location by referencing prominent landmarks, or, if he has a visual on your flight, by means of the clock code.

When both members of the flight have an eyeball on the FAC, the leader will nail down the positive identification by asking him to rock his wings. The FAC answers: "Roger . . . rocking left

. . . and rocking right," as he rolls the aircraft accordingly. This may seem to be exaggerating things a bit and belaboring the obvious, but with multiple FACs working fighters in the general area, you've *got* to be sure you're taking directions from the proper one.

After both pilots acknowledge a visual on the FAC, the latter proceeds with his target briefing. This will include the items listed below, plus any additional information he thinks necessary. Some of these things were covered by intelligence before takeoff; however, the FAC's briefing is the last—and the latest—word.

☐ Actual target description—Bunker complexes, truck hidden in the trees, storage area, food cache, etc.

☐ General location of the target in reference to easily identifiable landmarks such as rivers, valleys, open areas or roads.

☐ Active target defenses in the area—For example, a ZPU just east of the target, a 37mm site on the hill above the target, small arms fire from all quadrants, etc.

☐ Best bailout area.

☐ Run-in heading and weapons sequence—If friendly troops were near the target, the FAC would select an attack heading that would provide them with the greatest safety factor in case of long or short bombs. If troops were fairly close to the target, it was necessary to fly these headings quite accurately—usually plus or minus five degrees. The FAC also called the shot on what weapons he wanted first in the case of mixed loads, e.g., antipersonnel bombs before high explosives. These decisions were based on the type and disposition of the target and any time factors involved.

☐ Friendlies in the area—The exact location of these troops was spelled out very definitely by the FAC, such as: "Friendlies 200 meters west of the target and dug in." When they were very close to the target, the ground commander would often ignite a colored smoke grenade to show their exact position to the aircrews.

☐ Sequence on the target if other flights were scheduled to work the target first—In cases like this, the flight lead would have to decide if they had enough fuel to wait their turn, or to take the bombs home. Many times, a flight with a better cushion of fuel would allow a pair that was hurting to go ahead of them and make one pass on the target. Here, all ordnance would be dropped at once regardless of the sequence desired.

Naturally, if any member of the flight has any questions, or needs certain points amplified, this is taken care of immediately so that everyone on the mission has a clear picture of what the job entails.

When the FAC is ready to start working the flight, the latter begins a descent to bombing pattern altitude. Both fighters normally stay on opposite sides of their orbit during this letdown, and make any final adjustments that may be required to achieve the ideal spacing. This descent also allows the birds to build up their speed to at least 350 knots, in case they had gotten a little slow while waiting their turn on the target.

As they descend, the pilots go through the armament checklist, which sets up the aircraft's weapons system circuitry for the type of ordnance and delivery method desired. Usually the pilot recites this checklist to the GIB as he performs each switch action. This doublecheck ensures that the proper settings are being made, and that nothing is omitted.

The checklist covers the following items in the sequence listed, so that the pilot's hand and/or eye makes one sweep from the top of the cockpit to the bottom:

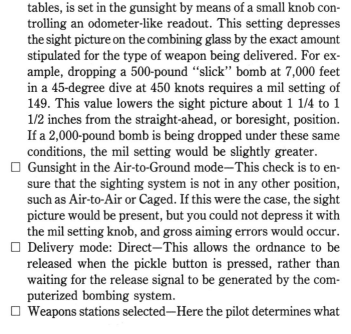

☐ Mil setting—This number, obtained from the bombing tables, is set in the gunsight by means of a small knob controlling an odometer-like readout. This setting depresses the sight picture on the combining glass by the exact amount stipulated for the type of weapon being delivered. For example, dropping a 500-pound "slick" bomb at 7,000 feet in a 45-degree dive at 450 knots requires a mil setting of 149. This value lowers the sight picture about 1 1/4 to 1 1/2 inches from the straight-ahead, or boresight, position. If a 2,000-pound bomb is being dropped under these same conditions, the mil setting would be slightly greater.

☐ Gunsight in the Air-to-Ground mode—This check is to ensure that the sighting system is not in any other position, such as Air-to-Air or Caged. If this were the case, the sight picture would be present, but you could not depress it with the mil setting knob, and gross aiming errors would occur.

☐ Delivery mode: Direct—This allows the ordnance to be released when the pickle button is pressed, rather than waiting for the release signal to be generated by the computerized bombing system.

☐ Weapons stations selected—Here the pilot determines what

stations, or bomb racks, the weapons will be released from; in the F-4, they are labeled center, right and left inboard, and right and left outboard. Stations may be chosen in any combination; however, if wing stations (inboard and outboard) are to be used, they are usually selected in pairs, such as inboard right and left. This is done to keep the bird more or less in balance as the ordnance is dropped on each succeeding pass. The net effect is that the aircraft is easier to fly and encounters fewer maneuvering problems in high-G, heavy weight conditions, such as jinking.

☐ Release sequence—With this switch the pilot selects how many bombs will be released from the aircraft when the pickle button is pressed. Three choices are available: single, triple, or ripple. When single is selected, one bomb will be released from each station selected; triple will drop a total of three bombs from the aircraft, and if the latter is chosen, all bombs will be dropped in rapid sequence.

☐ Fuse selection—Depending on the mission and the target, bombs may have fuses installed in the nose or the tail of the bomb, or in both places. The fuse selection switch gives the pilot the option of determining which fuse will be activated when the bomb is released. In Vietnam, except for special missions, this switch was usually left in the "Nose and Tail" position.

☐ Armament Master Switch to "Arm"—This oversized toggle switch, which locks in either position, is the real key to the entire release circuitry. Once in the "Arm" position, something will be dropped from one or all of the stations selected every time the pickle button is pressed. This occurs whether the aircraft is attacking a target or not. Thus, in order to preclude an inadvertent release due to switching hands on the stick and accidentally hitting the pickle button, this switch is the *last* one to be thrown before rolling in on the target.

It takes very little time to complete this checklist, since many of the settings can be made on the ground or enroute to the target. Such preset actions do not increase the possibility of an accidental release as long as stations are not selected, or the Armament Master Switch is not in the "Arm" position. These two items are the most critical in the sequence safety-wise, and thus are left until the final moments before the actual drop. One last thing is rechecked between the two cockpits after the armament checklist is finished, and this is the confirmation between the pilot and the GIB as to what the pickle altitude will be.

Working The Target

While all these checklist actions are going on in the fighters, the FAC has been setting up his own aircraft in a similar manner to fire the smoke rockets that will mark the target. After selecting the spot he wants hit, he alerts the fighters by calling: "Rolling in for the mark!" Once the white phosphorous smoke billows up from the marking rocket, the FAC gives the flight some last-minute instructions. In case the rocket went a little off from his intended impact point, he will tell the flight: "Hit 30 meters to the left of the mark," or "Target is 50 meters down the ravine from my smoke."

If the FAC has had a busy day and has run out of marking rockets, he has to describe the location of the target in relation to his airplane and various easily recognizable terrain features. This may take the form of: "Target is off my left wing, on the side of the hill, about 100 meters down from the ridgeline in the small ravine." This type of target identification requires the utmost attention and concentration from the fighter crews because they are quite a bit farther from the target than the FAC, and are usually seeing it for the first time. In situations like this, it always seems that the terrain below is maddeningly similar, and the landmarks so visible to the FAC are hard for the crews to pick out in a carpet of jungle. The FAC can help out here a little by flying directly over the target and waggling his wings. However, this can get a bit hairy if the defending gunners take exception to someone so blatantly pointing out their hiding place.

Let's assume that the FAC did good work (as was usually the case) and his smoke was right on the money. He lets the flight know this by calling: "Mark is good!," and, if he has a visual on the first bird to make a pass, he will add: "Cobra One, you're cleared in hot!" (Cobra was the call sign of all birds from the 12th TFW.)

Before either fighter can make a hot pass on the target, the crew must call that they have the mark in sight and receive clearance from the FAC to make the run. This latter condition is particularly important when random roll-in headings are being used to work the target. The FAC will only give clearance when he has a visual on the bird about to make the pass, and he is safely out of the attacker's way. There are times when this clearance for a hot pass, or permission to drop ordnance, may be delayed until the very last split second. This would be the case if the fighters were attacking through a broken deck of clouds, and might not have a chance to see the actual mark until late in the run. Also, the clouds might prevent the FAC from getting a visual until the fighter is on his way down the chute.

Once clearance has been received, the flight leader will normally be the first one in on the target if random roll-in headings are being used. However, if the attack heading is restricted due to friendlies, weather, or terrain, the first aircraft to approach the run-in heading from the orbit will be number one on the target. As described earlier, the roll-in is a hard diving turn utilizing a little bottom rudder to keep the nose from rising. In a combat situation, this turn takes a little more planning than it does on a practice range if you want to hit your attack heading with any degree of accuracy.

The reason for this is you must make allowance for the jink on the roll-in. (*Jinking* is rapid, random movements of the aircraft so as to make its flight path unpredictable to defending gunners.) The situation you want to avoid most is a long, straight dive on the target, which gives the bad guys ample time to solve the sighting problem and draw the proper lead on your bird. The idea behind jinking is to prevent the gunners from pulling the correct lead angle on your aircraft by allowing it to fly in any given direction only for the briefest of instants. The name of the game is to keep it moving, and the quicker and more violent the changes of direction, the better. This is no time or place for smooth, coordinated stick and rudder work. As an example, if the attack heading is 180 degrees and you are rolling in to your left, you may want to stop your turn at 210 degrees, hold this for an instant, then rack it over to 150 degrees, pause for a second, and then honk it around to 180 degrees for the last few seconds before release.

As you can well imagine, all this gyrating around the sky can play havoc with getting the initial pipper placement in the desired position. Ideally, the target should be about two inches above the pipper when the aircraft first rolls out of its turn and is diving straight for the target with no jinking. Since jinking in this situation definitely contributes to longevity, flying the proper orbit or base leg becomes critically important. If the orbit is flown at the correct distance from the target, the roll-in and jinks can still be accomplished, and the pipper will end up a little short of the target when you settle into the groove for those last few instants before the drop.

Circling the target in an F-4 maintaining about a 45-degree angle of bank, a good rule of thumb is to keep the target at eye level while looking along a plane parallel to the wings. This will put the target about halfway up the side of the canopy, and pretty well assures that you will be fairly close to the required dive angle as you head toward the target, as well as keeping the initial pipper placement where you want it.

What with all the thrashing around in an effort to fake out the guys shooting at you, there's a fair-to-middlin' chance that the delivery parameters may be a little off after the roll-in. As soon as the bird is established in its dive, the GIB calls out the altitude and dive angle to the pilot. The latter piece of information lets the front-seater know if the dive angle has to be corrected, and the former gives him an idea of how much altitude he has left before the drop in which to make the correction.

You might think that since the GIB cannot see the target once the dive is established, due to the ejection seat in the front cockpit and other aircraft structure, he would have very little to do. But, as in just about every other phase of operating the F-4, the back-seater's role is of equal importance to that of the pilot. A smoothly coordinated team effort here can mean the difference between a successful mission and a flop. While going down the chute, the GIB calls information to the pilot as to how well the delivery parameters are being met, and—most important—when to hit the pickle button. He does this by talking continuously to the pilot, feeding him vital information as to how things are going. This allows the front-seater to keep his eye on the target instead of both the instrument panel *and* the target. The conversation during a typical high angle dive bombing run may sound like this:

"Eleven thousand feet . . . dive angle a little steep . . . ten thousand . . . airspeed looks good . . . angle's good . . . eight thousand . . . ready . . . pickle!"

Naturally, the pilot will try to correct for any variances from the desired attack conditions, however, this is usually limited to a quick, one-shot stab, because time is so short. From roll-in to pickle usually takes only about seven seconds, and the pilot's main concern on the attack run is to get the pipper where he wants it at the last critical instant. There is no time for a systematic analysis of all the variances to determine the proper corrections. It has to

Fig. 9-2. View through an F-4 gunsight during a 60-degree dive bombing run in Vietnam.

be an almost subconscious reaction to the information coming from the GIB while your main attention is centered on the target and the jinking that must be done.

Once the selected ordnance has been released, the pilot immediately starts the pullout by laying a minimum of four Gs on the bird. If you've got a good head of steam built up, or have dropped most of your load, a few more Gs on the pullout might be advisable if they don't cost you too much airspeed. The idea is to rotate the aircraft out of the dive and into a climb as quickly as possible so as to minimize your altitude loss and thus lessen your exposure time to small arms fire.

As soon as the pullout is started, the G-suit inflates instantly and with considerable force, especially the part around your middle. It feels like you're being hit and tackled from all sides at once. As the G forces get up around six, the vision starts to dim, and both crewmembers must tense their muscles and strain while hunching over a little in the cockpit. This is known as the M-1 maneuver, and helps delay the grayout by keeping the blood in the head area. A combination of the M-1 maneuver and the G-suit is absolutely essential for dive-bombing hostile targets, since a bad grayout or momentary blackout at this critical juncture of the flight could ruin your whole day. Vision, and the awareness of the need

118

to keep the airplane moving constantly in this situation, are the key elements of survival.

Since the aircraft has been traveling in a relatively straight line for the last few instants before the drop, the pilot must jink on the pullout so as not to give the bad guys too easy a shot. The G-loading on the bird is quite high at this time, therefore, the jink here must be done by using the rudder rather than the ailerons. This technique allows the aircraft to be maneuvered quickly, and avoids setting up conditions that might introduce adverse yaw.

The pullout also brings to light another factor that accents the GIB as a full-fledged member of the team. While working a target, it is the front-seater who actually flies the bird, since only he has a clear view of the target and access to the necessary armament system controls. However, after calling "Pickle," it is not uncommon to feel the GIB on the stick in the back seat, gently starting the pullout action. Often there are times when the pilot wants to press a little below the pickle altitude in order to correct a delivery variance. This is normally a last-second decision, and more often than not, the pilot will not interrupt the GIB's calls to let him know that they will be pressing. Getting on the stick after the pickle call is the GIB's way of letting the pilot know that the press has gone too far, and that he, too, has a vested interest in getting the bird out of harm's way. Although this seems to be a violation of the "pilot in command" rule, it is not abused by the GIBs, and thus is tolerated. It also serves to keep some of the hot rocks honest, who, in their eagerness to "shack" the target, may press to the point where the chances of a safe recovery become marginal.

Once the nose of the bird is definitely in a climb, and the jink has been completed, the next two most important things to be aware of are to maintain your speed and keep a turn going. With the aircraft at a relatively low altitude, there is a decided tendency to try to climb the airplane as rapidly as possible, particularly until you are above 4,500 feet, the effective range of small arms fire. However, climbing too steeply at the outset will cause too rapid a bleed-off of airspeed. This in turn will make you an easier target, as well as fouling up the spacing in the bombing pattern. In all probability, you will have to resort to stroking the burner momentarily to keep things going as programmed.

Once established in the climbing turn back up to orbit altitude, the position of the FAC and your wingman must be determined at once. The FAC's location is the first order of business, since he is at or very near your altitude at this time. Often, he will be fairly close to the target in order to assess the effect of your bombs and make any corrections necessary. After the FAC has been eyeballed, the wingman is located and the pilot starts playing his turn so as to arrive at orbit altitude in the proper position with respect to the wingman and the target.

Maintaining the proper spacing in the bombing pattern is quite important for a number of reasons. Ideally, in a two-ship flight, as the first bird comes off the target and starts his climb, the other bird should be coming up on the roll-in point. If random roll-ins are being used, the second aircraft may have to wait for the first to clear the target before starting down the chute. One of the best reasons for this timing of bomb runs is to keep the defenders' heads down. If the troops are dug in when the first bombs hit, the idea is to have another bird rolling in before their ears stop ringing and they completely regain their senses and start to shoot. Seeing another F-4 roaring down on you, ready to drop a half-dozen 500-pounders, certainly discourages one from trying to be a hero by getting a few shots off. Here, the short time between runs is better spent digging your hole a little deeper. Another reason for keeping the spacing up to snuff is that the FAC may need a few seconds for the smoke to clear from the first run to see if a correction of the mark must be made.

During the climb to orbit, another job that must be done is to reaccomplish the armament checklist. This is particularly important if bombs are being dropped singly, or a different type of weapon is to be used on the next pass. In the first case, the chief concern is to ensure that the proper stations are selected so that ordnance is released from alternate sides of the aircraft on each succeeding run. As mentioned above, this procedure keeps the bird pretty well in balance and enhances its controllability in maneuvering flight. If another kind of weapon is to be dropped next—say, going from 2,000 pounders to 500-pounders—the pilot must make sure that the station carrying these bombs is activated. Here, a change of the mil setting would also be called for. Normally, if any switch action has to be made on the armament system between runs, the armament master switch is placed in the "Safe" position. This is a safety precaution to prevent an accidental release caused by a transient electrical pulse that may be generated when a switch is moved. In nearly all cases, it is usually best to run down the entire armament checklist to be doubly sure that everything is set up properly for the next pass.

As stated earlier, the FAC will often recheck the target and adjust the aim point for the next bird on the target. This call would be on the order of: "Number two, aim 30 meters short of lead's bombs." If the target is large and the FAC wants another part of it hit, he may even hold out the next bird until a new mark is put in.

When attacking a target from random directions, most jocks had a technique for keeping each other and the FAC advised of their position when starting the roll-in. The safety implications for the aircrews involved are obvious; however, another factor in the offense-defense equation established important ground rules for these calls. It was not uncommon for the bad guys manning the guns to have a radio on which they could monitor the pilot's conversations with other aircraft on the mission. These radios were either captured U.S. equipment or sets provided by the North Vietnamese for just this purpose. Someone fluent in English would listen in on the mission frequency and pass on to the gunners any information about our plan of attack. If a pilot called, "Rolling in from the north," or "Comin' in from the river side," the gun crew would be so advised and have the weapon swung around to the right direction, and be ready and waiting for the bird to come into range.

To avoid using references to commonly known directions, or prominent landmarks, aircrews normally used one of the following two ploys. Since clearance from the FAC was needed for the pass, using his bird for reference was a common technique. For example, the fighter would call the FAC: "Rolling in from your ten o'clock high." This would let the FAC know immediately where the fighter was, and also force the gunners into first locating the FAC, and then the attacking aircraft. Hopefully, by the time all this took place, it would be too late for them to solve their sighting problem.

Another method was to use cities in the United States as reference points. In this system, the target was always at Kansas City—that is, in the central U.S. However, this was never mentioned on the air, and the only calls the pilots would make referenced large cities elsewhere in the country. The relationship between these cities and Kansas City would indicate the direction from which the fighter was coming. Thus, "Rolling in from Chicago," or "Number one in from Philly," meant that these birds were approaching the target from the north and the east, respectively. It was our constant hope that the gunners lacked sufficient knowledge of American geography for these calls to do them much good. Of course, the major fallacy with this system was working with someone who had a mistaken impression of the importance of his hometown in the grand scheme of things. "Rolling in from Pumpkin Center" really wasn't too helpful to the other jocks working the target.

One cardinal rule that should always be observed when dive-bombing a hostile area is that no one makes any reference to their last pass on the target. Calling the FAC to tell him "This next pass will be our last," or "We'll be dropping everything on the next run," only gives the bad guys behind the guns some valuable information. A last pass usually means that the fighters have to leave the target area because of no more bombs and/or a low fuel state. This gives the gunners pretty much of a free ride, since they know you won't be coming back to work them over if they reveal their position by firing at your bird. A lapse of radio discipline that gives the gunners a clue that your next run will be the last will almost guarantee a good hosing down as you pass over the target.

However, once a bird has expended all its ordnance, is off target, and has climbed above the range of small arms fire, the pilot lets the FAC know his status by calling: "Number one-Winchester." This informs the FAC that as soon as number two is off target, he can move in for a close look at the results of the strike. Unless fuel is a problem, the flight leader will maintain a climbing turn in the general area of the target until the second man has finished his run and has joined up in close formation. Once this joinup occurs, the birds will roll out on a vector for home plate, and continue their climb to recovery altitude. This will usually be about 30,000 or 35,000 feet, depending on fuel and the distance to the home drome.

The reason for joining up in close formation is that a battle damage check must be made as soon as practical after coming off the target. If either bird took any hits that can be seen, the flight lead must know this immediately so that plans can be made for recovery at a closer base, if one is available. Should the damage be more serious and fuel, oil, or hydraulic fluid is leaking from the bird, the wisest move is to head for the coastline right away in case things turn to worms and a bailout becomes imminent.

The battle damage check is started by the wingman maintaining close formation but flying a little high so that the entire upper surface of the leader's airplane is visible. Both crewmembers in the number two aircraft look over the leader's bird carefully for any signs of damage and/or leaks. The wingman then moves straight down to look over the sides of the bird, then underneath and up the other side. If everything is okay, number two takes the lead position while the same inspection is performed on him by the flight leader. Once the checks are complete, both aircraft resume their original positions and continue the climb toward home base.

By this time, the FAC has had a chance to look over the target and determine just what effect the bombs had. He then calls the Bomb Damage Assessment (BDA) report to the flight leader, who must copy it down for the intelligence debriefing after the mission. BDA reports can also come from a ground commander, if friendlies are close to the target. Many times he is in a better position than the FAC to observe the effects of the strike. The report usually begins with the GEOREF coordinates of the strike, time on and off target, and the amount of the target destroyed or damaged. Examples of this last item would be 30 meters of bunkers destroyed; five hootches destroyed, three damaged; or two trucks knocked out. If the FAC cannot report actual figures such as these due to defensive fire or foliage, he may give the percentage of bombs within a certain radius of the target, such as 70 percent within 30 meters of the target and 30 percent within 50 meters. Naturally, these numbers are guesstimates by the FAC, but after directing a few missions, they become quite adept at "calling 'em like they see 'em."

Also given in the BDA report are the number of sustained fires or secondary explosions observed by the FAC. A secondary explosion is one that occurs as a result of an exploding bomb, such as would happen if you hit an ammunition cache.

Most of the time it was fairly difficult if not impossible for the FAC to give any report on how many troops were killed. A man's relatively small size, camouflage, and thick vegetation usually prevented getting an accurate body count from the air. If our ground troops moved into the area within a few days of the mission, they normally called back a factual report of the damage and included the number of troops Killed By Air (KBA). If the enemy was caught in a fairly clear area and were napalmed, some of the more macabre FACs referred to the KBAs as "crispy critters."

A Mission Example

The foregoing descriptions of how things were "supposed" to go on the mission, with respect to target briefings, checklists and required calls, did not always pan out strictly according to the book. In fact, the mission that went exactly as planned with no problems or changes was somewhat of a rarity. The following dialog serves to illustrate that point; however, it also shows that a lot of talk between the cockpits is usually eliminated when crewmembers fly with one another frequently. The conversations are taken from a tape recording made in the lead aircraft by means of a homemade adapter plug that tapped into the aircraft's radio and intercom system. The recording was the result of many tries by this crew to produce a tape that was suitable for mixed and young company. All too often, mission problems and excitement resulted in a more salty exchange between the participants than is transcribed below.

This mission was flown out of Phu Cat on April 14, 1971, with a takeoff time of 2:10 in the afternoon. The target was a truck park hidden in a wooded area next to a road. The general location of this target was 30 nautical miles west of Hue, in hilly terrain. The call signs of the two fighters are Cobra 43 (lead), and Cobra 44 (wingman), although as is the usual practice, Cobra 44 only uses his flight position number, which is "two." Cobra 43 also follows this practice and refers to himself as "lead" or "one," as does the FAC.

When 43 flight arrives at the rendezvous, the FAC is working another flight of F-4s out of Danang with the call sign of "Gunfighter." Because 43 flight was a little short of fuel, the FAC allowed the Gunfighters only one more pass so that he could put us to work quickly. The time covered by the tape amounts to about 15 to 18 minutes, of which only 10 were spent actually working the target. With the exception of the GIB reading back the BDA, all conversations between him and the pilot were on intercom. The pilot's calls to the FAC and to the wingman were radio transmissions.

It also should be understood that what is recorded below is just the conversations of the principles involved. The actual tape contains many, many other transmissions interlaced with those listed below. These include the FAC's instructions to the Gunfighter flight, calls on Guard Channel (which is always monitored in addition to the working frequency) about SAM activity at a certain location, notifications about "hot areas" due to artillery fire (also on Guard), and the usual grunting and puffing to counter the G forces during pullouts and jinking. The radio was alive with transmissions just about everywhere in Vietnam because of the heavy air traffic involved, and each crewmember had to be on his toes to pick out those that pertained to his flight.

As the mission progresses, there seems to be some uncertainty as to where the FAC wanted each load of bombs. This was not the result of confusion on the FAC's part, but stemmed from his efforts to move the impact points around so that the entire area of the target would be hit. Because of the smoke and dust from each bomb explosion, he often cannot see clearly where the next run should hit until the pilot is actually rolling in. This time compression only allows a very few seconds on both sides to make last-minute changes or corrections. The F-4 crews who flew this mission were: Major Frank O'Brien (pilot) and Major Paul Neihaus (GIB) in Cobra 43, and Captain Tony Gill (pilot) and Captain Bill Faust (GIB) in Cobra 44.

Pilot: "Bilk one three, this is Cobra four three." (*No answer, since the FAC was busy marking the target for another flight.*)

GIB: "We're right here in the SAM area, so I'm going to pay a lot of attention to that RHAW gear."

Pilot: "Roger. Bilk one three, this is Cobra four three."

FAC: "Cobra four three, Bilk one three roger."

Pilot: "We've got about five minutes of play time, if you'll get our FAC for us." (*Bilk 13 was not originally scheduled to be our FAC, but took over the mission because the other FAC was busy working a target.*)

FAC: "Okay, roger, come up on the two six zero radial for thirty—hold high and dry and I'll run you in after this last pass." (*Gunfighter flight was still working the target.*)

Pilot: "Two six zero?"

FAC: "Roger."

Pilot: "Four three at rendezvous, Bilk."

FAC: "Cobra four three, understand you're at the rendezvous?"

Pilot: "Roger—over rendezvous at this time."

FAC: "Cobra four three, Bilk one three—like to give you target briefing."

Pilot: "Ready to copy."

FAC: "Your target is a truck park—we've worked it over south but were unable to hit the exact spot, and we'd like to put you in on it too—elevation two thousand feet—uh—did you discuss run-in heading—understand you're going to run in south to north with a left hand pull—altimeter two nine nine two—terrain is high all around, going to five thousand feet to the—six thousand feet to east and forty-five hundred feet to west—bailout area zero six zero-feet wet—emergency airfield Channel seventy-seven Danang—friendlies are not a factor for this target—I'd like your ordnance—uh—like your lineup—over."

Pilot: "Roger, we've got twenty-four Mark eighty-twos with selectable fuses." (*500-pound conventional bombs.*)

FAC: "Okay—twenty-four Mark eighty-twos—uh—make 'em drop four at a time—that'll give you four passes and instantaneous (*refers to fuse setting*)—and I'd like to know your mission number."

Pilot: "Roger. Mission number five seven zero four, and we'd like to drop three at a time."

FAC: "Understand—three at a time—that'll give you four passes— five seven zero four, and I'm in a left hand turn in the target area, right in the area surrounded by an overcast and broken layer."

Pilot: "Roger—rock left."

FAC: "Understand you want me to rock—I'm rocking right, and back to left—and be advised I think I'm losing my UHF—I cannot hear you very well—over."

Pilot: "Roger—we have a tally on you, and we're ready to go to work any time—and understand target elevation two thousand feet, friendlies not a factor—and we don't have any particular preference on run-in—what would you recommend?"

FAC: "Run-in—like to run in south to north—that's going to give you a tailwind—I'd estimate about fifteen knots of tailwind, and uh—give you a left pull—over."

Pilot: "Roger—south to north with left pull."

FAC: "That's affirmative—I'll put my mark in."

GIB: "That'll be eight thousand indicated (*pickle point*), and you can take his wind with a grain of salt—it's forecast to be out of the east."

Pilot: "Yeah."

GIB: "He gave us the west, so you might as well split it the first time."

Pilot: "Okay—we'll put it right on the target then (*pipper placement*)—how about that?"

GIB: "Well, no—split it between the south and the east, which will be—"

Pilot: "Oh yeah—four o'clock to the target."

FAC: "Okay Cobra four three—lead—you can hit my smoke."

GIB: "Okay, it's at nine o'clock on the other side of the road" (*location of the target marking smoke*).

Pilot: "Roger—we have a tally on the smoke."

FAC: "Roger—hit my smoke."

Pilot: "Roger—and one is in."

FAC: "Roger one—you're in sight—cleared hot."

GIB: "South to north with a left pull—roger that—and we're thirteen thousand—coming up on ten—a little shallow—nine—ready—pickle!"

FAC: "I've got three away, one." (*He confirms the release of three bombs.*)

#2: "Two base."

FAC: "Okay two—lead hit short—if you still have my smoke, you can hit the origin of it—over."

#2: "Rog—I'm in—am I clear?"

FAC: "You're cleared hot—that's affirmative—you're cleared hot two."

GIB: "That's not too shabby—we need to be a little longer—maybe there was no wind from the south after all." (*Looking back and commenting on our hits as we climb out from target.*)

Pilot: "Yeah—we'll aim right for the target or just east from it." (*Discussing pipper placement for the next run.*)

GIB: "You got a good fix on where his smoke was?"

Pilot: "Yeah."

FAC: "Okay—you were long by about one hundred and fifty meters two—lead—I want you to hit between your bombs and two's—the smoke from your bombs has obliterated the target—I want you to hit southeast of the road—over."

Pilot: "Roger—and one is in."

FAC: "Roger one—you are cleared hot."

GIB: "Maybe up beyond that little bend just beyond the smoke." (*Discussing aiming point.*)

Pilot: "Yeah."

GIB: "We're comin' up on eleven—pretty good dive—we're at ten—nine—ready—pickle!"

Pilot: "Pretty good airspeed on that."

FAC: "One—I've got three away—okay—that's getting in there real close now—I'd like two—hit ten o'clock—thirty meters in the

128

general area where these three bombs hit, and smoke has obliterated the target—over—you're cleared hot."

#2: "Rog—say again exactly where you want it."

FAC: "Ten o'clock—thirty meters—just to the southeast of the road."

#2: "Rog—understand."

GIB: "I don't know where he wants them—ten o'clock is—"

#2: "Number two is in—am I cleared?"

FAC: "You're cleared hot."

GIB: "Long and to the left or to the left and a little long." (*Commenting on two's hits.*)

#2: "Two's off."

FAC: "Roger two."

Pilot: "Where do you want 'em from there, Bilk?"

FAC: "Make it four o'clock."

Pilot: "Four o'clock—one's in."

FAC: "I want it across the road—just across the road—over."

Pilot: "Roger."

FAC: "In fact, you can try to hit the road or the right side of it."

Pilot: "Roger."

FAC: "You're cleared hot."

Pilot: "Roger."

GIB: "Ten—nine—ready—pickle!"

Pilot: "I don't think they were too swingin'." (*Commenting on release.*)

FAC: "That's real good—uh—who's the next one in—over?"

#2: "Rog—two will be in."

FAC: "Okay two—from lead's hits—make it right down the road toward you—six—uh—make it six o'clock, thirty meters—that leads us right in there."

#2: "Roger—I'm in—am I cleared?"

FAC: "You're cleared hot."

GIB: "Last pass coming up."

Pilot: "Roger that—Where do you want 'em from there, Bilk, one is in?"

FAC: "Roger one—I want 'em across the road, four o'clock, fifty meters."

Pilot: "Four o'clock, fifty meters—one is in."

GIB: "We must have a bit of an east wind—ten thousand feet—a little bit shallow—nine—nine thousand—ready—pickle!"

FAC: "I've got three away—that's beautiful!—right in there!"

#2: "I've got lead's bombs—want me to hit 'em?"

FAC: "No—I want you to hit just a little bit short—let's work back—six o'clock about thirty meters, and you're cleared hot."

Pilot: "We're deselected and we've got sixty-four hundred over seventy-two hundred." (*Telling GIB that the armament stations are turned off and the pounds of fuel on board.*)

#2: "Two's in."

FAC: "You're cleared hot."

Pilot: "Do you have Tony?" (*Asking GIB for #2's position.*)

GIB: "Yeah—he's diving now—on final—pulling off."

FAC: "I've got three away."

Pilot: "Got 'im—Lead is Winchester now, Bilk."

FAC: "Understand—lead and two—you're both dry of bombs—is that affirmative?"

Pilot: "One is dry."

FAC: "Roger—one is dry—two, say your status."

#2: "Rog—I'm dry."

Pilot: "We're ten o'clock to you, Tony." (*Letting wingman know lead's position to expedite joinup.*)

FAC: "I'm kind of hurting for fuel here, so I'm not going to use any strafe passes—I haven't seen anybody shooting back at us— I'm going to BDA the area—stand by two minutes for your BDA."

Pilot: "Roger—we don't have any pistols."

FAC: "Roger."

Pilot: "Have you got us, Tony?"

#2: "Neg."

Pilot: "Keep your turn comin'—we should be ten o'clock high— now nine o'clock high."

#2: "Tally!"

GIB: "I don't see any truck park down there."

Pilot: "Is that what it was?"

GIB: "Yeah."

Pilot: "I've got to get a fuel check here."

GIB: "Okay."

Pilot: "Four three, fuel check—lead has sixty-four over sixty-nine."

#2: "Two has sixty-one over seventy-three."

FAC: "Cobra flight—this is Bilk one three with your BDA."

Pilot: "Ready to copy."

FAC: "You hit target coordinates Yankee Delta three three five zero five four—you were on target at three zero—off at four zero—one hundred percent of ordnance in target area—you had seventy-five percent of your ordnance within forty meters—negative duds—and we had eighty percent destroyed—you're working for the First Brigade of the Hundred and First—over."

GIB: "Roger—copy Yankee Delta three three five zero five four—on at three zero—off at four zero—one hundred percent in target—seventy-five percent within forty meters—negative duds—eighty percent of the target destroyed—workin' for the First Brigade, Hundred and First Airborne."

FAC: "That's affirmative—it's been a pleasure workin' with you—and I'm going to head on home myself—over."

Pilot: "See you another day, Bilk—thank you."

FAC: "Okay."

GIB: "Okay—one five zero." (*Heading back to Phu Cat.*)

Pilot: "One five zero?"

GIB: "Yeah."

Pilot: "We're heading one five zero now two."

#2: "Rog."

Pilot: "I guess button eleven would be appropriate." (*UHF channel change to "Panama's" frequency.*)

GIB: "Oh—yeah."

Fighter pilots, like everyone else, occasionally have a bad day when nothing goes right, including dive-bombing. At times like these you can't seem to hit the floor with your hat, and the mission results may be best summed up by: "All bombs hit the ground." It is probably a bit frustrating for a FAC to locate a target and work through small arms fire to mark it, only to have a couple of "turkeys for the day" come in and scatter bombs all over the landscape. Since professional pilots are highly competitive by nature, regardless of the type airplane they are flying, anyone who is having "one of those days" can expect a few more or less blunt comments from his fellow aviators.

After one such mission where both aircraft had dropped some less-than-respectable bombs, we were taken down a peg or two by some choice remarks by the FAC. He had finished his BDA report (what little there was), and thought we had changed to an enroute frequency. He then called another FAC in the area and said for all the world—and us—to hear: "Did you ever see such lousy bombing? I couldn't believe it! These guys were some of the worst I've seen!" And on, and on, and on.

After sitting there while these coals of ignominy were justifiably heaped on our heads, the flight lead called the FAC in an effort to rebut his cutting remarks. Lead was a senior officer who was not used to such caustic criticism, especially from a junior birdman. However, he realized the weakness of our case in light of the deplorable BDA, and wisely said: "Lets discuss it over the land line after we get back."

Of course the FAC didn't know the rank or position of anyone in the flight, and probably couldn't have cared less, since reprisals would be difficult if not impossible to inflict. The anonymity of the combat situation leaves only the results to be judged, and if they are found wanting, the man is taken to task by his peers. We deserved everything we got.

The reverse of the coin also occurs, when it is the FAC who is the goat. He can't pinpoint the target, his marks are wide, or the general handling of the mission is confused. Here again, he may have to take a few verbal lumps from the fighter jocks, but in the main, occurrences such as those described here were not too common. They would take place only if the mission really turned into a bucket of worms as a result of someone obviously not performing up to par. Certain givens that adversely affect a mission, such as low ceilings, poor visibility, or heavy ground fire are taken into account, and the blame for less-than-optimum results under these conditions is laid at no one's door in particular.

Don't get the idea from the above that only negative comments are passed between the aircrews working a target. There are those days when everything you touch is golden, and you slide right into the groove after some shifty jinking and pickle right on the money. The FAC's marks are true and he really has his act together in handling the flight. Fortunately, there are more of these days than bad ones, and it gives everyone involved a sense of professional pride to perform well what you have trained so long to do.

When things are going right, the FAC often becomes very expressive in his descriptions of the results of each run. It's like having a cheering section of your own on the sidelines. Also, after the "Winchester" call, the flight lead will normally give the FAC an "Attaboy" for a job well done. These plaudits, however, are not given lightly. Pilots are a professional group, and expect a high level of performance from every member of that group. Mediocrity, like second place, counts for little as they judge their own performance and that of others. To earn an accolade from a fellow pilot, one's job must be done in a near-outstanding manner.

As soon as the battle damage check has been completed, the leader will usually move the flight into spread formation for the trip back home. The pucker factor starts to ease off, and conversation again becomes animated. A switch is made to the appropriate GCI frequency, and the pair checks in for flight following to the recovery fix.

The usual traffic advisories are once more provided during the return trip. Upon arrival at the fix, the birds are cleared over to approach control by GCI. However, the leader switches them momentarily to a frequency monitored by the 12th TFW Command Post. Pausing here, they call in the status of each aircraft so that plans can be made for turnaround or maintenance action as required. Then it's over to approach control's channel, where each bird is given vectors for an individual letdown and handoff to GCA. A precision approach under their control completes the mission.

Again, the reason for no formation penetration to the field is to deny the bad guys an easy shot at two aircraft close together. If the weather was good enough for a VFR letdown to the field, this method was usually chosen since it was quicker and allowed less low-altitude exposure to ground fire. Also, most fighter pilots prefer an overhead traffic pattern to a GCA anytime.

Battle Damage Emergencies

If, however, the battle damage check on the climbout from the target revealed a problem—or a suspected problem—with either aircraft, the recovery procedures were decidedly different. The undamaged bird would usually fly a loose wing on the one with problems, so that the latter could concentrate fully on keeping things glued together as much as possible.

As previously mentioned, the flight would immediately take up a heading for the best bailout area, or "feet wet," and try to gain as much altitude as possible. A call was made to GCI to inform them of the emergency, and if bailout was imminent, to alert the SAR forces. If it came to pass that the crew and the aircraft had to part company, the other bird would circle the bailout point as long as fuel permitted. This would provide the SAR forces a definite fix on which to home and enable them to begin operations sooner. If the mission bird began to run low on fuel and had to recover, alert aircraft would be scrambled to take its place.

In the event that the damage was not too severe and the airplane could be flown, the flight would head for the coastline. The situation would be discussed between both aircraft and the best course of action decided upon. If the crew in the hurt bird felt that it could not be landed safely, they would proceed to a controlled bailout area over open water and eject. Pickup from these areas normally took only a very short time, since they were located relatively close to the shore and near a major rescue unit.

Should the aircraft be controllable to the point where the crew felt that a landing could be made, this would naturally be the most desirable route to follow. Once the decision was made to try for a landing, the GCI site would give a snap vector to the base designated by the pilot of the bird with the emergency. Conflicting traffic would be cleared from the area immediately, and when the flight got fairly close to the field, an enroute descent to a straight-in approach was commenced.

During the letdown and GCA, the other aircraft in the flight would fly wing on the one with the problems. By doing so, he would be readily available to visually check anything that needed checking. For example, if the emergency bird had lost its electrical system and hydraulics, it would be reassuring to have someone confirm that the gear had been blown down completely by the compressed air backup system.

Whenever an F-4 was damaged by flak and was going to attempt a landing, there was one procedure that applied in just about every case. The best way to land such a bird and get it stopped quickly, with minimum risk to the crew and the airplane, was by an approach end engagement. This was a technique that resembled an arrested landing on a carrier, and contained the emergency aircraft to a relatively small area where the firefighting and rescue equipment could be concentrated. Just about every military airfield that handles jet aircraft has arresting cables, more commonly known as "barriers," installed as standard equipment. These are heavy wire cables about 1 1/4 inches in diameter stretched across either end of the runway about a thousand feet from the threshold. The cable was raised approximately four inches above the surface of the runway by rubber disks positioned along the cable every fifteen feet or so. Both ends of the cable were attached to one of several devices designed to progressively increase the retarding force as more and more cable was payed out during an engagement.

By the mid-1960s, just about all Air Force fighters had tail hooks of one variety or another, similar to those used on Navy aircraft. Initially, these hooks were intended to catch the barrier at the far end of the runway. This was to prevent an airplane that had landed hot and long, or one that had lost its brakes, from going off the runway at the end of its landing roll. However, bringing in a bird with a blown tire or a partially extended gear would scatter wreckage over the entire length of the runway, and most certainly result in the total destruction of or extensive damage to the aircraft.

Stopping the airplane as quickly as possible was the solution to this problem, and catching the barrier at the approach end of the runway was the way to do it. Setting up for an approach end engagement began about ten miles out on a long, straight-in, final approach. The emergency bird would be in the lead with his wingman flying a loose position off to one side. Gear and flaps would be lowered farther out than on a normal GCA, just in case there were problems in getting "down and locked" indications in the cockpit. If there were problems, the gear could be cycled again without aborting the pass. Also, the birds would be high enough at this time in case the flak damage resulted in a split flap condition. This is where the flaps extended fully on one side but not on the other. The aircraft is not controllable enough to land under these circumstances, and if the one flap can't be retracted, the procedure is to climb to a safe altitude and eject.

Once the gear and flaps are down and look good to the wingman, the hook is lowered and checked for a "full down" position. From this point on, the bird is flown—or rather aimed—at the center of the runway just beyond the threshold. "Aiming" is a better description here, because in the Navy-style approach that will be used, the bird will hit the runway exactly where you line of sight over the nose intersects the runway. The ideal touchdown point is about 300 to 500 feet short of the barrier. This is preferable to trying to plunk it on the runway right *at* the threshold, since it provides a little cushion in case you underestimate things and drop it in a little short.

The approach should be flown with the angle of attack indicator pegged at 19 units, which is the optimum for any gross weight condition. Utilizing this standard Navy technique for carrier landings does not leave a wide margin for error. At 19 units the airplane is only a few knots above the stall, but this slower speed on final permits an accurate placement of the touchdown point and results in less energy to dissipate on the rollout. Throttle rather than elevator is the primary method of altitude control during this kind of approach. The pitch angle remains constant, and power is added or reduced to increase or decrease altitude in order to maintain the proper glideslope.

Once you're in the groove on this approach, everything must be held constant until the main gear hits. This is especially true of power, which cannot be reduced as the aircraft is flared in an attempt to "grease it on." If the throttles are reduced before touchdown, the bird will drop out from under you, and will most likely hit short.

Once the main gear impacts the runway (and impact it does!), the stick goes forward and the throttles are chopped to idle. This is to get the nosewheel on the ground before the hook picks up the barrier. If the cable were engaged with the nosewheel still in the air, it would be slammed on the runway with enough force to possibly break it off. A firm but controlled letdown to the runway is more desirable—and a lot safer.

If the airplane is a little off centerline at touchdown, it should be steered for the middle of the barrier. However, brakes should not be used for directional control at this time. Hard braking at this speed would probably blow a tire, and the possibility then exists that the wheel and brake discs will cut the cable as they go over it. One quick stab with the rudder is all the steering you have time for, because you're in the barrier in what seems like an instant after touchdown.

Once the hook grabs the wire, deceleration is fast and positive, with the bird coming to a full stop in only 1,200 feet. Just about every time an airplane takes the barrier, no attempt is made to taxi it after bringing it to a stop. Rather, it is shut down on the spot, its gear-down lock pins are installed, and it is towed back to the flight line.

All of this may seem like duck soup to the Navy jocks who do this sort of thing for a living every day. However, it was not the normal routine for Air Force pilots, and an approach end engagement was considered an emergency procedure that demanded care, planning, and deliberateness in its execution.

Every once in a while during a bombing mission, be it a high-angle, level, or low-angle delivery, a malfunction occurs that results in a hung bomb. This is where the bomb does not release, or only partially releases from the mounting shackle. The latter case is more serious, since the bomb is hanging on by only one lug, and is usually cocked at an angle into the airstream. There is no way of knowing in the cockpit just how secure the bomb is, or if vibration will work the shackles open and it will fall off unexpectedly—and on whom? If it *does* work loose, there is the added danger of it striking the aircraft, or other bombs, because of its skewed position.

The standard procedure for dealing with a hung bomb was to stay clear of any friendlies on the ground and have GCI vector you to the nearest jettison area. There the normal release circuitry would be tried a few times to see if you could get it to come off. If nothing happened, the same procedure was tried while putting a few Gs on the aircraft. Should the bomb still stay with the bird, it was assumed secure enough to attempt a landing, rather than jettison the suspension gear and the bomb.

As you might guess, landing with a hung bomb was treated a little differently from the normal routine traffic pattern. Excess fuel was burned off to reduce weight, and a long, straight-in approach was set up. The whole idea was to get the aircraft as light on the controls as possible and fly a power-on, controlled approach to a very soft touchdown. The name of the game here was to meet the runway "with a gentle kiss," and avoid dropping it in or any other banging around, that might jar the bomb loose. If this should occur, you had a definitely hairy situation with a 500-pound bomb skidding along the runway underneath the airplane at roughly the same speed.

If everything is in good shape after touchdown, the nosewheel is lowered carefully to the runway, and braking action is smooth and easy, again to prevent any jostling of the bomb.

Whenever a mission was cancelled entirely and the bombs had to be brought home, landing techniques again became critically important. Once more, fuel was burned down to reduce the landing weight, and a straight-in approach was planned. The best procedure was to fly a Navy-style approach at 19 units angle of attack. This resulted in the slowest practical speed on final, which in turn gave the shortest landing rollout. A soft touchdown was recommended to ease the strain on the tires, and the drag chute should be deployed immediately after hitting the deck. Smooth, steady braking was the proper method for trying to slow the beast down, which seemed like it wanted to roll forever.

If a drag chute failure occurred when landing with unexpended ordnance, it was a very good bet that you would have to take the barrier at the far end of the runway to keep the bird on the concrete. A wet runway—particularly one with standing water—compounded all of the above problems associated with heavy weight landings. Extreme care had to be exercised on the approach, touchdown, and rollout to ensure that everything was right on the money, and that nothing was done to induce the "free skating" tendency described in Chapter 2.

Dive Toss

Up to this point we have been discussing the events on a typical high-angle dive-bombing mission utilizing visual sighting and release. On the average, this method produced a CEP of about 250 feet in a combat situation. The large amount of jinking and the very short target tracking time were the main reasons for a figure this large.

However, the F-4 did have a system that produced highly accurate results when it functioned properly. This was the Dive Toss mode of the weapons delivery system, which used both visual and airborne radar information to achieve the exact release parameters. Hitting the precise altitude, dive angle, airspeed, and pipper placement is the biggest problem in a manual delivery, especially when you have to keep the airplane moving around. Dive Toss neatly solves most of this problem by using the radar and the computer to calculate the correct release point.

Airborne radar sets have scopes that display a vertical trace moving from side to side, known as the jizzle band. This trace "paints" the targets on the screen as it follows the radar antenna back and forth. Across the bottom of the scope the jizzle band will paint a solid area of ground return, which is the reflection of the radar beam from the ground just below the aircraft. The top of this ground return is a measure of the altitude of the airplane above the ground, and is the key to a successful dive toss delivery. The action on a typical pass using this method picks up as the roll-in on target is commenced.

Everything up to this point is the same as any other high-angle mission, with two exceptions: Dive Toss rather than Direct is selected as the delivery mode, and the pattern altitude is a couple of thousand feet higher than for a manual release. The increased altitude allows the GIB time to work the radar, and also keeps the bird farther away from the defending guns. As soon as the dive on the target is established, the GIB must quickly lock the radar on the top of the ground return line, which is now moving down the scope as the airplane gets closer to the ground.

Once a solid lock-on is obtained, the pilot puts the pipper directly on the target, presses and holds the pickle button, and starts an immediate, wings-level recovery from the dive. The computer now knows the position of the target in relation to the aircraft, the range, as well as the speed, dive angle and altitude of the bird. A release point is calculated instantly, and the signal is automatically sent to the ejector mechanism at the proper time during the pullout.

The greatest advantage of the Dive Toss method is its high degree of accuracy. If the pipper placement is correct, and the radar maintains a steady lock-on, you're just about guaranteed a "shack" on every pass. The higher orbit altitude and dive recovery altitude were added pluses. Much less jinking was required, and you stayed well clear of small arms fire throughout the pass.

With all this going for it, the obvious question is: "Why wasn't this technique used all the time?" To be successful, Dive Toss required two things: a fast and sharp GIB, and a good radar system. The first was usually not the problem, because with a little practice, just about any GIB could consistently hack the quick and solid lock-on that this method required. A properly tuned radar that included a stable tracking system was the key ingredient. The lock-on must stay right on the altitude line and not wander, as was the usual case when a lot of ground clutter was present on the scope. Breaking lock, or jumping lock to another, more prominent return, would abort the pass unless the GIB was really on his toes and could re-establish the lock-on quickly. Time became a limiting factor, not only because the bird was screaming toward the ground at 760 feet per second, but the long, straight dive made an inviting and easily trackable target for enemy gunners. Jinking down the chute while the GIB was trying for a relock made this an almost impossible task.

Another factor that resulted in the radars not being tuned to peak efficiency was that they were not used enough. Hardly any mission required the use of this system, and although it was turned on, it was not exercised thoroughly. Therefore, many malfunctions went unnoticed and thus did not get written up for maintenance action. And, since radar was not a mission-essential item, it was better to carry the write-ups and keep the bird in commission. This way the Wing would not come up short of airplanes to meet a heavy frag. If things got slow, then one or two aircraft with the more serious discrepancies could be pulled off the line and worked on.

Another big reason why Dive Toss did not get used more often is that either both aircraft in the flight had to employ this technique, or neither should. The rationale behind this is the confusion created by having two aircraft rolling in on the target from two very different altitudes. Achieving the proper spacing and timing under these conditions would be more trouble than it was worth.

LZ Prep

One variety of high-angle bombing that was a fairly common mission at Phu Cat was the LZ Prep. As mentioned earlier, this type of sortie was specifically designed to clear the trees and vegetation from a small area of jungle so that helicopters could land. These were always fragged missions whose purpose was to support a move by the Army into some new territory, or to establish a position of advantage in response to a move by the enemy. Once the ground was cleared, choppers would bring in men, equipment, and artillery pieces to set up a fire base and/or observation post.

The terrain selected for these missions was usually the classic "high ground" so favored by field commanders. The tops of small hills, a prominent bluff, or a ridgeline overlooking the area in contest were the most common examples. It might seem a bit extravagant to tie up a minimum of two fighters and a FAC simply to blow away some trees. However, if the Army thought that this particular piece of real estate was vital to their operations, airpower was the way to give it to them quickly—and with no loss of life. The alternative of cutting your way through the jungle, most likely fighting the VC along the way, makes an LZ Prep the only way to go. Actually, to use any method *other* than an LZ Prep to secure such a vantage point would be penny-wise and pound-foolish. Along with providing a quick, effective response to changing battlefield conditions, it nets a saving in a commander's two most precious resources—time and lives. Also, once the strike is over, the site is usable almost immediately.

This mission was the only one during the '70-'71 period that utilized 2,000-pound bombs. In order to carry these giants, the entire loading configuration of the F-4 had to be changed. The 370-gallon drop tanks attached to each outboard station on the wings were removed, and in their place was hung a 2,000-pounder. Each inboard station carried three 500-pound bombs, resulting in a grand total of 7,000 pounds of armament, all equipped with fuse extenders. The six-position bomb rack (MER) normally installed on the centerline station of the bird was taken off and replaced with a 600-gallon fuel tank. All this added up to a gross takeoff weight of 54,500 pounds, which, in the hot climate of Southeast Asia, resulted in a takeoff roll that seemed to last forever.

Once over the target, the delivery procedures were the same as for any high-angle bombing mission. Both 2,000-pounders were dropped on the first pass, and the bird seemed to have new life and maneuverability when all this weight and drag were gone. The six remaining bombs were released on the second run.

Two of these big bombs hitting at once created a striking phenomenon on days when the humidity was high, which was most of the time. The detonation of this large amount of explosives created a shock wave that raced outward from the impact point and was made visible by the high moisture content of the air. This, coupled with a great cloud of smoke and debris, made a scene reminiscent of the atomic tests in the Nevada desert. All in all, it was quite an impressive blast.

Since the objective of these missions was to clear out an area, the pinpoint accuracy required for smaller targets such as vehicles or bunkers was not needed. However, the idea was still to hit the FAC's mark, since he knew just where the grunts wanted their area cleared out.

The biggest difference between an LZ Prep and any other type of mission was the hung bomb problem. If one of the 2,000-pounders didn't let go, a *very* critical situation was created as far as aircraft controllability was concerned. This was particularly true if a jink was started into the heavy wing just after hitting the pickle button. The asymmetrical load and drag would have a marked tendency to roll the bird inverted during the pullout—definitely *not* the place for upside-down flying! An aircraft in this configuration required some very deft handling to remain controllable and going in the direction you wanted. The best remedy in this situation, if handling became a problem, was to hit the emergency jettison button, which cleaned everything off the bird immediately.

Overall, the LZ Prep was an effective mission since it allowed the Army to capitalize on tactical situations that would have otherwise been lost.

Night Dive-Bombing

Probably the hairiest mission of all those using high-angle delivery techniques was night bombing under flares. On these sorties, both aircraft had three flares mounted on one wing station instead of bombs. The rest of the load consisted of nine 500-pound slicks. The rendezvous with the FAC was the same as a daytime mission in that the fighters flew to a TACAN fix and set up an orbit at that point. Since the FAC would be flying blacked out, there would be no identification procedure like that used during daylight hours. On night missions he would be the only one down there, since all the other traffic usually seen around a target were strictly daytime operators.

Once contact was made with the FAC, he would proceed with the usual target briefing. However, there had to be quite a bit added to this briefing to describe the exact location of the target. At night, smoke rockets were not used to mark the target. Instead, the FACs dropped a device called a "log," which burned for quite a while with a fairly bright flame. These were very similar to commercial fireplace logs made of wax and wood shavings, except that they were fitted with an igniter to light them before impact. From the air, these burning logs looked like a pinpoint of light in an otherwise completely black landscape.

The FAC would get you into the general area by the TACAN fix, and would have two or three of these logs already burning on the ground. He would describe where they were, and (after a lot of heavy eyeballing by the crews) they were usually located without too much difficulty. Once the fighters were orbiting these references, he would describe where he wanted the bombs in relation to them. If things got too involved, he might even drop another log to clear up some of the confusion. Needless to say, with this method of locating the objective, these missions were only flown against targets that were fairly large, such as base camps or bunker complexes.

After both fighters had a definite picture of where the target was, one of the birds would descend to bombing pattern altitude. The other would set himself up at a higher altitude for a straight run across the target area to drop the flare. An important consideration here would be the winds between the flare ship and the ground. The proper wind corrections had to be made to ensure that the flare stayed roughly over the target while it burned.

The armament checklists were completed, and when everybody was ready, the flare ship called that he was heading inbound for the drop. This would alert the wingman, who was circling the target at a lower altitude, also blacked out, to get ready for his run. The flare was dropped strictly by a visual guesstimate of when you were over the target with the proper wind correction cranked in. This was done by repeatedly rolling the aircraft on its side so that you could look straight down to see just how close to the target you were. After the drop, the flare ship would set up a racetrack pattern so as to be ready to release additional flares if they were required, while the other bird worked the target.

The flares used on these missions were called Briteye, and were ignited a few seconds after release by a timer mechanism. The lightoff of a Briteye made it seem like a minor sun had suddenly blossomed in the night. These flares produced 5,000,000 candlepower of light and burned for about five minutes. This resulted in an illumination 20 times stronger than moonlight over the target area. The slow rate of descent that allowed the long burning time was achieved by the deployment of a hot air balloon, 19 feet in diameter, to support the flare. The hot gases produced by the burning pyrotechnic kept this balloon inflated.

The bird scheduled to hit the target first would be in his orbit and all ready to go when the flare went off. The main concern of the crew was to keep the target location definitely in sight at all times, and fine-tune their orbit to ensure the proper dive angle on roll-in. Keeping a visual fix on the target could be a little difficult, especially if the FAC wanted the bombs some distance away from the burning log. The whole idea was to start down the chute the instant the flare ignited so that you would be on and off target before the defenders had time to react. Random roll-ins were always used on these missions, and once the dive angle was established, normal high-angle bombing procedures were used from that point on.

After the pickle, the plan was to try to get the bird back up to pattern altitude as quickly as possible so that another pass could be made while the flare was still burning. However, if this didn't work out, or the FAC wanted another spot hit, the flare ship would set up for a second drop.

After the first aircraft was "Winchester," the two birds would switch positions and the whole process would be repeated. Usually, the second guy on target had an easier time of it because—hopefully—there were now some fires and smoke around the target from the first bombs. This made sighting a lot less difficult—unless, of course, the FAC moved you to another location.

Night bombing under Briteyes did present some problems that added to the pucker factor and the headaches associated with this mission. Probably the most aggravating was the aforementioned difficulty in getting an accurate fix on just where the FAC wanted the bombs. If other flights had worked the area earlier that night, there might be many logs and/or small fires burning in the general vicinity of the target. This required the FAC to have quite an imagination to describe the various patterns formed by these lights so that we had a mutual frame of reference. Not helping matters was the fact that the FAC had most likely worked the earlier missions and was quite familiar with all the logs and sustained fires still burning on the ground. From his lower vantage point he could distinguish which was which, but from our altitude, they all looked the same—just pinpoints of light.

After quite a bit of circling, conversation, and staring, the location of the target would finally be figured out, and we would go to work. By this time everyone's eyes had become pretty well night-adapted, with irises wide open to gather the maximum amount of light. At the moment of flare ignition, you could almost hear your irises click shut, so bright was the glare in contrast to the inky blackness of a tropical night—so much for your night vision for just about the remainder of the flight. This meant that a good bit of the flying on these missions was done with a heavy reliance on instruments, including the dive-bombing, jinking, and climb back to orbit.

The total impression produced by the flare light also caused another condition that did not help in the acquisition of visual references. This was known as the "fishbowl effect," and once your aircraft entered the sphere of usable light created by the flare, its illusionary influence became quite pronounced. Your whole world immediately became the globe of light you were diving through.

Everything took on the hazy shade of gray produced by the light from the flare, including the sky. There was no up, nor down, nor sideways. In order to keep from being disoriented by this visual misconception, the pilot had to keep his eyes riveted on the speck of light on the ground that designated the target. As soon as the bombs were pickled, it was back on the gauges for the pullout and climb to pattern altitude.

Along with the fishbowl effect, another sensation came into play as you went through the flare light. This was the realization that the same light that was illuminating your target also made *you* stand out like a sore thumb. Once the flare was lit, the gunners knew roughly where you were coming from, and that you would be in the light for the entire run. In your imagination you could almost see the gun crew pointing up at you and shouting to each other: "*There* he is! *There* he is!"

Another thing in the defenders' favor was that we generally worked at lower altitudes on night missions. This helped in identifying the various fires and lights used by the FAC to locate the target. However, it also resulted in bottoming out of the dive at a lower altitude, which put us in small arms range for a longer time. Another reason for working a little lower was that it allowed us to get in two passes during the five minutes the flare was burning.

When both birds had finished their runs, a joinup was accomplished and the climb toward home plate was started. The battle damage check was not done at night unless one of the aircraft had a problem that needed checking. The airplane's running lights gave off far too little light to detect holes produced by small arms fire.

J Runs

Once in a great while, FACs or the intelligence people would come up with targets that were mainly people. Although the guerrillas did not do it often, since it violated one of their basic principles, occasionally a mass movement or concentration of troops would be necessary to meet existing conditions. Because the VC normally operated in small, highly mobile units that could be dispersed quickly, any grouping of even company size was considered quite a lucrative target.

If such were the case, CBUs were called for. CBU stands for Cluster Bomb Unit, and was the official designation of the radar-fused clamshell container bomb described in Chapter 6. If the troops involved were fairly accessible—that is, they were not in bunkers or similar fortified positions—these munitions were quite effective.

As mentioned before, they are delivered by high-angle bombing techniques, and, since the target is usually spread out, and given the large impact area of the bomblets, precise accuracy is not essential.

This valuable a target usually meant that a considerable amount of flak could be expected. These factors, and the radar fusing used with the canister bomb, made a higher release altitude not only possible, but preferable. This was because these types of bombs could be released higher than general purpose bombs and still be effective. At the same time they permitted the bird to stay well above small arms range, even on the pullout.

If the troops on the ground were caught before they had time to dig in or take cover in prepared shelters, an attack with these munitions could be devastating. Since each aircraft dropped two canisters on every run, a large area could be saturated with these bomblets in a very short time. If other flights were attacking with napalm and high-drags, the consequences would be disastrous for the troops in the target area. Being exposed to this type of situation must be a completely unnerving experience—*if* you live through it. Even if you aren't hit by fragments, napalm, or pellets, the noise factor alone is crushingly overpowering. The jets by themselves scream down on the target area and seem to generate a solid wall of earsplitting sound just by their passing. Add to this the shattering detonation of a half-dozen 500-pounders and the roar of igniting napalm and you have a cacophony that is numbing and immobilizing in its own right—and any move to escape only exposes the individual to the withering hail of bomb fragments and pellets.

If a locality was to be used by the bad guys in the near future, or if the powers that be wished to deny its use to the enemy, a J run would be fragged to seed the area. As mentioned before, J missions were considered fairly hazardous because of the long, straight, and level delivery requirements of the weapons used. (The dispenser and the delay-fused munitions employed on these sorties were also described in Chapter 6.) Once ejected from the dispenser, the individual bomblets would be separated from their packets by the airstream and tumbling, and then fall free to the ground. Again, the sheer number of these weapons dropped on any given sortie would render a large area impassable to all except those in some sort of armored vehicle. It must have really watered the eyes of the guerrilla who was fortunate enough to find a foxhole during the attack, only to have one of these babies roll into his hole and just lay there, waiting to be disturbed in the slightest, which would cause instant detonation.

Self FAC Missions

On very infrequent occasions, missions would come up on the frag that did not have a FAC assigned to work with the fighters. These were designated "Self FAC" missions, which meant that the flight leader had the responsibility for identifying the target and controlling the strike. Targets selected for Self FAC sorties had two things in common: They were identifiable because of prominent landmarks, and there were no friendlies anywhere in the area. High-angle delivery methods were usually employed, and the weapons carried were normally 500-pound slicks and/or CBUs.

As mentioned in Chapter 7, aerial photographs were available for study during the mission briefing. These were sharp, clear pictures with an X or a circle inked in where they wanted the bombs dropped. Careful measurements were taken from the maps and photos to pinpoint just how far the target was from the bend in the river, the prominent ridgeline, or the road intersection. In the briefing room, the geography in the target area seemed so distinctive and easily recognizable that everyone left feeling that they could spot this place in the dead of night from 40,000 feet. Sketches and notes were made on the mission data cards; however, no one thought they would really be necessary because the target would stand out in conspicuous relief from its surroundings. Wrong! When you reached the TACAN fix over the target, the whole world below looked exactly the same—a carpet of green, devoid of anything resembling the maps and pictures back in the briefing room.

You circle a little lower, hoping that this will allow you to pick up a clue. Wrong again! The river with the prominent bend has either dried up or is overgrown with trees. The distinctive ridgeline looks like a million others, and what looked like roads on the map are little more than oxcart trails made indistinguishable by foliage and repeated bombings. Conversation is fast and thick between cockpits and between airplanes in an attempt to positively identify at least *one* feature. In many cases dusk is settling in, and the once-sharp landmarks become soft and diffuse in the fading light. Partial cloud cover obscures the target just when you think you've recognized something. And, in all cases, the fuel gauge moves relentlessly downward, telling you loudly and clearly that a decision must be made—and *soon*. Another orbit or so just to take the rough edges off your uncertainty, and then it's arm 'em up and go on in!

Because of all these problems, Self FAC missions were not too effective. Target identification was really difficult since you were seeing something for the first time and trying to pick out a distinguishing feature from what seemed like an ocean of sameness. No time was available for a lengthy study of the area, nor did fuel permit going down on the deck for a closer look.

Again, since these were usually large area targets, pinpoint accuracy was not a criterion. Since there were only bad guys down there, a bomb anywhere in the area could only do good work. Although not all Self FAC missions went as badly as described above, there was one benefit realized by everybody who flew one: It sure made you appreciate the FAC, and just how much easier things were by virtue of his knowledge of the terrain and his marking the target.

Low-Angle Bombing

Up till now we've talked almost exclusively about those missions that utilized high-angle bombing techniques. There were, however, a great number of sorties flown against targets that required the greater accuracy and/or the type of weapons delivered by low-angle methods. There was a standard load carried by all aircraft at Phu Cat flying this type of mission: six 500-pound high-drags and three cans of napalm. The only exception to this was the

Fig. 9-3. Standard load for low-angle bombing missions—three cans of napalm on the centerline rack and three 500-pound high-drags on each inboard pylon.

number one bird on alert, who carried a pistol and four fire bombs. The official nickname of the 500-pound bomb in the high-drag configuration was the Snakeye I. Consequently, low-angle missions were commonly referred to as "Snake and Nape."

The procedures used on these sorties were exactly the same as for high-angle bombing up to the point of the orbit over the target. Just before the FAC was ready to put the flight to work, they would spiral down to orbit altitude, which was 2,000 feet above target elevation. This height above the target would result in a dive angle of about 15 degrees from the horizontal.

This method of attack had some definite advantages and disadvantages. First of all, you were a lot closer to the target, and this made it easier to judge distances for corrections to the FAC's mark, or for winds. And the shorter time of flight of the bombs resulted in smaller offsets to counter the effect of the wind. These factors added up to a more accurate placement of the weapons on the target by low-angle bombing methods. This was particularly true of napalm, since its tumbling trajectory did not lend itself to exact predictions on a long drop.

There was, however, a price to pay for the accuracy made possible by this technique. The one of greatest concern was the increased exposure to ground fire. Even at orbit altitude, you were well within the range of everything the enemy had that could shoot. And since you were coming in at a flatter angle, it was much easier for the gunners to track their target and pull the proper lead. A lot of jocks resorted to higher attack speeds in an effort to swing the odds back in our favor. This in turn decreased the time available to track the target after rolling out from the last jink, just before hitting the pickle button. In this situation, pipper placement had to be just about perfect on the rollout because there was no time for any sizable corrections. Another disadvantage of low-angle bombing was the chance of ricochets and bomb fragment damage, as pointed out in Chapter 6.

The targets attacked by low-angle missions were mostly those that required the higher degree of accuracy possible. Examples of these would be a tank, a cave, a truck, or other such single objects, in contrast to a bunker complex or a truck park that might cover a considerable area. Probably the most common target for Snake and Nape was "troops in contact." This was a situation where the good guys would be pinned down in a firefight with the enemy, who were occupying positions of tactical advantage. If these positions had to be cleared, and if it looked like a ground assault would be too costly in time and lives, an air strike was called in.

Another consideration in selecting low-angle targets was the need for a relatively flat landscape in the area surrounding the objective. Karst formations and rugged mountainous terrain were more effectively attacked by high-angle bombing, which allowed more freedom to maneuver and still gave good results. The crews always hoped that, because of the higher risk from defensive fire, the frag shop at 7th AF considered the more lightly defended targets as candidates for low-angle missions. However, the bad news handed out at the intelligence briefing usually dispelled such ideas.

The fact that the fighter jocks "got no respect" from the guys in the frag shop was compounded by an even greater disdain shown them by the gods of war and weather. The collusion between these fickle and sometimes perverse deities was pointed out one day in the spring of 1971.

We were sitting alert as Cobra 01 and 02, which meant that we were configured with napalm, high-drags, and the gun, as described earlier in Chapter 3. Late in the afternoon the horn went off for our flight, and as we taxied out, our scramble instructions stated that the target was "troops in contact."

Such a mission usually caused the adrenaline to flow a little faster, since it meant that we would be working very close to friendlies who were hurting to get the bad guys off their backs. TIC also conjured up some unpleasant thoughts of restricted run-in headings, lots of small arms fire, and controlled pullouts as we came off the target.

The rendezvous with our FAC was 90 nautical miles northwest of Tan Son Nhut, and the weather on the way out to the fix did not look too bad. It was a fairly typical late afternoon in Vietnam—scattered variable broken fair weather cumulus and the usual haze at the lower levels. The mission went smoothly as we met and identified our FAC and received our target briefing. As expected, we were required to bomb on a given heading, and we could expect hostile fire from just about anywhere in the target area.

The one thing that made this mission a little dicey was that the friendlies were located very near the enemy positions, which meant that we had to stick to the run-in heading quite closely. It also necessitated breaking off the target in the same direction after each pass so as not to overfly the good guys with live ordnance.

As we let down to working altitude and took our spacing, another problem became apparent: The clouds over the target had become more broken than scattered, and a layer started to develop at and below pattern altitude. Just as soon as the enemy realized that an air strike was in progress, they pulled their favorite defensive tactic and moved in tightly around the friendly positions—*so* close, in fact, that the commander of the good guys started to voice his concern to the FAC. Quite a bit of discussion ensued as he tried to describe the orientation of his lines in relation to local geographic features. But since he and the FAC were viewing things from different perspectives, it took a while before the FAC had a pretty good idea where the troops were dug in. The ground commander, however, was still not entirely convinced, and, as a last stratagem, he decided to set off some colored smoke grenades to pinpoint his position.

The FAC agreed to this and positioned himself for his marking run while we armed things up and got ready to roll in as soon as we were cleared. The fighters had not heard any of the descriptions concerning the friendly lines because the people on the ground and the FAC utilized a different frequency (which was the normal procedure). Also, the descriptions would not have helped us too much, since at bombing pattern altitude we were popping in and out of clouds and did not have a clear view of the target area for more than a few seconds at a time.

As soon as the green smoke started to appear from the underbrush, the FAC acknowledged having an eyeball on it, and started his run. However, almost at the same time, green smoke appeared from a couple of other spots that did not correspond with the ground commander's previous briefing of where he was—more confusion on an already extended mission, with the fighters rapidly getting close to Bingo fuel. This latter problem was due to the fairly lengthy amount of time it had taken to get a positive identification on the exact target area. What had happened was that the enemy had been monitoring all the FAC's calls to us as he tried to keep the strike force abreast of what was going on. And they were sharp enough to know that setting off smoke grenades of their own might confuse the issue long enough so that the fighters would have to pull out for lack of fuel.

However, the FAC proved to be a lot sharper than the bad guys, because from the verbal description the ground commander had given him, he had a pretty good idea of just where the friendly positions were before the smoke appeared. Therefore, he discounted the smoke coming from locations that did not correlate with this picture, and put his marking rocket in the middle of the area defined by the bogus smoke grenades.

In situations such as this, where the friendlies were very close to the target area, it was standard procedure for the FAC to require each fighter to call a visual on the mark before he would be cleared to drop. Normally, this is no problem, because as you circle the target at pattern altitude, you can see the mark go in and receive any corrections necessary from the FAC. But such was not the case on this particular mission because a low deck of clouds had moved in over the target and extended back toward the base leg of our bombing pattern. This reduced clear area meant that we could start our run, but the target would not be visible until we were well into the final approach to the target and very close to the pickle point.

This allowed precious little time to find the mark, call it to the FAC, get his clearance, and then make the final sighting corrections before the drop point was reached. Fuel was getting to be a problem by this time, and if we didn't get rid of our ordnance, it would probably mean we would have to recover at a base closer than Phu Cat.

We eased down a little from the pattern altitude while turning base in hopes that we might get a glimpse of the mark, but still couldn't see a thing because of the cloud deck and the haze. As the run-in heading came up, I racked the bird into a hard left turn, rolled out short of the attack heading, and paused for just an instant; then a hard jink to the left, followed by another back to the right while the GIB was calling out our altitudes down to the pickle.

Finally, with only a thousand feet to go, the mark came into view and the FAC got an eyeball on us. He quickly acknowledged my visual call and cleared us hot. There was only time for one quick adjustment of the sight picture when the GIB called "Pickle!" As soon as we felt the cans of napalm go, I laid 4 or 5 Gs on the bird as we jinked up and to the left away from the target. It was only a few seconds until we had punched through the cloud deck and set up our downwind for another run.

Number two was just rolling in, but even with two cans of napalm burning on the ground, he still had the same problem we did in acquiring the target. Also, the FAC wanted the impact point moved slightly to ensure complete coverage of the target area. Nevertheless, he put his weapons right on the money, and as soon as he pulled off the target, the FAC was giving us instructions on where he wanted the next run placed.

Our second pass was a duplicate of the first—a hard roll-in, jinks, late target acquisition and clearance, with barely enough time to stabilize the sight picture before the drop. The FAC said we had put the nape right where he wanted it, and cleared us for one final pass with the pistol to strafe the entire area covered by the napalm.

By this time we knew when to expect a visual on the target, so we dropped even lower on base to get a slightly longer run since, because of fuel, this was definitely our last pass. Going down to a lower altitude meant that a few more jinks had to be thrown in on the way down the chute. The FAC called his visual on our bird and cleared us hot with a reminder to keep all the rounds in the napalmed area. By the time we rolled out of our last jink, the pipper was just approaching the edge of the target area, so I stopped the bird in a wings-level attitude and squeezed the trigger.

The Gatling gun roared into action, and I started to yaw the aircraft slightly from side to side by easing in a little rudder, first on one side and then the other. We gave the bad guys a full three-second burst before the pullout altitude was reached, and the high-explosive incendiaries and armor-piercing incendiaries swept across the target area like a buzz saw.

After the run, I pulled up hard with another jink to keep the defending gunners honest, and the GIB got an eyeball on our wingman as soon as we broke out on top of the lower deck of clouds. Considering the distance we had to travel back to Phu Cat, we made an enroute joinup and battle damage check rather than the usual climbing orbit over the target.

As we were looking each other over for holes, leaks, or other evidence of taking a hit, the FAC called to relay the ground commander's thanks, and his report that we had put the bombs just where he wanted them. He also observed a secondary explosion after one of our passes, which was probably the ammunition the enemy was planning to use against the friendlies.

As we cruised back to Phu Cat at 30 grand, the adrenaline flow started to ebb, and we had a chance to review the last 20 minutes or so in a little more detached perspective. Despite the lousy weather and the restrictions imposed by a clever enemy, we had done the job and done it well. That small bunch of grunts who were pinned down by the bad guys could now move out and get on with the rest of their mission.

It was a good feeling!

The different techniques required for delivering Snake and Nape start to show up after the fighters are in orbit around the target. Because of the lower altitude, a lot more jinking is done, and a higher pattern airspeed is used. The latter was needed not only to fool the gunners, but also to keep you closer to delivery airspeed, since the bird does not accelerate as rapidly in a shallow dive. The armament checklist is accomplished the same as before, and once again clearance from the FAC is required before any ordnance can be dropped on any run. Since friendlies are usually a factor, the chances of having a restricted run-in heading are much greater on this type of mission.

The same techniques as used in high-angle deliveries apply here for leading the desired attack heading on the roll-in, and jinking on the rollout. Flying this close to the ground, which you visualize as just crawling with people trying to shoot you down, lends an air of reality and urgency to your defensive maneuvering. Unlike at higher altitude, where the threat seems a little more remote, being down where you're practically eyeball-to-eyeball with the gunners definitely increases the pucker factor and makes everyone a real believer in jinking—and lots of it.

The GIB makes the same calls going down the chute as he does for high-angle bombing, and the same corrective actions apply if you are off in any of the release parameters. However, it is a little easier to track the target on a low-angle mission because of the shallow dive, but because you are closer to the target, things seem to happen just as fast.

After the pickle, it is *de rigueur* to rack the bird over in a hard jink, and then immediately reverse it in the other direction as you climb back up to orbit altitude. Once again, the presence of friendlies might force the FAC to restrict the turn off target to a single direction, thus more or less limiting any fancy jinking you might have in mind. The reasons for this are sound, albeit unpopular with the aircrews. The idea is to avoid overflying friendly positions with a load of bombs on a bird that is all armed up. An inadvertent release, caused by any number of reasons, could be disastrous for the grunts. The climbing turn back to orbit must be played as before to maintain the proper spacing and to keep the FAC in sight.

Low-angle missions usually go a lot quicker than other types because of the higher airspeeds and the shorter time required to get back up to orbit and around the pattern.

Strafing

Strafing runs are a variety of the Snake and Nape mission that utilize exactly the same procedures as described above. If you are shooting at a point target such as a truck or a cave, the pickle altitude is where the trigger is squeezed. Naturally, the pipper must be kept on the target as long as the trigger is depressed.

If, however, the target is an area that must be hosed down to keep the bad guys honest, no sighting techniques are needed. As soon as you roll out of the jink on the attack heading, the trigger is depressed and held for a maximum burst of three seconds. (This time limit is imposed to reduce damage to the gun barrels caused by overheating.) The correct procedure for area targets is to yaw the aircraft gently back and forth while the trigger is squeezed. This, and the high rate of fire produced by the Gatling gun, combine to create a scythe effect that sweeps across the target. A veritable shower of armor-piercing and high-explosive projectiles ravages the entire area, making a shambles of all except moderately armored equipment. Such a totality of destruction also discourages any would-be heros from standing up to take a shot at the attacking bird.

As you might guess, this kind of attack is very effective against troops unless they are quite well dug in. Adequate fortifications might protect the individual, but he cannot be spared the terror of being strafed repeatedly by an F-4 with a pistol.

The devastating nature of this weapon was vividly demonstrated one afternoon while on a scramble mission from alert. The target was a rocket launching site that was being readied by the Viet Cong for an attack against the airbase at Phan Rang. Probably to facilitate the launching of the rockets, the spot was unique for Vietnam in that it was an area relatively clear of trees and vegetation on the top of a small hill.

The Nape and Snake went well, and after our last pass, the FAC asked the flight leader if he had any "twenty mike mike," which was the code name for 20mm ammunition. You could almost hear the leader grin as he answered: "Roger that! Am I cleared in hot?"

We held high, orbiting the target, as the FAC cleared lead for as many passes as he wanted. As he rolled out on the attack heading and started to fire, the effect was awesome, to say the least. Instantly the entire hilltop was bathed in destruction, a myriad of flashes as high-explosive shells raked the area, detonating as they hit. Not visible, except for the dirt and fragments they kicked up, were the armor-piercing rounds interspersed with the former.

All told, it was a spectacle that boggled the mind with its display of power and havoc. Needless to say, Phan Rang was not rocketed that night, or for a long time thereafter—at least not from *that* site.

Gunship Escort

The supplies necessary to sustain the activities of both the North Vietnamese regulars and the Viet Cong operating in South Vietnam were nearly all delivered by truck via the Ho Chi Minh Trail. By day this tortuous system of roads, trails, and stopover points was as quiet as a graveyard, because that's just what it would have become if the trucks dared to venture forth when they could be spotted and bombed. At night it was a beehive of activity, with truck convoys of every size and description heading south with needed supplies or going back north to get more. Trucks traveling in either direction were almost impossible to detect, since they operated exclusively at night and always drove just about completely blacked out.

Stopping this traffic was the job assigned to the "Stingers." This was a group of Fairchild C-119 cargo aircraft specially modified to work this mission. This modification converted these aircraft from cargo carriers into gunships, and was done by installing four 7.62mm GE miniguns and two 20mm cannons in the cargo bay with their muzzles pointing outward from the left side of the fuselage. These guns fired the same ammunition mix as did the F-4s, that is, high-explosive incendiary, and armor-piercing incendiary. (Tracers were not used because their telltale stream of fire would pinpoint the position of the gunship.) The combined rate of fire of all these guns was 36,000 rounds per minute. This was impressive indeed, and it really must have watered the eyes of the VC truck driver who got caught in this withering hail of steel and explosives.

The guns filled the bill as far as providing enough firepower to kill a truck instantly once it was spotted. However, *finding* a

Fig. 9-4. Fairchild C-119G, the type of aircraft used on "Stinger" missions, after being modified to carry the rapid fire guns. (courtesy National Air and Space Museum, Smithsonian Institution)

blacked-out truck moving under jungle cover on a dark, moonless night was still a problem. This was solved by a high-technology device called a Starlight Scope, which, through a combination of optics and electronics, allowed a visual search to be made of the ground under extreme low-light conditions. A crewmember on the gunship would lean out the window with his scope and scan the trails below until a truck was located. Target information would be taken from the Starlight Scope, run through a gunsight computer, and presented to the pilot in the form of aiming information.

Unlike other aircraft, the image of the gunsight reticle was projected on the side window of the pilot's compartment on the C-119. Once a target was located, the Stinger would go into an orbit around it while final sighting adjustments were made. When everything was ready, the pilot simply lined up the aiming information and pressed the gun button. In the truck, it must have seemed like the whole world had come to an end—which for the driver it did when all this firepower struck at once from out of nowhere. The intelligence reports, briefed each day before every mission, gave the number of trucks destroyed by the gunships the previous night, and the figures were truly astounding. For the truck-killing mission, the Stingers were very effective.

The procedures that the gunship followed were essentially those of visual reconnaissance, except that it was done at night. They flew along the main truck arteries of the Trail, with the scanner hanging out his window, eyeballing the landscape below through the Starlight Scope. Their route paralleled the Trail off to one side so that if a truck was discovered, the guns were already trained in its general direction.

The Stinger was completely blacked out except for a row of dim blue lights along the upper surface of the wing. This is where the fighters came in, since these lights were installed to enable the fighter escort to maintain a visual on the gunship. As might be expected, the VC did not sit idly by while the gunship turned their truck convoys into flaming junk night after night. A lot of 37mm guns were moved in along the Trail to even things out a little. Since these missions were only flown beneath a middle to high overcast, or on moonless nights, these gunners definitely had their work cut out for them. Unless they could silhouette the gunship against starlight or a bright spot in the clouds, they were pretty much aiming on sound. However, if the Stinger was spotted, it really took a hosing due to its lack of speed and maneuverability.

The fighter escort's job was to suppress any flak batteries at-

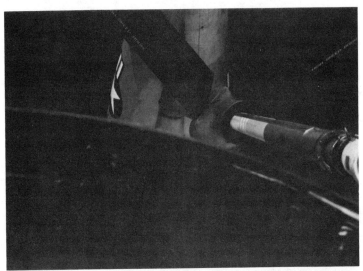

Fig. 9-5. Cockpit view of mid-air refueling from the back seat of an F-4. The refueling boom extending down from the tanker is just passing over the cockpit to the receptacle located immediately behind the back seat. At night, all that would be visible would be the dim outline of the tanker and a small purple light on the end of the boom.

tempting to down the gunship. This was done by maintaining a position off to one side and to the rear of the Stinger about 10,000 feet higher than his altitude, which put the escort at about 15,000 feet ASL. (However, most of the time a middle layer of clouds forced the fighters down to around 12 or 13 thousand feet in order to keep him in sight.) The escort position was fairly difficult to fly because the Stinger would be constantly twisting and turning in random directions to follow the trails, and your job was to stay to the rear and to the outside of his turns.

Not knowing which way he was going to go, and trying to weave just enough to make up for the difference in airspeed so that you could stay in position, caused an occasional wrong guess on the turns. He'd zig and you'd zag, and before you realized it, the Stinger was out of sight beneath the nose of your bird. About the time you rolled in 90 degrees of bank to look straight down, you'd pop into some ragged clouds hanging below the general ceilings. By the time you were in the clear, the Stinger had reversed his turn—and so it went. However, after a few steep turns and some anxious looking, you picked him up again and resumed your position to await his next whifferdill.

While on station, the fighter worked completely blacked out.

This did not create any problems because the gunship and its escort were the only two aircraft allowed in the sector being patrolled. All traffic in the theater was under positive radar control, and the GCI sites would vector any conflicting tracks around the area.

As mentioned earlier, every combat mission was flown in flights of at least two aircraft, and Stinger escort was no exception. But when the two birds approached the reconnaissance area, one would proceed to rendezvous with the gunship while the other would be vectored to a refueling track to meet the tanker. After a prearranged time, the latter aircraft would top off its tanks and head for the gunship to take over for the bird on station. Once over the designated TACAN fix, they would stay at altitude with all lights on and call the escort aircraft to let them know that they were relieved. The escort would then begin a climb to a different TACAN fix, and when above the other bird's altitude, would give them a call and clear them down to the escort position. Then they would head for the tanker to gas up and wait their turn to go back on station by repeating this procedure. GCI monitored these exchanges, but usually stayed out of the conversation unless they were asked to help.

Since flak suppression and people-killing were the name of the game, each bird on an escort mission carried four CBUs with radar fusing. If you did get a chance to work while on Stinger escort, two of these weapons were dropped on each pass.

The procedures that were followed on these missions were a little cumbersome; however, for safety reasons they had to be adhered to exactly. Since the gunship was between you and the bad guys, a bombing run could not be started until they were well clear of the target area. A typical mission where the escort got some action is as follows:

Once the bird was in position, the armament checklist was accomplished, except for the "Arm-Safe" switch. This was left in the "Safe" position until you were cleared in on the target by the gunship. While you were weaving around on what always seemed to be a totally black night, trying to keep an eye on the Stinger, a flak battery would hose off a clip or two at the gunship. Orange-colored tracers would suddenly start arcing upward, and then just as suddenly disappear.

This all happened in an instant, and it was the job of the crew in the fighter to get a visual fix on the position of the gun. This was a very difficult proposition for a number of reasons. First, you are looking down at a totally black landscape; there are no identifying features visible, no reflection of moon or starlight, and no ground lights to help orient you to the flak battery, not even in the distance. The darkness is complete, and obscures any and all clues as to the location of the target. Secondly, the lines etched in the night by the tracers do not start at the muzzle of the gun. The tracer part of the shell does not ignite until the round is a few thousand feet above the ground. This makes it necessary to form a mental picture of the tracer arcs in your mind's eye and then extrapolate these lines back down to where you *think* the ground is. This "simple" procedure should give you the position of the gun, which can then be related to some part of the aircraft structure, such as the leading edge of the wingtip, or the nose of the drop tank.

Such a precise fix on the target might have some value if you could roll in for a pass immediately, while all this is fresh in your mind. However, the gunship has to get out of your way, and because of his slow speed, this does take a few moments. This brings into play the third problem in establishing an accurate aiming point: You have moved considerably since the original sighting of the tracers, and are continuing to move. Naturally, an orbit around the estimated spot is set up right away; however, the longer you must wait before rolling in, the less positive you are of the target's location.

The gunship might be of some help in this situation, if he is still in the right position. If his scanner has a visual on the flak battery, they might fire a short burst in that general area to "sparkle" the target. This would occur when all the high-explosive incendiary shells hit the ground with a bright flash. However, expecting the Stinger to hang around for a shooting match with a 37mm gun is asking a little much.

Regardless of the help that the gunship can give, the fighter crew's job is to keep an eye on their best guess of where they think the target is located. During these few moments while you're circling, waiting for the Stinger to move off to one side, the GIB is an invaluable asset to the team. He can concentrate his attention on "the fix" while the front-seater arms up the weapons system and makes sure everything is ready for the drop.

Finally, after what seems like an eternity of waiting, filled with a million second guesses as to the exact location of the target, the gunship calls that he is clear. As soon as this confirmation is received, the fighter rolls in immediately. Achieving the exact bombing parameters in this situation is a little difficult, primarily because the dive angle will probably be shallow. This is usually due to where the escort position places you in relation to the gun when it starts firing. In order to keep a visual on the Stinger, you are normally a little too far out from the gun to roll into a 60-degree dive on the target.

The easiest way to keep track of the estimated target position is to maneuver the aircraft to put it on a wingtip, and then stabilize your bank to keep it there. Then, after the gunship is clear, your roll-in is simply a 90-degree diving turn. The rest of the bombing run follows the usual procedures.

Admittedly, when comparing this type of mission with the standard daytime bombing techniques, it all seems very imprecise. However, working on a good estimate is better than nothing, and the large dispersion pattern of the weapons helps to offset sighting inaccuracies. One pass is all that is made, because trying to relocate the target after climbing back to altitude would be all but impossible unless he opens up again.

Therefore, the next order of business is to find the gunship—which could be just about anywhere after all your gyrating around the sky. In order to save time and get on with the mission, the fighter usually asks the Stinger for a short count. The latter responds by counting from one to five and back again while the GIB uses the UHF/DF to get a magnetic bearing on the gunship. Once a visual is obtained, the fighter gets back into the escort position and the mission continues.

After being on station for a given length of time, the relief bird shows up and the exchange is accomplished as described above. Once clear of the reconnaissance area, the aircraft coming off escort would be vectored to the tanker by GCI. Normally they would bring you in on the shortest route, and then swing you in behind the tanker so you could approach it from a dead-astern position. The fighter then closes on the tanker slowly until a visual is obtained. They would then switch to the refueling frequency and follow the boom operator's instructions from that point on.

The resources devoted to a Stinger mission were considerable: two fighters, the gunship, a tanker, and all their aircrews, along with the required ground support. Given the inaccuracies of the bombing phase of the mission, the obvious question arises: "Was it worth all the effort?" Considering the probability of actually knocking out a large number of flak sites, the answer has to be "No." The areas worked by the Stingers were very sensitive to the guerrillas, and thus were occupied by a large number of troops. Therefore, getting our people in to follow up the attack, or to confirm the destruction of the flak batteries, was much too risky to be practical.

However, when the entire mission is viewed in the light of its objective—killing trucks—the answer to the above question is a resounding "Yes!" It is all conjecture, but the presence of fighters armed with antipersonnel weapons undoubtedly served as a deterrent to the defending gunners.

Because of the sighting problems affecting both the fighters and the gun battery, luck played a large role on each side. The likelihood of the gunners hitting anything when they were aiming mostly at shadows or sound was fairly small. Should they take a chance and hose off a few clips? The odds of the fighters actually dropping one in on them weren't too good, but then again, if the birds got lucky, it was curtains.

Based on the number of times the guns actually came up against the Stingers, the threat of taking a pounding from the fighters must have been effective. At least it kept the gunners honest to the point that if they didn't have a good clear shot at the gunship, they wouldn't risk giving away their position.

Radar Bombing

Another bombing technique used in Southeast Asia was high-altitude level delivery. This would normally conjure up visions of a sky black with B-17s and B-24s pushing their way eastward to pound *Festung Europa*. This was not the case, however, in Vietnam. Because of the small size of the target, such missions consisted of the usual flight of two; on certain occasions, a third airplane was added. The drop altitude on these sorties was normally between 20,000 and 25,000 feet, and they were just about always flown at night. They were also a good method of delivery during the monsoon season, when a target needed attention but was too clobbered-in with clouds to attack visually. Weather in the target area was not a mission factor, since all steering and aiming information was acquired electronically.

Normal procedures were followed up to either an initial point or a TACAN fix, after which some sort of precision guidance was used for the final attack heading. Once established on this vector, airspeeds, altitudes, and headings had to be flown exactly in order to meet the close tolerances needed by the computer to generate a release signal. The wingman's job on these missions was pretty much reduced to just flying good formation. He would keep it tucked in on the leader's wing and drop his bombs on command, or when he saw the leader's go.

Except for the usual thrills of flying night weather formation, these sorties were not too exciting. They did, however, provide a means of keeping the pressure on the enemy during conditions that would preclude the normal dive bombing methods.

Despite the precision steering required on these missions, the accuracy achieved was not as good as by visual methods. Consequently, only large area targets such as truck parks, base camps, or bunker complexes were hit by high-altitude level bombing. This method was also well-suited for interdiction sorties against the Boxes, again because of their large size. The bigger impact pattern of the bombs, coupled with the lesser degree of accuracy, dictated that no friendlies could be near targets attacked by this method. In almost every case, the standard load on these sorties was twelve 500-pound slicks, although on rare occasions "J" munitions would be used.

The first type of high-altitude level bombing we'll discuss was code named "Combat Sky Spot." On these missions the final attack steering was provided by high-precision ground-based radar. They knew the coordinates of the target and the direction to approach it that would optimize the bomb impact pattern. The controller would lock his radar on the bird making the run and let the computer solve the problem. Any variances from the ideal track would be given as readouts from the computer and appropriate corrections would be radioed to the aircrews. In many respects it was like flying a GCA, except that it was level and the directions were far more precise.

The takeoff and enroute procedures on a Combat Sky Spot were the same as for any other mission, with GCI vectoring the flight to the handoff point. Once in orbit over the fix, the ground site would be contacted, and from then on, all you did was follow their instructions. Only one bird at a time would be vectored down the attack heading, so after lead started his run, the wingman did another 360 to achieve the proper spacing.

The first thing to be done after rolling out on the desired vector was to go through the armament checklist, with the exception of the "Arm-Safe" switch. Steering instructions on the attack heading were very exacting, with commands like: "Increase airspeed two knots," "Down twenty-five feet," or "Left one degree" being fairly common. The F-4's navigation computer provided a true airspeed readout that worked like an odometer, making airspeed corrections fairly easy. However, altitude changes of less than 50 feet were just about anybody's guess, along with one degree and one-half degree heading changes. With directions like these as the normal order of business, it didn't take much more than thinking about it to achieve the desired correction.

As the release point was approached, you were instructed to accomplish final arming action, at which time the "Arm-Safe" switch was placed in the "Arm" position. Small corrections continued to come until the countdown to the drop started. As the count from ten to zero began, no more corrections were given, because by this time the bird should be right on the money. The entire load was dropped on the "Pickle" call, after which the aircraft was passed back to GCI control for recovery.

There were many reasons for aborting the run once the attack had started, and this was not an infrequent occurrence. The usual ones were: Loss of radar lock-on, computer malfunction, or (most commonly) the aircraft had drifted outside the release parameters. The latter would usually result in an abort late in the countdown, which meant that you had to go back to the initial point for another try. If things kept going haywire, the flight could get below Bingo fuel before getting their bombs off, which meant going into an alternate recovery base. If everything went right the first time, a Combat Sky Spot was an unusually short flight.

The area around Pleiku was frequently hit by this method, and often the number three and four birds on alert would be used for these missions. Since Pleiku was only about 60 miles from Phu Cat, the flight time on these sorties was normally less than an hour from takeoff to touchdown, and usually included at least one repeat run on the target. (One tiger, who must have been in afterburner to and from the area, had the record at 25 minutes.) Since there were no FACs used on Combat Sky Spot, nor were there any friendlies around the target, there was no BDA reported on these strikes.

Obviously, there were only so many areas where the sophisticated radar used for Sky Spot missions could be set up and adequately protected. This in turn limited the number of targets that could be hit by this method. In order to interdict areas that could not be covered by this radar because of enemy activity, the offset bombing capability of the F-4 was used. These sorties were called "Commando Nail," and a combination of the aircraft's inertial navigation system, radar, and computer were used to generate steering information and the bomb release signal.

This was pretty much an all-GIB mission, since the front-seater had little else to do but fly the aircraft according to the steering commands developed by the weapons release system, and hold the pickle button until the bombs were dropped by the computer. A lot of the GIB's work started before takeoff in the flight planning room. The selection of Commando Nail targets was based on the availability of some prominent landmark in the same general area as the objective. This would be a mountain peak that was much higher than the surrounding hills, or a coastline feature that stuck out like the proverbial sore thumb. These landmarks were picked not so much for their visual distinction as for their ability to be unmistakenly identified on the radar.

The GIB would then measure the distance either north or south and east or west from the landmark to the target. Thus, if a target was in a generally northwest direction from a particularly high peak, the distance from the peak directly west to a point south of the target would first be measured. Then the distance from the peak to a point directly east of the target would also be calculated. These distances would then be converted to feet for entry into the navigation computer.

The general approach heading to the target would be that which gave the best radar picture of the landmark being used. Photographs of how this feature of the land looks on a radar scope were also available for study. At this time, a TACAN fix would be selected that would put the aircraft in the best position to fly the selected inbound heading to the target.

After the bird is airborne and navigating toward the fix, the distances mentioned above are dialed into the computer, along with other bomb release data affecting the run. Upon reaching the TACAN fix and turning toward the target, the armament checklist is accomplished except for the Master Arm switch.

Now the GIB's work really begins as he radar-scans the area ahead to pick out the landmark on the scope. The set might have to be tuned a little to maximize the radar return of the landmark and identify it properly. Once he is satisfied he has the correct image on his scope, he locks the radar on it and the system then tracks this feature automatically. Now the computer knows the location of the landmark in relation to the aircraft, and also the location of the target.

The rest is just geometry. When the aircraft gets closer to the landmark, its radar return on the scope sharpens appreciably, and then the lock-on can be refined to the exact center of the image. This provides more accurate information to the computer, which will result in more accurate bombs.

With an updated lock-on and good, steady tracking of the landmark, the GIB switches the system to the bombing mode, and steering information is supplied to the target. The pilot merely flies the aircraft to maintain level flight and center the vertical needle on his attitude indicator. If a turn is required, he banks the airplane until the needle again centers on the instrument. As the on-course is approached, less bank will be required to keep the needle in the middle. Once the bird settles out on the desired attack heading, final arming action is accomplished, and the pickle button is depressed and held until the computer releases the bombs automatically at the correct spot.

The major problem associated with this type of bombing is the difficulty in tuning the radar to produce a sharp, identifiable image on which to lock the system. Fuzzy, ill-defined radar returns will cause inexact lock-ons, resulting in bad information being fed to the computer. In some cases, this type of return will also cause the lock-on to wander as strong adjacent returns come into view. This will also cause erroneous data to be entered into the bombing problem. In general, though, with carefully chosen landmarks, an average GIB could put the bomb load right where he wanted it by using this method.

Loran Bombing

A third technique for high-altitude level bombing utilized Loran as a guidance system. This mission was called "Pathfinder," and was one of the few occasions when another F-4 was added to the normal flight of two. This bird was a special version of the Phantom that was outfitted with Loran equipment. Utilizing this gear, the GIB in the Pathfinder could navigate to the intersection of two Loran lines of position that intersected over the target. Again, knowing the position of the target, the bombing computer could convert this information into the required steering and release data needed for this mission.

All of the Pathfinder birds were based in Thailand, therefore the two fighters out of Phu Cat had to meet the Loran aircraft at a TACAN fix designated in the frag. This rendezvous was normally accomplished quickly by a combination of GCI vectors and airborne intercept radar. Either of these methods would bring the flight in behind the Pathfinder, who would be in orbit at the TACAN fix. As soon as visual contact was made, the flight would split, and each aircraft would take a wing of the Pathfinder and fly close formation for the rest of the mission.

The GIB in the Loran bird, which was now leading the flight of three, took over control of the mission as they headed for the drop point. Periodically, he called out distances to the target just to keep everyone advised of what was going on. About 15 or 20 miles from the release point, he would call for the flight to "Arm 'em up!" Both wingmen would slide out just a tad, so that the pilots could make sure of the settings and switch selections for the armament check. After the "Arm-Safe" switch was in the "Arm" position, they would call "Armed Hot" and would move back into close formation.

About this time the lead GIB would start his countdown to the drop; on his command, all three birds would release their entire load. As soon as the bombs were away, the Pathfinder would take up a heading for his home base and the other two fighters would break off, reform as a flight, and head back toward Phu Cat.

Although most fighter jocks don't really enjoy night weather formation, these Loran birds were modified with a new development that made it almost easy. This was the installation of electroluminescent lighting panels on the fuselage, wingtips, and fin. These panels, which measured about 2 by 36 inches, were considered as a quantum leap in technology as far as night formation flying was concerned. When turned on they glowed with a soft green light, and their placement on the airframe seemed to give substance and dimension to the otherwise dark shadow you were flying wing on.

Heretofore, the only things you had to help you stay in position were the regular navigation and position lights on the wingtips and fuselage. As you moved in on someone's wing at night, these seemed to glare with the brilliance of a spotlight. If you were in the weather it was even worse, since they lit up the entire cloud with their glow. When the wingman thought he had a good visual on the leader's airplane, he would call and say: "Go dim." The flight leader would then switch his lights to the dim position, and usually the next words between the cockpits in the wingman's bird were: "Where'd he go?" It was fairly difficult to maintain a good wing position on a dark night, or when the two birds were muckering around in the clag. This was because your only frame of reference was to line up the wingtip light with another light on the fuselage. Such a drill put your depth perception to a real test in order to keep from sliding in too close to the leader.

Also, things do not improve after long periods in the weather, when the autokinetic phenomenon sets in. This is a visual illusion that occurs when you stare at a point source of light against a completely dark background. After a while the light appears to move even though you know it's stationary. While flying on the wing in thick clouds, you sometimes find that the fuselage light you are lining up on becomes quite obscured at times. Thus, you are forced to put a heavy reliance on the wingtip light as your only source of reference to maintain position—and you stared at it, and stared at it, and stared some more to make sure you didn't lose the one fix that kept you from falling off the wing. Even the steadiest of jocks can't prevent a little bobbling of the wingtip, and this only added to the problem when all the staring finally took its toll. The wingman would swear that the leader was doing slow rolls as he struggled to stay lined up with a pair of what he thought were wildly gyrating lights.

After doing this number a few times, it can be easily imagined what a Godsend the new lighting system on the Pathfinder was to all concerned. Gone were the problems of bright and dim, and gone were the problems of lights that didn't seem to remain still. Electroluminescent lighting made night formation flying almost as comfortable as flying wing during the day.

Smart Bombs

There was one other type of mission flown in Vietnam that was not high-altitude level bombing, nor was it full-fledged dive-bombing. This was a "smart bomb" mission. Because of the newness of the equipment required for this method and a scarcity of aircrews trained in this technique, smart bombs were used rather sparingly. None of the aircraft at Phu Cat were modified to drop these weapons, and the few that were used in the theater were normally based in Thailand.

During that period of time, smart bombs were considered high-technology items and were limited to targets that could not be destroyed by conventional bombing methods. Terrain features such as karst formations, very concentrated defenses, or a combination of these were the usual factors considered in earmarking a target for smart bombs. In most cases, the target had been attacked many times by normal dive-bombing with little or no success.

By far the most common variety of smart bomb used in Southeast Asia was the one that was laser-guided. These weapons were nothing more than regular free-falling iron bombs fitted with a guidance and steering device. This mechanism, which also incorporated

Fig. 9-6. An F-4 dropping a laser-guided bomb. The guidance and steering unit is the pointed, winged device attached to the nose of the bomb. (courtesy Defense Audiovisual Agency)

the fuse, was screwed into the nose of a 2,000-pound bomb, and was a completely self-contained unit. Mounted on this contrivance were small vanes that would steer the bomb in response to commands from the guidance system. Power sources for both the guidance and steering circuits were activated upon release from the aircraft. In order that this bomb would "fly" a little better than the unguided version, the tailfin assembly was about 80 percent bigger.

The ability to steer these bombs while in flight had two major advantages. First and foremost was the phenomenal accuracy made possible by this system. Targets that seemed to elude the best efforts of all comers were dispatched in quick order by a smart bomb mission. The other big plus for using these weapons was that this accuracy could be obtained by conforming to only very general release parameters. There was no requirement to hit the exact airspeed, altitude, and dive angle called for at the release point with regular bombs. This in turn allowed the weapons to be dropped from a lot higher altitude than that necessary for conventional dive-bombing. The reduced exposure to small arms fire was greatly appreciated by all smart bombers.

Along with its accuracy, this mission was somewhat unique in that it required two aircraft to get the weapon on the target. One bird dropped the bomb; the other provided the guidance. Either could perform both roles, since each airplane carried two bombs, and both were equipped with the laser gun to illuminate the target.

Once over the objective, the setup was fairly similar to a regular dive-bombing sortie except for the pattern altitude being about 5,000 feet higher. Both aircraft orbited the target on opposite sides of the circle and went through the usual calls and checks.

When the one dropping the bomb had everything ready, he let the wingman know that he was set to roll in at any time. The latter then illuminated the target with a low-energy infrared laser. This light would be reflected back upward in a funnel-shaped pattern toward the bomb-carrying airplane on the other side of the circle. This bird would then roll in on a normal dive-bombing pass and release the weapon into this funnel of reflected light, or "basket" as it was called.

The bomb's sensors would pick up the infrared radiation and steer the weapon to the strongest area of reflected light. Thus the bomb would slide right down the inverted cone of invisible light to its source, which was the target.

Naturally, the bird illuminating the target had to keep the laser centered on the objective until the bomb hit. This requirement for constant target illumination limited the Laser Guided Bomb (LGB) to targets that were not obscured by clouds or smoke. Getting the weapon into the "basket" only required an abbreviated dive-bombing run, which allowed both aircraft to stay well out of range of all but the heavier guns.

Watching a flight at work using smart bombs is a little embarrassing—and also makes one green with envy. One afternoon our flight was fragged to knock out an underwater ford used by the guerrillas to cross a small river. It was not visible from the air, but from the FAC's directions relative to his mark, we had it pretty well pinpointed. We both made two passes and dropped six 500-pound slicks on each run. The gods of luck were not smiling on us that day, because while the bombs were good, they were not good enough. It was a case of close-but-no-cigar as we churned up the river all around the ford, but left the target relatively unscathed.

We had just finished copying our BDA (which was nothing to write home about) and were climbing out of the target area when a smart bomb flight checked in with the FAC who had just worked us. This target was not too far from our base and fuel wasn't a problem, so we decided to hang around and watch these guys work. After what the next few moments did to our egos, we realized that we should have gone home when we had the chance.

The FAC put in a new mark, the wingman set up with his laser, lead rolled in, and bang—no more ford. The bomb was right on the money, just as if it had traveled down a set of rails. It really watered your eyes to see how easy they made it all look, and definitely gave us the impression that we were living in the Stone Age as far as weapons delivery was concerned.

The other type of smart bomb was the EOGB, or Electro-Optical Guided Bomb. On this weapon the guidance device was an integral part of the bomb, and was not mounted on the nose of a regular slick, as was the laser-guided bomb. The EOGB weighed 2,000 pounds and was steered by small control surfaces similar to the laser weapon.

The method of target acquisition and tracking is what set this bomb apart from other weapons in this category. A small TV camera was mounted in the glass nose of the bomb, and it was through this that the GIB located the target and set the aiming parameters in the weapon. The camera would transmit a picture of the target to the radar scope in the cockpit, and on this picture was superimposed a set of crosshairs.

Once again, the setup over the target was the same as for the LGB, except each aircraft could operate independently of the other. After the FAC had put in his mark, the bird was rolled in for a normal dive-toss delivery. When the aircraft was pointing at the target, a TV picture of the objective was shown on the radar screen. The GIB would center the crosshairs on the target and lock this image into the bomb's guidance system, and then the pickle button was pressed. The bomb's on-board computer would then supply steering signals to keep the crosshairs centered on the target image as the bomb fell. After bombs-away, the delivery aircraft could immediately pull out of its dive and return to orbit.

Up to this point we have been looking at the various types of missions flown out of Phu Cat and the other bases in the theater during 1970-1971. Although each was treated individually here, things were never that compartmentalized during an average day's operations. The wide variety of targets usually found on the frag meant that missions of all kinds would be called for in any 24-hour period. Aside from being shot at and rocketed, the diversity of the job alone kept things from ever getting dull.

Probably the best example of sustained operations involving just about every type of mission occurred during Lam Son 719. As we shall see, this operation brought into play the multiple roles of the fighter pilot on a daily basis. With the exception of Stinger escort and night bombing under flares, the hungry tigers had many opportunities to ply their trade in all its varieties.

Chapter 10

Lam Son 719

Lam Son 719 was the code name of a large ground offensive into Laos that started on January 30, 1971. The scope of this operation was somewhat limited in that plans only called for a penetration of about 25 miles as the crow flies to the village of Tchepone. The invasion route would generally follow Highway 9, which ran between Khe Sanh and Tchepone, and the Ye Pon river, which roughly paralleled the road. The corridor would also be restricted to 15 miles either side of the highway.

The reasons for this incursion were based on intelligence reports that showed an unusually heavy stockpiling of materiel by the enemy in the area around Tchepone. From this base area, North Vietnamese Army (NVA) regiments threatened the key provinces of Quang Tri and Hue. In the past, assaults from this area had been thwarted by the presence of American troops in these northern provinces. However, by late 1970 the process of Vietnamization was well under way, and the American forces had begun to withdraw, hence the large buildup by the enemy.

The overall objective of Lam Son 719 was not the acquisition of territory, but rather to spoil the enemy's plans for an attack against these strategic provinces. The specific goals of the operation were threefold: Interdict the North Vietnamese supply and infiltration routes, destroy their logistical facilities, and inflict losses on NVA units.

Lam Son 719 was named after a North Vietnamese village

where the legendary hero Le Loi inflicted a crushing defeat on an invading Chinese army in 1427. Unfortunately, things did not turn out quite that well for his 20th century counterparts. This operation was the first time in ten years that South Vietnamese troops had fought without their American advisors—and there would be no U.S. combat troops assisting on this drive. On the ground it would be a completely ARVN (Army of the Republic of Vietnam) show.

Other factors did not augur well for the success of this venture. The communists were ready and waiting with over 20,000 men in the area, including 13,000 firstline combat troops. Ammunition had been stocked, plans for a counterattack had been made and rehearsed, the access roads to the area had been improved, and the antiaircraft defenses were heavily reinforced. Even the terrain was a forbidding obstacle, as it lent itself to easily prepared fortifications by the enemy along the line of advance. The NVA capitalized on this natural advantage by overlaying the area with an excellent in-depth defensive system.

Planners in the south were relying strongly on the one thing in their favor to counter all these negative aspects of the mission: U.S. airpower would be available in just about unlimited amounts to support the ground operation. And, with the exception of a few days lost to weather, this support was delivered as requested from just about every base in the theater.

Initially, things progressed well—perhaps too well—as the ARVN advanced steadily with no serious resistance. They entered Laos on February 8th, and continued their push while establishing fire support bases along the way. All thoughts of an easy operation were quickly dispelled on the 12th, when the enemy defenses stiffened considerably. Airpower was called in to deal with this problem, and even though it was more concentrated than ever before, it did not provide the decisive hammer blow that the southern planners had hoped for.

There were two reasons for this: First, there were no U.S. advisors with the South Vietnamese army to coordinate the attacks. What was heretofore a smooth-running operation broke down in the face of language problems, confusion, and coordinators who were new at the job and unfamiliar with the required techniques. This critical shortage of key advisors was discovered too late to be remedied in time to change the course of the operation.

The second reason for airpower not providing all the answers was a shrewd tactic employed by the North Vietnamese. They knew that air strikes would not be called in if friendlies were within so many meters of the point of the attack. Therefore, the enemy stayed in extremely close contact with ARVN units and fire bases—so close that the friendly commanders could not call for air support without endangering their own people and positions. This ploy diffused the usually neat line of battle that demarcated friend from foe, and the uniformly jungled terrain only added to the problem in favor of the enemy. Since the FACs were not given clear-cut information as to *who* was *where*, the ARVN was unable to use the most potent weapon in their arsenal—the one on which they had relied so heavily.

The bitter slugfest, often involving hand-to-hand combat, continued until the 6th of March, when Tchepone was finally occupied. Southern forces spent the next ten days ravaging the area, clearing supply dumps and destroying all facilities. At this point the operation could be considered a success since the objectives had been achieved. The base area around Tchepone had been severely damaged, and the NVA had suffered heavy casualties. But this had not been a free ride for the ARVN, who took quite a beating during the drive to Tchepone. The latter also had to face the problem of getting back to South Vietnam through the same gauntlet they had just traversed. Stung by the loss of a key base area, the North Vietnamese were poised for an attack on the withdrawing troops. They had amassed 36,000 men including two tank regiments along the road back to Khe Sanh. Both sides took a severe mauling during the withdrawal, with the ARVN losing about 50 percent of their force and the NVA suffering an estimated 10,000 killed.

Crowded Skies

The air operations associated with Lam Son 719 were indeed massive, particularly in the area of close air support. Almost the entire effort of the 12th TFW, along with that of other bases in the northern half of South Vietnam, was devoted to this operation. Relatively few night missions were scheduled against other target areas so that just about all the available aircraft could be utilized to fill requests for daytime strikes against the forces opposing this invasion. And, based on the number of sorties flown, 7th Air Force must have been swamped with requests from the beleaguered South Vietnamese.

During the early days of the campaign, the most common mission flown was an LZ Prep. Even before NVA resistance became a major factor, ARVN ground commanders were very tentative in their advance. Before pushing forward, they insisted on having fire support bases established to cover the move.

In an effort to meet these requests so that the operation could proceed on schedule, 7th AF, if anything, overreacted. Everybody and his brother was in the air over Route 9, hauling 2,000-pounders with fuse extenders. *Way* too many aircraft were scheduled for the available FACs, and it was a common occurrence for flights to be stacked up, waiting their turn to work with the controller.

The language difficulties mentioned above compounded the problem, because the FAC could not get clear, concise instructions from the ground as to where they wanted the area cleared. The lack of American advisors to coordinate the air strikes proved to be a definite shortcoming right from the outset.

The delays in getting on target soon had everyone yelling about fast approaching Bingo fuel. Knowing the urgency of the situation on the ground, it was most probable that these Bingo fuel calls were stretched to the absolute limit. A good number of times the fuel crunch got so tight that each aircraft was permitted only one pass on the target, regardless of the armament carried.

As mentioned earlier, the normal load on an LZ Prep mission consisted of 2,000-pounders and 500-pounders. These two different types of bombs required two different mil settings to be dialed into the gunsight in order to aim them properly. Thus, when the FAC wanted everything dropped at once so that things could be expedited, about all you could do was to average out the two settings and hope for the best. This less-than-optimum solution was only possible because the target did not require pinpoint accuracy and because there were no friendlies to contend with.

The FACs who worked Lam Son 719 were responsible for a large portion of whatever success airpower achieved during this operation. They virtually did the impossible in handling the swarms of fighters fragged by 7th AF. It was the normal order of business for the FAC to be giving one flight a target briefing and interrupting it every few moments to clear another flight in on a hot run. These jocks really did good work in keeping things flowing as smoothly as possible, especially considering that all their instructions had to be relayed through the Vietnamese observer who rode along on these missions.

Another problem cropped up when the fighting became more intensified, due to the high state of flux in the ground situation. From moment to moment, targets and their priorities would change;

as each new one appeared, the FAC had to mark it with another smoke rocket. It wasn't long before he was out of rockets and was forced to describe the target position to incoming fighters. This usually took a fair amount of time whenever the objective was anything but an LZ Prep. Nonetheless, the FACs got the job done, often by flying dangerously low in the face of heavy ground fire and rocking their wings over the point they wanted hit. All of this consumed time, which was really at a premium if all the fighters in orbit were to get a chance at the target.

Once the North Vietnamese started to resist the invasion in earnest, most of our missions were to support troops in contact with the enemy. Again fighters were committed in abundance, with some coming from as far away as Phan Rang. These were F-100s, whose shorter range did not allow them to normally work such a distance away from home. The "Huns" were each armed with a pair of thousand-pounders, and in order for them to take these all the way to Tchepone, they had to stop at Phu Cat for refueling. This top-off of gas would give them that little extra cushion over the target area, which certainly came in handy as this operation developed. After dropping their ordnance, these birds would head for altitude and recover directly back to their home base.

All of the airpower involved in helping to pave the way for the South Vietnamese once more resulted in very crowded conditions in the air, similar to the LZ Prep missions. Fighters in orbit waiting for their turn on target had to keep one eye on the FAC and the other on a flight of fighters orbiting nearby. Most of the time these other birds were being worked by a different FAC and would not be on the same frequency. Both flights would be intent on keeping their FAC in sight, unaware of each other's presence until their orbits overlapped and one suddenly flashed by in front of the other.

After a close one like this, the GIB in the lead bird would keep his pilot advised of the whereabouts of the other flight so that they didn't tempt fate too often on the same mission.

The targets on nearly all of these sorties were quite small— gun position, a bunker, or a tank. This, coupled with the close proximity of friendly troops, meant that low angle bombing had to be used to obtain the accuracy needed.

The standard load carried on these missions was three cans of napalm and six high-drags. If you happened to luck out and catch the FAC when he didn't have three or four flights waiting to go on the target (a rare occurrence), you had a couple of options as to how the ordnance would be dropped. The usual sequence would be for each bird to make a napalm pass first and drop all three cans. The six fire bombs would cover quite a large area and pretty well immobilize everything within it. The napalm would be followed by each bird making three passes where a pair of high-drags would be released each time. These bombs would do a good job of knocking out vehicles or artillery made stationary by the napalm. Lam Son 719 took place close enough to Phu Cat that if there were no delays in getting on target, there was enough fuel to make this number of runs.

Most of the time, however, it was just the opposite, with everybody stacked up and complaining about low fuel. On an average day, the best you could hope for was the FAC allowing each bird in the flight to make two passes. Again, the order would be the same—all the Nape on the first run and the Snake on the second. In spite of the difficulties of working through an interpreter and shuffling flights in on the target depending on their fuel state, the FACs did a great job of keeping things sorted out.

In the interest of time, some regular procedures had to be modified a bit so that everyone would get to drop his bombs. One of the first to be changed was the use of TACAN fixes for rendezvous points with the FAC. If he was busy in the target area, he would instruct the flight leader to bring his birds to a certain loca-

Fig. 10-1. Two distinctive landmarks formed by the Ye Pon river, known as "the Heart" and "the U," that were used extensively during Lam Son 719 as rendezvous points between FACs and their fighters.

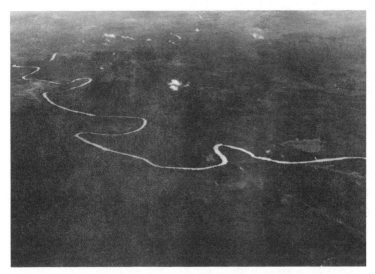

Fig. 10-2. Another landmark on the Ye Pon river known as "the Anvil."

tion where he wanted a target hit. More often than not, the target was in a completely different area than that designated by the fix because of the rapidly changing conditions on the ground. Rather than compute a new TACAN fix, which would have taken too much time, the FACs made considerable use of prominent landmarks to identify the new meeting place.

Fig. 10-3. The "Catcher's Mitt," formed by another river in southern Laos.

As mentioned above, the Ye Pon river generally followed the invasion route planned by the South Vietnamese. This stream twisted and turned into a few very distinctive patterns along its east-west course. Two of the more popular sinuations used by the FACs because they were so easily identifiable were "the Heart" and "the U." These could be spotted from the air at a considerable distance, and certainly expedited getting the flight joined up with the FAC. The latter's directions to his location were quite brief, such as: "I'm two clicks north of the heart." Nonetheless, this was sufficient to get the flight in the ballpark before starting more specific identification procedures.

Getting a positive ID on the FAC during this operation was a little more difficult than on most other missions flown in 'Nam. This was because the air support for Lam Son 719 was so complete, and the majority of this support was aircraft other than fighters. Looking down on any given sector of the operation, you could see dozens of aircraft—fighters working a nearby target, choppers of every size and description scurrying back and forth at treetop level, liaison birds, artillery spotters, and, of course, FACs. Usually none of these aircraft were on the strike frequency, so a controller had to be on the lookout constantly for helicopters suddenly crossing the target area just after he had cleared a fighter for a hot run. Working in and around crowded conditions definitely increased the pucker factor on these missions.

Another contributor in this area was the fact that friendlies were a definite consideration on just about every sortie. The North Vietnamese tactic mentioned earlier of sticking very close to Southern units necessitated very restricted run-in headings and no option on the direction of your turn when coming off target. As the battle got more desperate on the ground, strikes were called in closer and closer to friendly lines, which meant that each jock had to be right on the money on every run. In this situation, if the pipper wasn't exactly on the target at pickle altitude, it was better to go through dry because a bomb that was off in range or azimuth could spell trouble for the wrong folks.

Tough Targets

The target parameters associated with a typical mission during Lam Son 719 were not the type to make one stand up and shout with joy. Invariably the target was on the floor of a valley, which had a number of unpleasant connotations. First of all, the attack heading had to follow the valley, which gave the defenders an advantage as to the placement of their guns and the length of time they had us in their sights. Secondly, a target altitude that was lower than a good bit of the surrounding terrain brought our orbit altitude down fairly close to the tops of the hills in the target area. This put us in range of just about every type of small arms fire they cared to use. The gunners on the hilltops also had another advantage in that they could fire *down* on the fighters making runs along the length of the valley. Not having to aim while looking up into the sun, and knowing that the target would fly a predictable path, resulted in a real field day for the gunners.

Losses and incidents of battle damage started to climb as a consequence of this increased exposure. One of our birds took a very bad hit just after coming off target, and the crew barely had time to eject before the aircraft went in. Both the pilot and the GIB made it to the ground okay; however, they were separated from each other. It was very late in the afternoon when they punched out, and the other strikes fragged into that area, along with the SAR effort, kept the bad guys pinned down for the remaining daylight hours.

The SAR forces finally pinpointed the location of both crewmembers, but darkness fell before the area could be sterilized and a pickup attempted.

The guys on the ground were told to sit tight until dawn, when the rescue would take place. It was a traumatic night to say the least, as they both lay hidden in the jungle while all around them they could hear the North Vietnamese searching for them, and could see the beams of their flashlights probing into the brush. They came very close to the pilot, who was lying under some bushes, clutching his .45 automatic to his chest. He was prepared to blow away the first guy who poked his head into his improvised hiding place.

Luck was with them both as the North Vietnamese finally decided to call it a night, and gave up the search until morning. But at first light, the SAR birds were back in force, and the bad guys were stymied in their attempts to locate the downed crew. While the Sandys kept the communists pinned down, the Jolly Greens moved in and made the pickup of both people. After the pilot was hoisted up on the cable and helped on board the chopper, he immediately ran to an open window and fired a clip from his .45 at the North Vietnamese down below. Needless to say, there was a great sigh of relief at Phu Cat when we found out that these guys had been picked up okay.

It soon became apparent that we had to make some changes in our delivery procedures or continue to take damaging losses in the less-than-optimum conditions of Lam Son 719. However, there weren't too many things that could be changed without affecting the only reason we were there—to put the bombs on the target. Higher releases and steeper dive angles didn't solve the problem because they detracted from the level of accuracy we needed in this operation.

The only thing left was to up the delivery speed from the almost-standard 450 knots to something faster, which lessened our exposure time to the defensive fire. After flying a few missions where you looked *up* at the guns firing at you, most people figured that if faster was good, fastest was best. The name of the game quickly evolved to: "Throttles at full military power," which resulted in speeds of 550 knots or better going down the chute. Pushing the speed up to this range did more than act as a counter to the enemy's defensive efforts. Diving on a target at that speed made the ground almost seem to leap up at you after rolling out on final. This resulted in less time to achieve accurate pipper placement and to properly track the target before release. If things weren't close to being exactly right when you finished the last jink on the attack heading, it was necessary to press in order to realize the correct release parameters.

The problem of minimum time between rollout and drop was further compounded by another difficulty that was commonplace on these missions. More often than not, the target would be obscured by fire, smoke, and haze, particularly if you were last in a string of fighters to hit the target. However, in spite of the problems encountered, these higher speeds did work.

This was brought especially close to home one day while we were working over a target just east of Tchepone. A South Vietnamese unit on a small knoll was being hammered by the bad guys, who had brought in a tank to help them out. The tank was approaching the knoll on a road along the floor of the valley, and our job was to knock it out. The FAC called for the Nape first to slow things down a bit for the high-drags, and after each bird had made a pass, the whole area was awash with burning napalm.

Because of the limited time on target and the restricted run-in heading, the wingman, Capt. Tom Skanchy was the first bird through on each run, and he did some real good work with his high-drags. As we rolled in for our last pass, the entire target area was covered with flames and smoke, so aiming was pretty much by guess and by God. As soon as the bombs were gone, we rolled into a hard jink and started a climb out of the target area.

At that instant the master warning light came on, indicating that we had a problem somewhere. A quick check of the idiot panel showed that the utility hydraulic system was out. This system controlled everything hydraulic on the airplane except flight controls, such as landing gear, flaps, brakes, speed brakes, power rudder, etc. Utility failure was not an uncommon problem with the F-4, since the seal on the pressurized reservoir had a tendency to blow out every now and then. We assumed that this was our trouble, and since the bird was handling okay, we continued our climb to join up with the wingman. After getting together, the battle damage check was started, and it was then that we found out that our assumption had been wrong.

The wingman reported that the underside of the wing in the area of the flaps was covered with hydraulic fluid. This is easy to spot because of its bright red color, and a blown reservoir seal does not result in the loss of so much fluid. It finally dawned on us that we had taken a hit on the last run over the target. Since we had no idea of how much other damage had been done, it was decided to recover at Da Nang, which was quite a bit closer than Phu Cat.

A straight-in approach was made to the field, during which the gear and flaps were blown down by the emergency air system. The wingman checked us over and said that everything looked down and locked, so the hook was lowered and we landed by making an approach end engagement.

After the maintenance people had gone over the bird, they told us that we had taken three hits by small arms fire, one of which had nicked a utility hydraulic line. What made us feel better was that all three of the holes in the bird were aft of the cockpit area. It didn't take much imagination to figure out where these holes would have been if we hadn't been flying the attack at the higher speeds.

When Lam Son 719 ended on March 24th, the tallies on both sides were impressive, but grim. The casualty figures mentioned earlier for the seven-week operation seemed to be a throwback to wars of a bygone era, when frontal assaults on fortified positions were the normal way of doing things. The close air support flown by tactical aircraft in the theater amounted to over 10,000 sorties, and even the B-52s made a high-altitude contribution of 46,000 tons of bombs.

Despite the staggering cost, the objectives of this spoiling operation were achieved; however, it did bring to light several shortcomings on the part of the ARVN. Overall, their performance did not measure up to expectations, especially when confronted with a determined opposition. There were many telling weaknesses in command and control that resulted in numerous serious errors being committed along the way. Planning had been faulty in that the enemy had been underestimated, and an overreliance had been placed on tactical airpower.

Regardless of the problems encountered and the losses incurred, by far the most significant outcome of Lam Son 719 was that it delayed the possibility of an invasion by North Vietnam for almost a year.

Thus far we have only talked about the close air support mission in a conventional war, where the use of tactical nuclear weapons was not a part of the game plan. However, if war broke out in Europe, it is unrealistic to believe that nukes will not be employed. The basic mission will still be the support of troops facing the enemy, but, as we shall see, the delivery of tactical special weapons is a different breed of cat.

Chapter 11

A European Accent

The mission of the tactical air forces in the European theater has an additional component that is unique to that area. Along with supporting NATO ground units with conventional weapons as described earlier, fighter squadrons in Europe are also charged with the delivery of tactical nuclear weapons.

Normally, the targets for such a mission would be semi-strategic in nature in that they would have a direct affect on the enemy's ability to wage war. However, in this case, their influence would be more in the realm of tactics than of grand strategy. The differences here would be likened to the scalpel as compared to the ax. Whereas a strategic nuclear strike is designed to cripple a country's total ICBM and bomber capability, tactical special weapons are used to neutralize lesser objectives, such as a given airfield or missile site. Smaller targets, whose weapons systems are a potential threat to friendly forces in the immediate area, are earmarked for the smaller nukes that can be carried by fighters.

It is also a distinct possibility that these less-powerful weapons could be used against an armor assault massed by the communists. Indeed, such a tactic may be NATO's only counter when facing the marked superiority of the Warsaw Pack countries in the areas of tanks and manpower—and it may be the only way of stalling a determined offensive by the communists long enough to allow a regrouping of forces to preclude another Dunkirk.

In any event, tactical nuclear weapons are a fact of life as far as operations in Europe are concerned. The war plans of both sides must consider their employment by one another, and have to contain provisions on how to survive and fight in this environment.

The game plan for conducting tactical operations involving nukes is completely different from that associated with the types of missions described in earlier chapters. The destructive power of the weapon carried, and the large size of the target, whose location is known precisely, does away with the need for a FAC. Also, these missions can either be a one *or* a two-man show instead of the usual flight of two normally utilized for close air support work.

Specific targets are designated for each crew assigned to this mission, as well as a very definite ingress and egress route. The flight path for each aircraft is meticulously planned so that the aircraft's timing over the various checkpoints along the way is coordinated with other strikes in the same general area. These times must be adhered to *exactly,* and there is ample rationale for hacking them to the second. Anyone who is early or late may suddenly find himself flying into the fireball of a weapon delivered by another bird along this same route.

Thus it can be seen that navigation is of primary importance on these sorties, and this is where the GIB really earns his coins. Getting from A to B with a tactical nuke requires an intimate combination of the inertial navigation system, radar navigation, and some good old-fashioned pilotage between visual checkpoints.

In these days of electronic navigating, not too much attention is paid to utilizing time and distance calculations as a means of getting from one point to another, but if the balloon went up in Europe to the extent that tactical nukes would be employed, any airplane that could get airborne and drop the weapon would be used. A bird that was out of commission for radar or the inertial system would certainly be flown if the weather permitted at least a partial VFR penetration to the target. This is why pilotage assumes a much more critical role on these missions than as a casual backup on a routine cross-country.

This is also the reason why this facet of the mission is honed to a fine edge on innumerable practice runs. These simulations of the real thing are laid out just as carefully as the actual route. They are designed to duplicate, as much as possible, the terrain features found on the ingress route to the target, especially those used for radar checkpoints.

Ingress Problems

The one common denominator found in the flight plans of all the birds assigned to this mission is altitude—or rather, the lack of it. The universal doctrine is to stay low anytime you can. This, plus speed, are the two primary ways of improving the odds of getting into the target and back out again.

Staying low in this case means less than 500 feet above the ground. Whipping along at 500 knots this high over the trees and rocks definitely keeps your mind on the business at hand. The landscape goes by at a rate just this side of a blur, which makes the acquisition and identification of visual checkpoints fairly difficult. Therefore, these features must be chosen carefully, with an eye toward permanence and easy recognition. Things that are manmade are, for the most part, not counted on too heavily because of their susceptibility to destruction and/or change. Natural attributes that have been a part of the topography for generations, and are not likely to be altered appreciably, even in a limited nuclear conflict, are the ones sought after. Tree lines that have been in place for years outlining sections of property are very useful, along with any features exhibiting vertical development. Examples of these would be prominent peaks, ridgelines, or hilly areas in otherwise flat terrain. These checkpoints cannot be too far apart, because at the altitude you are flying, the ability to pick out and identify objects at a distance is fairly limited.

The hungry tiger delivering tactical nukes in the European theater has two major problems confronting him that must be considered as givens on every mission. The first of these is the weather, which in Europe is lousy a good percentage of the time. Therefore, although visual navigation is stressed, each practice run is conducted as if the whole world was zero-zero. Navigating and flying by instruments is the primary means of getting to and from the target. This type of training ensures that the mission will be accomplished even in the worst possible situation. Should the gods of weather choose to smile on us, then the cross checks provided by visual navigation are looked on as a bonus. Ceilings that are low enough to preclude running the route VFR underneath would force the bird up to the absolute minimum enroute altitude dictated by the terrain along the flight plan.

Weather bad enough to require a completely IFR run tips the scales a little in favor of the opposition. To the radar defense network and the radar-equipped interceptors, it's business as usual as they scramble to meet our inbound birds. Their job will actually be a little *easier*, because the incoming force will most likely be flying a little higher than they would in VFR conditions. This gives the ground radars a better chance to detect and establish tracks on the ingressing fighters and thus vector their interceptors with more certainty. Even intermittent contacts on the approaching aircraft would give enemy controllers enough information to get their birds into the general area of the raid. Then the sophisticated radar used in modern all-weather interceptors could take over and complete the mission.

This leads us to the second major problem associated with this mission. All the way to and from the target you are flying in a high-threat area. The enemy knows where you are based, and undoubtedly has a pretty good idea as to what targets of theirs are worth dropping a nuke on. With this in mind, they can place their radars, SAM units, and defensive fighters in the best possible locations to thwart our attack.

When the battlefield situation in any given area deteriorates to the point where the employment of tactical nukes becomes a good possibility, the bad guys will be monitoring the level of activity at all our airfields. In this type of situation, any unusual increase in the traffic from any of these fields would instantly alert them that our tactical nuclear force was being scrambled. Therefore, before your flight is more than a few minutes old, the enemy knows you're airborne and is activating a considerable number of defenses specifically designed to ruin your whole day. Along with radar and infrared guided SAMs, and fighters carrying more of the same plus a gun, flak batteries of every size will be ready and waiting in case you pop out underneath the weather in an attempt to get as low as possible.

It may seem like the odds are stacked somewhat against the good guys when considering all these advantages held by the enemy. However, even though they know you are up and have a general idea of the route you must take to the target, there are still a few things going for the guys in the white hats.

First of all, they have to find you, and even under the best of conditions, detecting and intercepting a target at extreme low levels is not an easy task. Electronic jamming of enemy radars would be used extensively in this situation, both by the fighters carrying the special weapons and by any ground stations whose location would make them effective. These jammers would saturate the opposition's radar scopes with electronic "noise" and literally mask off a given area to their radars. However, because of the limitations of power output and the effects of distance, plus countermeasures employed by the enemy, no jammer can totally deny radar information in the jammed area. Their controllers may get an occasional "paint" on an incoming fighter, but with the profusion of returns on the scope under these conditions, it will hopefully be too intermittent for effective tracking.

These jammers would also be directed against SAM sites and the missiles they fire. A couple of other factors enter the equation here that, when coupled with the jamming, help considerably to negate the SAM threat. These are the high speed and low altitude used by the ingressing fighters. The detection and guidance radar used by the missile sites has a relatively short range, and operates strictly on a line-of-sight basis. These limitations prevent the radar from seeing very low targets, except when they are fairly close to the site. If the birds are picked up, then it is hoped that their speed will carry them through the coverage of a particular site before the latter can react and get a missile off. Thus, if it is a total IFR mission, the combination of speed and jamming help to offset somewhat the disadvantage of probably having to fly a little higher than desired. Should the weather be good enough to allow the fighters to operate VFR underneath, then low altitude is the best counter to the enemy's efforts to find you. Nap-of-the-earth flying would be the technique utilized here if forward visibility was good enough. This would in turn act as a multiplier to the advantageous effects of speed and the line-of-sight problem associated with opposing radar.

Even if the weather turned out bright and clear, this would still be the preferred method of getting to and from the target. Knowing that we would be coming in eyeball-to-eyeball with the trees to prevent radar detection, the enemy would have to rely heavily on their interceptor force to find us before bombs-away. Spotting a camouflaged fighter against the mottled landscape typical of Europe is a tough job. In many cases, only a sun flash off a wing or the canopy will provide a fleeting clue as to the whereabouts of the quarry. Then it becomes a problem of keeping him in sight while closing to a range where the air-to-air missiles can be used. This by itself could present a significant difficulty, because the fighters used by both sides would of necessity be in the same general performance category. This means that if one of the inbound birds was sighted by a defender and the latter gave chase, it would take him a considerable amount of time to close the range to a point where armament could be launched. Naturally, quite a bit depends on the geometry of the defender's attack, but if he had to turn much over 90 degrees to roll out behind the inbound fighter, that might be all she wrote. Both aircraft would be maxed out, and in all probability the one with the nuke would be into his delivery maneuver before the defender could catch up.

Let's suppose that the bad guys are having a good day and things are breaking in their favor. They pick up one of our birds and have enough altitude and/or airspeed to close the gap to missile range. What options are open to the guys in the friendly fighter? If their opponent elects to try a radar missile pass, the RHAW gear will alert them to his presence and intentions. In order to deal with these missiles, the bird is equipped with a device that dispenses small bundles of chaff into the airstream.

Since the supply of chaff is limited, the timing on its use is critical. A bundle could be dropped as soon as he is locked on to your bird, just to see if he can be suckered into firing on the chaff. Only a real greenhorn would be faked out by this move, but if it works even for a few moments, it will buy you some extra time. Weather permitting, the best way to combat a radar-guided missile is to drop a bundle of chaff, make a turn about 45 degrees from your old heading, and get as close to the ground as you can. The idea is to catch his attention with the chaff drop, and while he's investigating that, dive down and to one side of the area where he'll be expecting to find you after checking out the chaff.

If the boy behind you has done his homework and is still on your tail and closing after all this dazzling footwork, a missile launch can be expected shortly. Now is the time to keep a close eye on the bird in your six so that the instant the missile is fired, you drop a couple of bundles of chaff and start a hard turn *into* the missile, pulling as many Gs as you can. Hopefully, the narrow look angle of the missile's radar will only see the chaff and home in on it.

If the attacking fighter opts to use IR guided missiles, the problem for the good guys is a little more difficult. Here a clever attacker will silence his radar once he has a visual on his target so as not to give away his presence by activating the RHAW gear. He will then close until his missiles tell him that they can see the target by introducing a growling tone into the headset. Then it's missiles away, and the good guys lose another one.

Since the crew in the friendly fighter has no way of knowing that someone is attacking with IR missiles, getting a visual on the opponent is an absolute must. Seeing someone behind them with no activation of the RHAW gear is a pretty good indication that an IR attack is under way. Therefore, about all they can do—besides firewalling the power—is keep the bogey in sight, and as soon as they see the missile launched, take immediate defensive action. In the case of IR missiles, this would consist of dropping a flare and starting a maximum-G turn in the direction of the missile. The flare serves the same purpose as the chaff during a radar missile attack—that is, it offers a more inviting target to the missile guidance system and thus decoys it away from the airplane.

Delivering the Nuke

Along with the problems of navigation and enemy defenses, the crew of the inbound fighter has a few other mission procedures to contend with. The first of these is a careful monitoring of the fuel gauge to determine exactly when the drop tanks are empty. The fuel in these tanks is the first to be used on the mission, since they are sequenced to replenish the internal tanks at a rate equal to engine consumption. There is no fuel gauge or indicator for the drops, and the only way the crew knows that they are feeding is a constant reading on the internal fuel quantity gauge.

As soon as this needle starts to move downward, it is an indication that the external tanks are empty, and they are jettisoned immediately. The decrease in weight and drag—especially the latter—causes a significant increase in the range and endurance potential for a bird on this type of mission. Consequently, this change in performance has to be figured into the flight plan quite carefully.

The second, and probably the most important, is the correct execution of the weapons delivery procedures. In the latter part of the mission, the data initially fed into the offset bombing system of the airplane are updated and refined. The procedures used here would be the same as those described in Chapter 9 for the Commando Nail mission. Radar and/or visual reference points would be cross-checked with the aircraft's actual position, and any corrections needed would be cranked in.

The closer the bird gets to the target, the more dense the defenses will become, which makes flying as low as you can get more important than ever, but the delivery procedures for the special weapon call for a set amount of time that the weapon must fall before detonation. This short delay allows the aircraft to achieve the minimum distance necessary to stay beyond the lethal radius of the bomb. The type of maneuver used to release the weapon is determined largely by the target being attacked; however, the one most often employed is the LADD, or Low Altitude Drogue Delivery.

Using this method of attack, the pilot follows the steering information generated by the offset bombing system. While approaching the target, this involves keeping the vertical needle on the attitude indicator centered—again, the same as for a Commando Nail mission. But at this point the aircraft is still on the deck; therefore, the LADD computer programs a pullup to the bomb release point so that the weapon achieves the minimum free-fall time. The system gives the pilot a signal at the exact time the pullup should be started. The bomb button is depressed and held, while the aircraft is rotated into a climb by the application of the prescribed amount of Gs to achieve the required release parameters.

Directional control during the climb is maintained by keeping the vertical needle centered on the attitude indicator. At the computed release point, the system automatically sends a signal to drop the weapon, followed by an indication to the pilot that the bomb is gone. At this instant the pilot initiates the follow-through maneuver, which is a carefully planned action specifically designed to ensure the survivability of the crew. The proper execution of the follow-through is essential if the aircraft is to avoid the fireball and shock wave generated by the weapon. The time, fuel, and distance involved in this maneuver are all considered in the flight planning for the mission.

The procedures followed on egressing from the target are the same as those used on the way in—stay low and check your six! The pullup and escape maneuver must be accomplished with quite a bit of precision to satisfy the close tolerances involved in this critical juncture of the mission. For this reason they are done almost entirely by instruments. Although this requirement amounts to doing mild acrobatics on the gages, with sufficient practice, these unusual attitudes can be mastered.

The prospect of both sides launching tactical nuclear strikes at approximately the same time is indeed a hairy one to contemplate. A situation that involves bad weather and low ceilings, along with our birds going out, theirs coming in, and interceptors on both sides chasing down all of the above, coupled with flak and SAMs, to say nothing of the nuclear detonations, pretty well boggles the mind. Then throw in the effects of communications and radar jamming on both sides, as well as the normal confusion predicted by Murphy's Law in this setting, and you come up with a *real* can of worms. Yet this is the environment in which a modern fighter pilot must function—and function well. Having the knowledge, competence, and heart to cope with the myriad problems faced on such a mission is the stuff that makes a hungry tiger.

Considering all the difficulties of getting to the targets, and given that their locations are known with a fair degree of certainty, a logical question is: "Why not do the job with missiles?" Their size and speed negate the flak and interceptor problems, and their completely self-contained guidance systems are immune to jamming. Weather is not a consideration, and their accuracy and reliability put them on a par with a manned aircraft. Even more important, the lives of highly trained aircrews would not be risked.

Granted, all of these factors are correct, and are certainly valid portions of the total equation. However, there are two major reasons why missiles are not the complete answer in tactical nuclear warfare. The normal chain of events leading up to the use of special weapons would be the escalation of tensions on both sides until one or the other makes the fateful decision. As each side ups the ante in this war of nerves by moves, feints, and countermoves, their nuclear forces—both manned and missile—would be poised for instant action.

There are countless situations in this scenario where he who hesitates is lost. Opposing commanders cannot afford to wait until every decision factor is clarified in this all-or-nothing game. *The one who feels he must strike and chooses missiles has in essence triggered World War III.* Once launched, the missiles cannot be recalled, and the other commander has no choice but to launch his force in return. The use of missiles introduces a factor of finality into the decision-making process. There is no more buying time in which to consider other options or new information, nor can you change your mind once the button is pushed. The only thing left to consider is how many weapons you can get off the ground before the other guy's missiles hit.

Along with the lack of a recall capability, the other reason for using manned aircraft instead of missiles in this situation is that the former are retargetable. Once a missile is off and running, its target is fixed and that's where it will impact, regardless of any last-minute changes in the tactical circumstances on the ground. Consider the use of such weapons against a moving target, such as a massed armor thrust that imperiled our strategic position. The lack of exact target coordinates could result in the waste of a weapon—or, worse yet, having it drop in on our own people.

The nuclear-armed fighter plane neatly solves both of these problems. Like a missile, it too can be advanced to higher states of readiness as tensions increase. But it goes the missile one better in this situation by giving the commander a little more time to consider more options while maintaining a creditable yet flexible posture. The birds can be launched on their routes with orders to hold at some checkpoint on our side of the fence. This would demonstrate our resolve in this confrontation and give the enemy a chance to back down before it is too late. It also keeps our aircraft poised at the brink for a quick thrust to the target, should the bad guys persist in their actions. Another plus that airplanes offer in this area is that they enhance the survivability of the strike force by getting airborne in response to both real threats and feints by the enemy.

During the struggle that would ensue once the nuke force was launched for real, the manned fighter again proves its superiority over the missile. This would occur if the priority of targets changed after the fighters were airborne. Secondary targets, or areas that were not previously considered as targets, may become critically important as the overall situation develops. Last-minute changes of this nature can be accommodated with no sweat by a crew of tigers already in the air.

This adaptability to changing conditions assumes even greater significance when these fighters are launched to counter an overwhelming ground offensive by the enemy. Given the uncertainties and conflicting information that usually abounds in such a drama, it is essential to have a decision-maker on the scene to observe what is actually happening. Only the aircrew in position over the battlefield can determine just where so powerful a weapon has to be placed to achieve the desired results. In this type of environment, the man's the thing! No computer or missile can observe and assess what is really going on at that instant, arrive at a rational decision, and put the weapons where they are needed most. This is a job made for the hungry tiger, where smarts, guts, and skill combine to hack the mission.

The foregoing has been an overview of what it takes to be a fighter pilot as far as the air-to-ground role is concerned. However, before control of the ground can be accomplished, control of the air must be achieved. This brings into play the traditional mission of the fighter jock: air-to-air combat.

Part II:

Air-to-Air

Chapter 12

The Counter-Air
Mission: Overview

The contribution of airpower in modern war is of even greater significance today than when this doctrine was originally espoused by Alexander P. deSeversky in the 1930s. The quantum leaps in aircraft/missile design, weapons development, communications, and detection devices have made this facet of war-making the keystone upon which the success of land and ocean forces depend. Control of the air is absolutely essential for effective surface operations of any size. Without it, such activities take on the aura of a kamikaze mission.

The successful prosecution of a war requires that air supremacy be maintained in three areas. The most obvious is over the actual battlefield where the contest is being fought by surface forces. However, in order to sustain these forces, the area behind the lines where such support is generated must also be protected. This requirement establishes the need for a system capable of defending this territory against strikes by opposing air elements, i.e., an effective air defense network. Lastly, our control of the air must extend beyond friendly lines and over the enemy's domain. This requirement would be transitory in nature, since it would only apply during the time we were conducting air strikes into that area. Also, it would be somewhat localized geographically in that only the airspace occupied by the strike force going to and from the target would be considered.

The effectiveness of modern offensive and defensive weaponry establishes the need for specialization in both these areas. This specialization is not a singular activity; rather, it is a team effort. The enemy has so many options with which to counter our bid for air supremacy in any given sector that no one aircraft has the capability of meeting such a diverse threat. This is where the teamwork involving quite a few unique activities comes into play. Not only must these teams work in harmony with each other to be effective, the teams themselves must meld with the other facets of the mission if the overall objective is to be attained.

On the defensive side, there must be a smooth blending of command and control, interceptors, radar surveillance and control sites, and SAM/flak batteries for the air defense network to function properly. Imperfect teamwork here could create holes in the net through which disaster could easily slip.

Offensively, the problem becomes even more complex. Here, each pair of fighters engaging enemy aircraft have to function as a coordinated unit, where every move and countermove is planned to maximize the offensive potential of the basic fighting unit. In addition, the actions of individual elements and flights must contribute to the integrity of the total force and the realization of its objectives. Thus, if the mission is just the destruction of enemy fighters (such as in MiG Alley during the Korean War), then the combined effort should work toward that end. However, if a strike force is being escorted on a raid into enemy territory, then the priorities are changed somewhat. Job number one is keeping the bad guys off the backs of the people carrying the bombs. If this can be done by shooting them down, so much the better. But given the high speed maintained by the strike force, it might be sufficient to divert the opposing fighters away from their objective for just a relatively short time. This could be done by forcing them to turn away from their attack vector to keep from being shot down. If this parry to their initial thrust causes them to lose considerable Mach and/or altitude, the strike force will be long gone before they can recover sufficiently to pose another threat. Things move so fast in this situation that just making them execute a hard diving turn to avoid a missile launched by one of our birds might be all that is needed to effectively put them out of the fight.

Air Superiority Requirements

The enemy, of course, will not rely only on fighters to counter a raid into their area of interest. SAMs, flak batteries, and their radar defense network will also play a vital role. Consequently, other members of our team must be earmarked to nullify such potential threats. These would be aircraft specifically equipped for these roles—some with chaff dispensers and others with jammers. Their task would be to blind and confuse enemy radars trying to detect and intercept our force. The problem of SAMs would be dealt with by "Iron Hand" flights, whose special detection gear and armament allow them to home in on and destroy these sites.

In addition to the main strike force and its supporting elements, any large offensive maneuver such as this should be covered by friendly surveillance radar to warn them of approaching interceptors. This could take the form of land or ship-based early warning radar, or preferably an AWACS bird on station near the area of hostilities.

It can be seen from the foregoing that modern air operations require a variety of skills, techniques, and equipment in order to achieve superiority over the numerous counters posed by the enemy. And all of these separate and distinct facets of the overall mission must function as a team both individually and collectively if we are to optimize the effectiveness of our weapons systems.

The successful employment of fighters in today's tactical environment involves quite a few considerations, including some givens. First and foremost among these would be the absolute requirement for search and track radar systems in every aircraft. These must be capable of locating, identifying, and tracking fighter-sized aircraft well beyond the launch envelope of today's air-to-air missiles. This means that, as a *minimum*, the system should be able to consistently pick up enemy fighters 50 miles away. Along with a good detection range, this radar should have circuitry that enables it to function in a heavy electronic countermeasures (ECM) situation. This would include at least the ability to combat barrage jamming, angle receivers, gate stealers, and chaff drops.

Since very low level tactics are pretty much the name of the game in modern war, these weapons systems have to have a good "look down" capability. Before the new generation of fighters appeared in the '70s, the best radars of the day could not "see" targets flying below them close to the ground. Therefore, the only way to detect such targets was to fly lower than the opposition and use a slight "look up" angle on the radar. The best way to approach this problem is to have radars capable of blanking out the ground return and only "painting" the returns of actual targets on the scope. With this type of system, the offensive and defensive potential of the fighter force is maximized, since they can operate at higher altitudes and thus cover more territory.

The radar in today's birds should also have an infrared subsystem that can both detect and track enemy aircraft. At any given time the constant seesaw battle between radar and the countermeasures designed to thwart it may be favoring the latter. Therefore, an IR backup system might be the only way to hack the mission if the enemy's ECM denies us radar information. Even if the scales were more or less balanced, there are many times when IR is the only way to go. An example of this would be if you wanted to approach a target undetected and have to put your radar in "standby" so as not to activate his RHAW gear. Another comes into play when the enemy's jammer overpowers your radar and the IR system provides a method of finding your target and launching the weapons. An additional advantage of having an IR subsystem with tracking capability occurs in a dogfight against an aircraft that can turn better than yours. If you get behind him but can't pull enough lead to let your missiles acquire the target, you simply raise the IR detector head until it sees the bogey, initiate system lock-on, and launch the armament.

The limitations of size, design, and power output restrict the operation of radars in fighters to a relatively short range, and pretty much to a one-vs.-one type of situation. Birds involved in fighter sweeps looking for enemy aircraft, or those escorting a strike force, have radar coverage only in a 120 degree cone in front of the flight. They are essentially blind to the approach of opposing fighters from either side and from the rear, which are the two best areas from which to launch an attack.

Therefore, if the force is to operate effectively as a coordinated offensive unit, this vulnerable area must be covered—and this coverage must extend beyond the normal range of the radar in the fighters. This is necessary because of the high speeds at which today's aircraft operate, which often results in closing rates in excess of Mach 2. The requirements for long-range radar coverage around the fighter/strike force translates into time, i.e., more time to react once the hostile force is detected. At these speeds, even an extra minute would enable the friendly fighters to position themselves in the most advantageous alignment to meet the attack.

From this it can be seen that some form of long-range radar capable of providing both early warning and snap vectoring to friendly fighters is an urgent necessity in any operation involving control of the air. Such a requirement can be met in one of two ways. If the area of interest is within range of a ground-based radar station, this is probably a good option. GCI sites are not restricted by size and weight limitations on equipment, and thus can utilize larger antennas, generate more output power, and bring into play a large number of backup/alternate systems. These advantages provide for excellent control of fighters out to its *effective* range of coverage—"effective" is emphasized here because this range will be determined by the distance from the site at which enemy fighters can be picked up. The problem is further compounded by the fact that these aircraft must be detected by a "skin paint," probably in an ECM environment. A skin paint is the actual image on the scope made by the radar energy reflected by the target, not the enhanced, coded return produced by transponders. The small size of fighters and the presence of jamming combine to reduce the radius of effective control of any radar installation. The job of the hungry tiger is to carry the war to the enemy, and this usually requires deep thrusts into hostile territory to strike a telling blow. These strikes usually range far beyond the coverage of friendly GCI sites, thus pretty much limiting their role in the battle for air supremacy to defensive situations.

Another problem with fixed locations is that they are subject to destruction by an enemy ground or missile attack. Portable tactical radar control sites provide partial answers to the permanence and distance problems of regular GCI stations. However, these units lack the versatility and redundancy needed for the type of operation under discussion.

All things considered, the most effective way of providing the required radar coverage for a fighter sweep or a strike force is through AWACS. The Airborne Weapons And Control System is actually a GCI site with wings. Miniaturized and sophisticated design has enabled powerful radars incorporating advanced ECM features to be packaged in such a way that they will now fit into a relatively small multi-engined airplane. (The particulars on the types of AWACS birds currently in use will be covered in Chapter 14.)

The primary advantage offered by AWACS over a ground radar site is mobility. These birds can be positioned along a line parallel to the route of the strike force, but well beyond the range of enemy fighters. This was the tactic used in Vietnam, with the radar birds on station over the Gulf of Tonkin. On raids deep into an extended land mass such as Europe, the AWACS aircraft could go at least part of the way to provide radar coverage to the maximum possible range. In this type of situation, some fighter protection would have to be provided for the AWACS bird while operating near or over hostile territory.

The role of the fighter forces in modern warfare also includes some considerations that are less specific. Their increased range and ability to survive in a combat environment, plus their capability of carrying both nuclear and conventional weapons, make the fighter plane a major instrument in the waging of any kind of war. No longer is their task just to fly top cover for strategic bombers and provide air defense over friendly areas. They now give the theater commander the ultimate in mission flexibility, enabling him to maintain control of the air while at the same time affording the potential for a nuclear strike on intermediate-range targets.

The expansion of the role of fighters to include the semi-strategic mission frees up our long-range bomber fleet for raids into the enemy's heartland. This is the mission that these aircraft were designed for, and the one they do best. And the mission of the strategic forces is, in many respects, incompatible with the quick response to rapidly changing requirements that is the essence of any tactical situation. During a limited war—even one that has escalated to the level where tactical nukes are being used—fighters will most likely constitute the total air arm of the theater commander. Long-range bombers will undoubtedly be held in reserve until circumstances deteriorate to the point where a World War is imminent. Therefore, a basic consideration in any future conflict would be the inclusion of the fighter mission as a major instrument of national policy.

Another factor that influences any situation involving the air forces of other services is autonomous vs. non-autonomous operations. In most cases, strikes by Navy, Marine, or Army aircraft are coordinated with similar activities being conducted by the Air Force. However, the word on last-minute changes in response to rapidly developing conditions may not filter through to adjacent services. Marine aircraft scrambled from a carrier to support the "Mud Marines" ashore would be a good example of this. The necessarily hasty preparations to get this flight airborne might not have included a call to the Air Force radar site controlling the area through which they must pass. When these birds are picked up on the radar, they would be declared hostile immediately. Interceptors would be sent after these tracks, and if weather or darkness were a factor, they could be shot down before anyone was the wiser. A straggler egressing from a hostile area after being separated from the main force could trigger the same reaction. Although every joint operation calls for coordination between all participants down to the lowest levels, there are times when something slips through the crack and some folks don't get the word.

After a few near-misses such as those just described, it became apparent that the rules of engagement in every theater had to take these possibilities into account. What evolved were policies that were code named "Guns Free" and "Guns Tight." If an area or time period were designated "Guns Free," it meant that targets could be fired upon without first being identified. On the other hand, if "Guns Tight" was in effect, no target could be fired upon until it was positively identified as hostile. This meant that someone had to get an eyeball on the bogey and declare it hostile to the controlling agency before anyone was cleared to squeeze the trigger. These rules applied to both aircrews and the people manning the flak batteries and missile sites. (Fighter operations under both these conditions will be detailed in the next chapter.) Even though the procedures established for "Guns Tight" put us at a slight tactical disadvantage, they were considered necessary in order to make us safe rather than sorry.

An additional tactical consideration that applies to all actions involving modern fighters is the extreme speed and altitude at which they operate. These factors come into play particularly during engagements between aircraft on fighter sweeps and strike escort missions. The attack patterns normally used by opposing forces at the outset of these clashes generate closing rates in the neighborhood of Mach 2. Such speeds only permit the barest minimum of time in which to assess the situation, select the best attack option, acquire the target, and launch the armament. Decision time is reduced to an instant, and if the instant is lost due to hesitancy or incomplete information, so too is lost the advantage. A delay of even a few moments will allow the enemy to flash by and gain the upper hand while maneuvering into your six, or find easy pickings among the bomb-laden strike force.

The high speed coupled with the thin air at altitude make early and correct decisions an urgent necessity. These factors combine to reduce an aircraft's maneuverability while maintaining the speed necessary to stay in the fight and win—or even survive. Gone are the days of the hard break into the attack where the aircraft seemed to swap ends. The hard break is still there, but today's fighters need many miles of airspace just to make a 180-degree turn while keeping their Mach up to fighting speed. Dogfights between modern airplanes cover huge areas of the sky, and given the speed and small size of the participants, it is extremely difficult to keep a visual on the opposition. Losing the enemy, even for an instant, at the long ranges brought about by the wide turns dictated by high-altitude maneuvering could be fatal. The loss of a visual on your opponent allows him to maneuver for the kill with impunity, while your counters are reduced to guesses and luck. By the time he is close enough to catch sight of him again, it is too late.

Combat Maneuvering

The basic requirement in any hassle of keeping your Mach up, along with the climbs and turns necessary to maintain the tactical advantage, oftentimes dictates that the aircraft be continually flown on the feather edge of its controlability envelope. Extreme altitudes, tight turns, and high G loadings are the usual keys to success in any fighter engagement. The bird that can zoom higher and pull tighter turns has a significant advantage over his opponent.

But achieving top performance from an aircraft under these conditions requires a velvet touch on the controls. The pilot has to develop an instinctive sense of how the bird is handling at every instant during any maneuvering. This is very much a seat of-the-pants type of flying, because you have to feel through body sensations just how the bird is reacting to your control inputs. Of course, the instruments provide all this information in very precise terms, but glancing at them to find out what's going on will almost guarantee losing your eyeball on the opponent in a hard turning engagement.

This is where the seat of the pants and the velvet touch combine to allow you to coax the maximum performance out of the airplane while keeping a visual on the enemy. A light nibble at the wingtips while turning in either the horizontal or vertical plane most likely indicates that you aren't pulling it tight enough. On the other hand, reefing it in until the whole aircraft is bucking all the way around the turn means that you have gone too far and are in imminent danger of a complete stall, or an out-of-control condition.

Maximum-performance flying while in maneuvering flight puts the airplane just a tad away from this latter predicament, yet this is where it has to be to do good work. However, if these limits are exceeded, the aircraft "departs the controlability envelope." This is the term the engineers use to describe what is probably the hairiest ride imaginable in any airplane. Once the aircraft "departs," it becomes a wildly gyrating thing with a mind of its own—violent excursions about every axis that pin you to the seat with positive Gs one instant and in the next throw you up against the top of the canopy with gut-wrenching negative Gs. Control inputs to counter all this thrashing about have no effect whatever, and even though the engine is at full power with afterburner, you are probably registering zero airspeed. The bird is completely stalled out, and unless something can be done to break the stall, it will probably start tumbling in space and recovery will be all but impossible.

This relatively narrow area between effective performance and departing the controlability envelope is a very real tactical consideration for today's hungry tigers. This is the region in which they must operate if they are to win—anything less and they become a statistic.

Combat maneuvering along this fine line demands a constant awareness of the energy level of the aircraft at any given moment. Energy level, or energy maneuverability, is a fairly recent concept that deals with an aircraft's ability to perform combat maneuvers by utilizing the interchangeability of the bird's potential and kinetic energy. More simply, if you are above your opponent (higher potential energy), you can dive to generate sufficient airspeed (increased kinetic energy) to press home the attack. Conversely, if you are Maching along at a good clip, the high airspeed gives you the ability to zoom to a greater altitude if the tactical situation so dictates.

This might sound like pretty basic stuff that would be quite obvious to any throttle-bender. However, the tiger who enters an engagement with a game plan that is not based on energy maneuverability is soon a dead duck. Every dive, climb, turn, and roll must be planned and executed with an eye toward gaining or conserving the maximum possible amount of energy. The ham-handed jock who horses the bird around with no regard for these important principles quickly reduces the energy level of his bird to the point where he is no longer able to maneuver. He is then at the mercy of his foe, because once lost, energy is tough to regain. In this situation, the throttle is already wide open, so little help can be expected from this area. The only thing left to do is to dive—preferably in a zero-G condition—to gain enough airspeed to get back into the fight. The pilot who understands the concepts of energy maneuverability, and employs them properly during an engagement, will most likely be the one who does the victory roll back at the home base.

Weapons for All Seasons

One last topic to touch on in this overview of the counter-air mission is the capabilities of the modern fighter plane. The aircraft of the Vietnam era typified early attempts to make the fighter into a machine that would be all things to all people. Design requirements were laid on specifying that a bird had to excel not only in the air-to-air role, but also do equally well at all-weather intercept work and the close air support mission.

The F-111 was the first attempt to design a multimission fighter from the ground up. This "Edsel of the Airways" soon proved what the pilots knew all along. Given the state of the art at that time, an aircraft designed for the multimission role performed no task very well. Too many things had to be added to the basic airplane—which was probably well suited for *one* of the roles—in order to make it meet the requirements for all three. Each of these "mods" increased weight, drag, and complexity to the point where all missions suffered.

Reason and common sense prevailed when the F-111's forte was finally realized—night low level interdiction. The bird took to this mission like a duck to water, and was able to do it better than other aircraft in the inventory at that time. Up through 1970, the McDonnell F-4 Phantom II was probably the closest thing we had to a good multimission fighter.

About that time, a new generation of aircraft started to appear—and because of recent technological developments in airframe and engine design, along with improvements in the weapons systems, the true multimission fighter had arrived. Airplanes such as the F-15 and F-16 perform all roles well (more will be said about their individual capabilities in Chapter 14). Existing firstline aircraft are, as might be expected, wonders of complexity and performance. They have the radar, missiles, and guns that make them tough customers in any air-to-air situation. These birds also have the capability of carrying a large amount of external stores of any variety, including nukes. This, coupled with their excellent speed and maneuverability, makes them ideal for the close air support and interdiction missions.

Perhaps more than anything else, their radar and weapons delivery systems enable these birds to be categorized as the all-around threat. The versatility, power, and reliability of modern airborne radar make the systems found in fighters of the previous generation seem almost primitive. The variety of roles performed by the modern fighter all require some specialized input from the radar system. Included among these would be airborne search and tracking for all missions (but particularly all-weather interception), missile preparation and guidance at the culmination of a radar pass, and ranging information while pressing home a gun attack.

The radar also plays a key role in the ground support phase. Many delivery methods from Dive Toss through the various offset bombing techniques need (or can be enhanced by) good radar information. Standoff, or "shoot and leave," weapons also utilize this system. The manufacturers of radars in the older airplanes always claimed that the set could be used as an aid to navigation. If you happened to be flying up the Florida Keys, around Cape Cod, or over some other very distinctive coastline feature, the radar might be of some help—if you could interpret it correctly. If you found yourself over Kansas or Nebraska, forget it! However, the newer systems provide better target resolution and increased discrimination between dissimilar areas. The result is a sharper and more understandable ground-mapping capability, which can be used for both navigation and locating targets.

Despite their sophistication, the radars in this new breed of fighters will, on occasion, most likely be jammed by enemy countermeasures. Therefore, in order not to jeopardize mission accomplishment, some form of backup system must be available. Infrared is the answer here, yet surprisingly enough, neither the F-15 nor F-16 have a fully developed IR search and track system.

They do, however, have the capability of carrying the AIM-9 Sidewinder missile. This weapon uses a self-contained IR tracking unit for guidance during its flight. But since the look angle of the IR detector in this missile is fairly narrow, the airplane itself must be pointed just about at the target before the missile is able to "see" it. This could present some added maneuvering requirements during a hard turning fight. In some instances, the lack of a complete IR subsystem limits the options of a pilot who wishes to approach his target without triggering their RHAW gear. He must have a visual on his adversary if he is operating with his radar in "standby" before he can maneuver in for a kill with the Sidewinder. Of course, if the bad guy has a little keener eyesight, he may be able to successfully counter the attack before he is spotted. IR missiles such as the Sidewinder cannot be jammed like those guided by radar; however, they can be faked out and drawn off target by a well-timed flare drop.

The Human Factor

The imposing blend of performance, weapons, and delivery systems, plus a hungry tiger at the controls, would seem to form an invincible combination. Nonetheless, it is conceivable that the tiger himself may be the biggest limiting factor of all. Although the airplane is quite capable of performing all its various missions, it requires a skilled hand at the helm to optimize that performance.

The acquisition of these requisite skills is not an easy nor a quick task. The air-to-air game is so complex and filled with so many variables that many, *many* months of practicing two-against-two and four-against-four are required just to learn how to operate effectively in this environment. Then at least a couple of tactics sorties each week are needed to maintain a hot hand. The close air support mission, with its many different ways of delivering ordnance, is another area that requires constant practice. Like air-to-air, this facet of the fighter pilot's business is more an art than a science. As such, it, too, requires that a few bombs be dropped on a regular basis in order to keep the eye sharp. Naturally, the more precise techniques used in offset bombing—particularly where nukes are concerned—need periodic honing to stay proficient in this area. Add to this the regular practice necessary to hack the all-weather intercept mission, along with instrument flying, formation work, and midair refueling, and it's easy to visualize the scope of skills needed to fly today's fighters.

Given the natural order of things, it is unrealistic to think that everybody in a fighter squadron is equally proficient in all the areas mentioned above. Some people will be better at dive-bombing, while others excel in air combat tactics, while yet others find that night and precision instrument work is their bag. Much like the barnyard residents in *Animal Farm*, all the jocks in any unit can perform each facet of the total mission, but some are better performers than others in certain areas.

In the event of hostilities, a prudent commander would certainly assign his "top guns" to that portion of the mission that each does best. However, as attrition begins to take its toll, lesser qualified people will be forced to fly missions they are not comfortable with. This is where the potential of the machine is limited by the skill of the man. Also, even in wartime, this situation is not likely to improve because of the normal rotation of personnel in and out of any squadron. There are rare occasions when all the crews in an outfit become equally proficient in every aspect of the mission, or nearly so. This usually occurs following an intensive training period that prepares a unit for some specialized deployment. A squadron in this situation is a tough bunch to beat, and will remain so until new people are brought in.

Chapter 13

Air Engagements: Vietnam Era

The discussion of air-to-air engagements in this chapter will be more concerned with the overall tactics employed during the Vietnam era than with the individual maneuvering of one fighter against another. The latter topic is much too broad for the scope of this book, and is better covered by those who actually flew the missions.

By the time we became involved in the Korean War, engagements between fighters only took place as a result of planned actions made up of relatively large numbers of airplanes. Gone were the days of the solo patrol over enemy lines at dawn, where an unwary opponent could be pounced upon. Modern tactics called for massed fighter strength when opposition by the enemy was even a remote possibility.

This was the doctrine that prevailed during the 1960s, when fighter engagements could or did occur as a part of the following types of missions: Strike escort, Barrier Combat Air Patrol (BARCAP), and intercepting an unknown intruder. Pure fighter-vs.-fighter missions, such as were flown over Europe in the latter days of World War II and over the Yalu during the Korean War, were not a vital consideration during this time period. Enemy fighter strength in Vietnam was concentrated around Hanoi and Haiphong, and was only used for the defense of this area. Therefore, just about all engagements occurred as a result of these fighters trying to break through the birds flying top cover for the strike force.

BARCAP

BARCAP missions became routine after the North Koreans shot down one of our aircraft that was on an electronic intelligence gathering flight, and was over international waters. Specially equipped birds from both sides have been flying this type of mission for many years. They parallel the coastline to sample defensive radar frequencies and monitor any communications traffic they can pick up.

After the Korean incident, fighters were deployed along the line of flight of the Electronic Intelligence (ELINT) aircraft. Numerous flights would be positioned between the coastline and the ELINT bird so that any attempt at interception could be met and defeated. These missions were usually quite a bit longer than a normal sortie, and in most cases required two midair refuelings.

The entire area over which the BARCAP was flown was also covered by GCI radar. This was accomplished by using picket ships or an AWACS bird. The radar controllers kept everyone advised of the whereabouts of other flights on the BARCAP, as well as the position of the ELINT aircraft. They also provided vectors to and from the tanker in order to expedite this phase of the mission. Most important of all, they kept the BARCAP apprised of any fighter activity along the coastline that looked like it might be a threat to the operation. If enemy fighters headed toward the ELINT bird, these controllers gave immediate directions to the good guys to intercept the hostiles. Their job was only to give snap vectors and target range and bearing to the various flights. Once pointed toward the enemy, the fighter's airborne radar would be used to acquire the targets and complete the intercept.

Of course, whenever an unknown aircraft was detected approaching our airspace, only a flight of two would be scrambled to intercept it. This would be sufficient to handle a situation of this type where only one or two hostiles were involved. Should a larger force be picked up heading our way, the principle of massed fighter strength would once again be applied. Nearly all the bogeys intercepted on this type of mission would be single aircraft, and would probably fall into one of two categories. They would either be an enemy bird on an ELINT mission, or a fighter-bomber on an interdiction sortie.

Strike Force Escort

Each of the three situations mentioned above that led to fighters battling fighters was governed by rules of engagement formulated for each type of action. These rules again came under the general heading of "Guns Free" and "Guns Tight."

Let's first take a look at the conditions where the former would apply. As mentioned in the last chapter, operations under "Guns Free" meant that unknown targets could be fired on without first having to be identified. Application of this policy was only practical up through the first head-on pass of opposing fighter forces. After that, things would break down into a series of dogfights between elements from each side, and quite a bit of discretion had to be used before any armament was launched. AWACS or GCI is unable to distinguish friend from foe during this melee; therefore, no one would consider firing a missile at any target unless they could positively identify the bird as hostile.

This type of situation is typified by the strike escort mission. During these operations, the fighters assigned the job of protecting the strike force had to be ready to engage the enemy at any instant. For this reason, elements and flights would normally maintain an almost line abreast formation. This arrangement proved to be the most flexible for offensive maneuvering, as well as affording the highest degree of lookout coverage to the rear of the formation. Line abreast required a little more adroit flying by the wingmen to stay in position during the weaving and turning required when flying escort, but the tactical advantages gained were well worth the effort.

A typical strike force was made up of a number of components, each of which was vital to the success of the mission. At the center of it all were quite a few flights of fighters that carried the bombs. These birds would be flying a variety of the line abreast formation known as "Pod." This got its name from the ECM pod that each bird carried to counter the SAM threat. These pods did a good job of jamming the SAM radars; however, in order to provide protection for a flight of four, their radiation patterns had to overlap slightly. This meant that the aircraft had to fly fairly close to one another so that this mutual coverage was realized.

If this formation was maintained, it resulted in pretty good protection from SAMs, but it was not the best arrangement to be caught in if you were bounced by MiGs. The close quarters necessary for effective jamming allowed no room for quick maneuvering if a MiG managed to slip into your six. In order to reduce the odds of this possibility, flights of strike escort fighters were positioned on either flank of the bomb carriers. The mission of these birds was to take care of any MiGs that were able to get by the MIGCAP. (More will be said about this latter group shortly.)

Out in front of the bomb carriers and their escort by a mile or two were the chaff bombers. These birds, also flying line abreast, stretched across the entire front of the strike force, and each was loaded wall-to-wall with chaff dispensers. Their function was to spread a carpet of chaff in front of the strike birds to deny enemy radars information on the size of the force and the position of the flights within it. The position of the chaff bombers, however, was fairly precarious, since the bad guys knew that they were right at the forward edge of the chaff stream. This gave their GCI controllers some pretty solid information on which to base the vectoring of their fighters. Such a tenuous situation soon resulted in escort fighters being positioned near both ends of the line of chaff bombers to pick off any MiGs trying to break down the protective shield.

Iron Hand

Even farther out in front of everybody would be a couple of "Iron Hand" flights. These were birds with special equipment that could detect and home in on SAM radars. As soon as any site directed its radar at the strike force, the Iron Hand aircraft would pick up their signals and get a fix on the position of the launch complex. A quick turn in that direction, and a weapon designed for just this type of mission was launched to destroy the facility.

It took an especially gutsy bunch of individuals to fly in the Iron Hand flights. While they did carry ECM pods, they were quite a distance in front of the strike force, and thus could expect little help from the fighters assigned to protect it. In addition, the essence of their mission could be likened to flying down the muzzle of a loaded gun and hoping to destroy it before it went off—just another example of a nasty job that was taken in stride by the hungry tigers, and done well.

MIGCAP

The MIGCAP, or MiG Combat Air Patrol, was the final unit that went to make up a typical strike force. The MIGCAP would consist of two or more flights of fighters (depending on the situation) that were strictly configured for the air-to-air role. The only armament they carried were various combinations of Sparrow, Falcon, or Sidewinder missiles, and a Gatling gun. (When the F-4E came into the inventory, the gun was no longer housed in a pod mounted on the centerline station, as described earlier. Miniaturized electronics had reduced the size of the radar to the point where the gun could be mounted in the bottom of the nose compartment. The reduced weight and drag realized by an internal gun gave this model of the Phantom a boost in performance capability.) The MIGCAP's primary job was to roam over the entire area covered by the strike force and act as the first line of defense against attacking enemy fighters. Based on the information received from AWACS or GCI, they would position themselves in the best location to meet the incoming threat.

Now that we've got a general idea of how the various parts of the strike force are arranged with respect to each other, let's take a look at the game plan that would be followed if they got bounced. The MIGCAP would be the first to make contact with the enemy, so the discussion will center on their actions. The strike escort birds would react in a similar manner; however, since they must stick close to the bomb carriers, their freedom to maneuver is a little more restricted. The guys with the bombs would maintain formation until they were actually under attack, at which time they would execute the required defensive maneuvers.

Let's assume that the strike force is heading due north, and the AWACS has reported MiGs inbound from the northwest. On this attack, the MiGs will pass to the west of the strike force and then angle in, aiming for the left rear corner of the formation.

The radar controller would only broadcast very generalized information to the entire strike force, such as: "Bandits, ten o'clock at 70 miles." Even this sparse amount of data is enough for the MIGCAP, and they immediately wheel around to a heading that hopefully places the enemy at 12 o'clock and closing. At this point the MIGCAP birds must get a radar contact on the MiGs if they are to successfully counter their attack. If everything is going right, they should pick up the MiGs a little to the left of center on their scopes at a range of about 30 miles.

The GIB has to be sharp here and get an immediate lock-on despite the high closing rate of the target. As soon as radar contact is obtained, the pilot must also start a moderately hard turn into the target to keep him on the scope and allow the GIB to get a lock-on. The ideal situation here is to achieve an early lock-on so that a Sparrow can be launched on the initial frontal pass. If these missiles connect, fine, but if some of the MiGs get through, the attack must be continued by keeping the hard turn going to retain the bogey on the scope.

However, things are not that simple, and all this good work is easier said than done. By now the target is crossing the scope at a high angular velocity, and is probably diving to pick up a good head of steam for the final attack maneuvering. Even though an early lock-on was not obtained, this turn into the bogey must be kept going, and must be kept tight.

As the MiGs get closer to the strike force, they will have to start a turn that will bring them in behind, and probably below, the rear of the formation. The middle of this final turn by the bogey is where the MIGCAP will make its kill. When the MiGs are about halfway through this turn, they will be canopy-up to the approaching MIGCAP birds, who have just about completed their turn and are starting to accelerate. This planform view of the MiGs provides an optimum radar return, and if the attack geometry worked out, the good guys will see a bright radar target in their twelve o'clock position, and should have no trouble completing a beam attack to the weapons launch point.

While the MIGCAP birds are in their hard turn to cut the bad guys off at the pass, the strike escort aircraft would be kept advised of the threat approaching from their beam or rear. These flights really can't do too much until they know just where the enemy plans to commit himself. Turning away from the strike force prematurely to meet this threat is not too advisable. A poor guess as to the position of the approaching MiGs will have the escort birds pointing in the wrong direction—most probably away from the airplanes they are supposed to protect. It is also a good possibility that their turn has to be relatively tight, which would leave them in a less-than-desirable condition energy-wise. The AWACS radar would not be of much help by this time, since all the blips would be too close together to pick out the good guys from the bad. Therefore, it is pretty much of a judgement call as to when the strike escort starts its turn, but they can get a lot of help from the MIGCAP, who are closing in on the bogeys and can see how the attack is developing.

Another type of situation is possible where the strike escort would be in the thick of it a lot faster, with little or no help from the MIGCAP. This would occur if on the initial pass the bad guys and the MIGCAP passed each other head-on. Here, getting a lock-on in time to launch a Sparrow might be difficult because of the high closing rate and the small frontal area of the approaching targets. If our missiles did not score a kill on this pass, the enemy would streak by the MIGCAP, who now have to make a 180-degree turn to get back into the fight. Considering the time, space, and energy consumed during this turn, it is doubtful that the MIGCAP will get to the strike force in time to do much good unless the enemy decides to stick around and play.

On a direct frontal pass as just described, there might be some benefit in hosing off a missile at the approaching MiGs even if proper guidance may be lacking. The idea here is to hope that one or two of the enemy pilots are nervous types who, upon seeing a missile heading in their general direction, will immediately break down and out of the fight.

Last Ditch Maneuvers

Regardless of the crossing angle that develops on the initial pass between the opposing fighters, the MIGCAP's job once this first run is complete is to provide mutual support to the strike escort in any way they can. By this time the fight will have broken down into engagements between flights or elements from both sides, with each attacking targets of opportunity. Flight integrity and mutual support become the key words here as the tactics shift from radar to basic fighter maneuvers. The name of the game becomes: "Get on the enemy's tail and hammer him, while your wingman covers your six!" The offensive and defensive maneuvers and counter-maneuvers used during a dogfight are a book in themselves, and much too complex to be described here.

In the wild hassle that ensues, there is always the possibility of a MiG slipping into your six and trying to close for a gun attack. If your wingman is similarly occupied or is otherwise unable to help, something has to be done to shake this guy before he reaches firing range. Obviously, the first things to try are the standard defensive maneuvers such as the Break, Scissors, or High-G Barrel Roll.

However, if the guy has done his homework and successfully counters all your fancy gyrations, the situation starts to get a little dicey. You must keep the airplane turning as hard as you can, pulling at least six Gs, or more if you can squeeze them out without a total loss of energy. But a turning fight is a MiGs forte, and it won't be too long before he is pulling the proper lead to lay a lot of hurt on your bird.

Something must be done to destroy the tracking solution provided by his gunsight. Now is the time to try a last ditch maneuver, a few of which every fighter pilot must have in his repertoire. These maneuvers are resorted to only when you have an attacker behind you that you can't shake, and he is at—or very close to—gun range. Four of the more common ones used are the high-G rudder roll over the top, the high-G rudder roll underneath, the jink, and the negative-G maneuver. In nearly every case, the situation where any of these is tried is the same. The bird is in a hard diving turn, pulling about six or seven Gs, and with full afterburner power.

Assuming a turn to the right, there would normally be no control inputs except full back stick, and maybe a little bottom rudder. To start the rudder roll over the top, left rudder is applied while holding the G load on the bird with back stick. The nose starts to rise and more rudder has to be put in to keep it describing an arc across the horizon. As the maneuver progresses, back stick and rudder have to be played to keep the bird rotating in the vertical plane. The G loading is particularly important here, and has to be handled very carefully or the aircraft will suddenly depart the controllability envelope. Control inputs are maintained until the nose completes 360 degrees of rotation, or until the energy level of the airplane is depleted to the point where you must break the maneuver or go into an out-of-control situation.

The rudder roll over the top makes for a pretty hairy ride all the way around, with the entire airplane bucking and shuddering on the verge of a complete stall throughout the maneuver. The whole idea of both high G rudder rolls is to present your adversary with a target he cannot track with his gunsight, while at the same time decreasing your velocity along your flight path rapidly, causing him to overshoot. These maneuvers accomplish both these ends extremely well.

Following someone who goes into a high-G rudder roll over the top is an eye-opening experience. The defender would normally not try this gyration unless you were fairly close on his tail—say, about 1,500 feet. Naturally, you are concentrating on trying to get the pipper settled down on his midsection, when all of a sudden his nose starts to rotate upwards. His aircraft seems to stop dead in the air as his energy level is dissipated in a rush, and your overtake rate instantly jumps by several hundred knots. One instant he is 1,500 feet away, and the next he is filling your windshield. Your gun pass quickly deteriorates to a collision avoidance maneuver, as you must break off the run and take evasive action to keep from having a midair. Your aircraft's high energy level squirts you out in front of your opponent before any successful counter can be made.

However, there is not too much of a problem in being in front of someone who has just completed a high-G rudder roll. After finishing this maneuver, his aircraft has absolutely no offensive potential remaining, and he is probably sitting there with barely enough airspeed to keep the bird flying. Once one of these rudder rolls has been executed, the only thing left to do is dive for airspeed on a heading 180 degrees away from that of your opponent and head for home.

The high-G rudder roll underneath is much the same as the one just described, except that the aircraft rotates in the opposite direction. It is entered by the application of full bottom rudder while again maintaining the G loading with aft stick. The first 120 degrees or so of rotation really gets your attention, since the nose is pointing almost straight at the ground and you are upside down for a portion of the time. You would almost swear that you are in an inverted spin until the nose of the bird struggles up above the horizon in the second half of the maneuver. Once again the objectives are achieved, since the attacker cannot follow you through the roll and keep his gunsight tracking you properly. An overshoot occurs, and once this happens, the defender's options are the same as before—dive for airspeed and separation and make a dash for home.

The jink is a violent last ditch maneuver whose objective is to destroy the enemy's tracking solution while attempting to generate some lateral separation between the two aircraft. It is not as costly in terms of energy maneuverability as the high-G rudder rolls; however, it also does not get the attacker off your tail immediately.

Let's go back to our previous situation, where the defender is in a hard diving turn to the right but his opponent is still outturning him and is able to pull lead. The defender has got the stick back in his gut and may have a tad of bottom rudder in to keep the nose down. When he decides to jink, full opposite controls are applied, and the aircraft is unloaded for just an instant. This is done by slamming the stick full forward and full left in one motion, while at the same time jamming in full left rudder. The aircraft's response to this just about loosens your fillings, as it goes instantly from a hard turn to the right to one in the opposite direction.

As soon as 180 to 200 degrees of roll have been completed, the stick is again reefed in and the G loading goes from a negative one or two to a positive six or seven. The bad guy on your tail, trying to draw a bead on your airplane for the kill, suddenly finds his target going the other way, and he is forced into a similar maneuver to maintain the advantage. However, the split-second delay in his reaction to your turn reversal causes him to lose a little ground. Before he has a chance to gain it back, you lay another jink on him to force him out a little farther. After a few of these gyrations you hopefully have him zigging while you're zagging. Although he is still in a position of advantage behind you, he is not able to get his pipper on your bird long enough to get in a telling shot.

As can be imagined, the jink produces a wild and tumultuous ride for the pilot, banging him around in the cockpit while at the same time requiring him to make an accurate assessment of the offensive moves of the fighter behind him.

The final last ditch defensive action is the negative-G maneuver. Admittedly, this is not a very effective counter against a determined and even moderately skilled opponent. However, since most pilots dislike negative Gs, it might be worth a try before resorting to other options.

A jock who suddenly finds someone on his tail may try pushing the bird over into a negative-G condition in an attempt to lose his adversary. If it is done quickly and in an unexpected direction, it will probably gain the defender a little time and space in which to try something else. At the very least he should be able to increase his airspeed quite rapidly, and with the resulting higher energy level, might be able to try a more involved maneuver.

Tactics and Rules of Engagement

The tactics used on a BARCAP mission are very similar to those described above for the MIGCAP. Probably the biggest difference is the problem of maintaining good position in the line abreast formation during a BARCAP.

Each flight of fighters has a definite area to patrol, which necessitates them flying a racetrack-shaped pattern. The 180-degree turns at each end of the pattern require quite a bit of jockeying to keep the flight in a tactically advantageous alignment. Anyone who slips behind soon learns that it takes quite a long time to get back in position, because the flight is holding about .9 Mach. This speed is the minimum desirable for this type of mission in order to keep the flight's energy level as high as possible for maneuvering. And with everyone going at .9 Mach, there isn't much throttle left to help you catch up.

Another point worth noting about these turns at the ends of the racetrack pattern is that they are always made in the direction of the threat. The purpose of this is to prevent the BARCAP fighters from being caught in a turn pointing 180 degrees away from the enemy when he is first detected. By the time they would get turned around, the bogeys would have the upper hand tactically, and would probably have a field day. As soon as the enemy fighters are picked up, the BARCAP birds turn to position themselves for a direct head-on pass, where radar-guided missiles will be fired. If the bad guys are coming in utilizing a spread formation, it might even be possible for the BARCAP fighters to pick out individual aircraft on their radars. This of course is an ideal situation, where the flight leader can assign targets to each of his birds to ensure that all are covered.

After the missiles are fired on the front pass, the BARCAP birds would start an immediate 180 degree turn and try to catch up with the bogeys for a follow-on missile or gun attack. However, the time and space problem described above again comes into play, and the enemy fighters might be all over the ELINT bird before the BARCAP aircraft can get turned around and catch up to the action. Because of its lack of speed and maneuverability, the ELINT aircraft is quite vulnerable should one of the enemy fighters break through. Its only defense is to head away from the approaching fighters at top speed just as soon as they appear on the radar screen.

The "Guns Free" rule applies during a MIGCAP or a BAR-CAP only up to the time of the initial pass. Once the enemy fighters are engaged, there are too many aircraft wheeling about to be sure that the one on your scope is a bad guy. Therefore, even though the missiles are able to hit something beyond the range where visual indentification is possible, no one can risk firing any armament until they know they are locked on to an enemy aircraft. This does not present too much of a problem once the dogfight begins, because with everybody mixing it up, just about all of the attacks will take place in the rear hemisphere of the target aircraft. In this situation, missile launch range is inside visual acquisition range, and the attacker can be sure of just who he is shooting at.

The rules of engagement that govern just about all air defense operations would be considered "Guns Tight." There is simply too much air activity by each service in the theater to be absolutely sure that an aircraft penetrating our airspace is hostile. As mentioned earlier, there are numerous situations where lack of coordination or overlapping raids going to and from a hostile area could cause one of our birds to be misidentified as an enemy. But the air defense system must also provide protection from interdiction missions, and prevent ELINT aircraft from having a free ride. Therefore, the Identification and Attack pass was developed to provide a method of positively identifying an unknown while at the same time having the capability for an instant kill.

The ID and Attack sortie is flown by two aircraft scrambled to intercept a bogey approaching our airspace. These birds utilize an in-trail departure, which means that the number two aircraft releases its brakes about ten seconds after the flight leader starts his takeoff roll. Once airborne, number two locks his radar on the leader and adjusts his power to achieve a five-mile separation between the two birds. He also steers his aircraft to place number one dead ahead, in his twelve o'clock position. During the remainder of the enroute phase of the mission, he maintains this position by keeping the jizzle band centered on the scope and the overtake rate adjusted to zero.

The flight leader's responsibilities during an ID and Attack sortie are to follow GCI's instructions and locate the target on his search radar. The radar controller will bring the flight in on a direct head-on pass, and if possible, a little below the target's altitude. When the unknown is about 50 miles in front of the flight, the controller will start calling its range and bearing about every ten seconds. As soon as number one gets a good "paint" on the target, he will obtain a lock-on and steer to center the jizzle band on the scope. He will also adjust his altitude to maintain a slight "look up" angle on his radar. Although the leader's bird is loaded, no armament is selected on this pass since his primary job is to get an eyeball on the bogey as it flashes by overhead.

When he sees and identifies the unknown, lead calls "Hostile" or "Friendly" to number two, who reacts accordingly. If the aircraft is hostile, number one pushes over to a zero-G condition and accelerates as much as possible down and away from the target. He holds his heading for about 15 seconds and the starts a hard turn back in the direction of the enemy aircraft.

While all this is going on, number two also has his work cut out for him. When the controller starts giving target information to the leader, the wingman breaks his lock-on and returns to the search mode. His radar will then "paint" number one on each sweep, and he maintains position by keeping this blip centered on the scope at the five mile range mark. Radar-guided missiles are selected, and as soon as he gets a contact on the bogey, a lock-on is obtained and he begins following steering information generated by the weapons system computer. If lead calls the bogey hostile, the trigger is squeezed and the missiles are launched at the correct time by the computer. If the bird is friendly, the lock-on is broken and the weapons systems is safed up.

Given the geometry of this intercept, where all three aircraft are in a straight line, there comes a point in the attack when the blips from the target and the flight leader will merge on number two's scope. This is the reason why the leader dives slightly after IDing the bogey. It carries him out of number two's radar beam and minimizes the chance of the wingman's radar jumping lock to him as the two blips cross.

Since the ID and Attack mission will only work in the daytime when the weather is fairly good, what would happen if the bogey spotted number one coming down the pike? His RHAW gear would let him know that he was being tracked by an interceptor's radar, and chances are he would get a visual on the flight leader as he passed by underneath. With an enemy aircraft behind him, the bogey cannot afford to do less than turn into the threat before his advantage is lost. He may even surmise that the interceptor's radar malfunctioned, which would make for even easier pickings.

In any event, it would be almost instinctive for any fighter pilot worth his salt to start an immediate hard diving turn to give chase. Should this happen, it really simplifies things for the wingman. As the bogey turns, his bird will be belly-up to number two, and all the flat surface of this planform view makes an excellent radar reflector. This, coupled with the reduced overtake caused by the turn, enhances the probability that the missiles will guide successfully, and if things work right, they should catch him just about in the middle of his turn.

Even if the worst occurs and the missiles fail to launch or guide, the bogey is now sandwiched between number one and two, and a follow-up attack can be executed. By now the flight leader has started his turn back toward the bogey, and the latter must also turn if he wants to stay in the fight. This turn by the bogey allows the wingman to establish a cutoff angle on him, whereby he can press home an attack with either IR missiles or the gun.

Our discussion of the air-to-air game thus far has made frequent mention of the IR and radar guided missiles that were the standard armament found on fighters of the '60s and '70s. A little closer examination of these weapons is appropriate, because their capabilities and effectiveness have definitely made them the primary weapons of the modern fighter pilot.

The Sidewinder has been around for quite some time, making its debut in 1953, and is one of the simplest and cheapest guided weapons ever produced. Its manufacturer claims that it has less than two dozen moving parts and no more electronic components than a domestic radio. Yet its accuracy and reliability have made it a popular weapon in the air forces of some 16 countries. The Sidewinder is 9 feet, 3 1/2 inches long, has a diameter of 5 inches, and a fin span of 1 foot, 10 inches. It weights 159 pounds at launch, and its solid-propellent rocket motor gives it a range of two miles. The missile is guided by an infrared homing device mounted behind the glass nose of the weapon. When this detector is pointed at a source of infrared energy, it informs the pilot that it "sees" the target by introducing a growling tone into his headset. The Sidewinder's bite is provided by a 25-pound high-explosive warhead.

The Sparrow is another old-timer, having been designed as the primary air-to-air weapon for the first production models of the F-4, which rolled out in 1961. The Phantom carries four of these weapons in semi-submerged mountings along the fuselage bottom. The Sparrow is 12 feet long and 8 inches in diameter, with fins spanning 3 feet, 4 inches. It too is powered by a solid-propellent rocket motor that enables it to achieve a speed of better than Mach 3.5 and a range of eight miles. The missile weighs 450 pounds at launch, and incorporates a radar homing guidance system. This requires that the aircraft's radar stay locked on the target during the time of flight of the missile, since it homes on this reflected energy.

The last of the missiles in common use during the Vietnam era was the Falcon. This too is a vintage weapon, being a little older than the Sparrow and the Sidewinder; like the latter, it utilizes an IR guidance system. Overall it is a little smaller than the other two, being 6 feet, 7 1/2 inches long, about 6 inches in diameter, and having fins 1 foot, 8 inches wide. It weighs only 134 pounds and is effective out to six miles. The initial versions of this missile were the first air-to-air guided weapons adopted by the Air Force, and follow-on models are still in service today.

By the time of the Mideast war in 1978 and the Falkland Islands scrap in 1982, the airplanes that had served us so well in Vietnam were just about passé. Giant strides had been made in the development of airframes, engines, and weapons systems, and when these wars were fought, the new items were already in the inventory.

Chapter 14

The Mideast and the Falklands

The impressive new weapons systems that appeared on the scene in the early 1970s did not get an all-out test of their prowess until the decade was nearly over. By then the Israelis had purchased enough F-15s to permit them to be employed in sufficient quantity to support or conduct large tactical operations. Over the years since these birds entered the inventory, just about all the bugs that initially plague any new airplane had been worked out. This fairly well precluded any glitches or excuses from mitigating the validity of a true operational test of their capabilities. During the latter half of 1981 Israel also acquired the F-16, and by the end of that year had over 50 assigned to active squadrons.

Both these birds were given a good workout in the Middle East theater, being used on missions that exercised every facet of their design potential: air-to-air, air-to-ground, interdiction, air defense, and employment with AWACS. The air-to-air and air defense sorties were no "piece of cake" missions, since in 1979, Israel's enemies were flying the MiG-21 and MiG-23. A year later—probably in response to Israel having the F-16—Syria added the Mig-25 to its inventory.

Judging by the lopsided score run up by the Israelis, the F-15 and F-16 were living up to their press releases, even when tangling with some of the opposition's top-of-the-line fighters. Naturally, a good deal of the credit for achieving these scores has to be attributed to the continuous and intensive training received by the Israeli jocks. Their excellent state of preparedness undoubtedly allowed them to outfly their opponents, even if the aircraft were more or less evenly matched. Another segment that must share the limelight here is the Israeli AWACS, whose presence definitely shifted the overall advantage in these battles to Israel.

The high level of performance delivered by the F-15 and F-16 in all tactical areas made for an instant love affair between these aircraft and the pilots who flew them. They were designed from the ground up with the fighter pilot in mind, and toward a singular end: *air superiority*. Everything that anyone who had ever flown fighters wanted was there, in spades—an engine that made it seem like the airspeed indicator was connected directly to the throttle; the ability to sustain a high-G turn without a disastrous loss of Mach; a weapons system and armament that could handle all comers in any kind of weather, and cockpit visibility that hasn't been available for decades. Add to these a Heads Up Display (HUD) to facilitate weapons delivery, plus long range and good load-carrying ability and you have a real tough customer for the air superiority game. Previous fighters were built with an eye toward doing their primary mission well, but this meant compromising on certain desirable features in other areas. Through advanced technologies, the F-15 and F-16 have achieved new heights in "getting it all together," thereby providing today's hungry tigers with a bird that has true multi-role capability.

Today's Fighters

In order to better understand just what it is that places these fighters a quantum leap beyond their predecessors, a little closer look at their vital statistics is necessary.

The F-15 was the first to emerge from the high-tech aerie, and was appropriately named the Eagle. Designed in 1969 and first flown in 1972 by McDonnell-Douglas, the Eagle was just what the doctor ordered to counter the threat to air superiority posed by the Mig-23. Compared to the F-4, it is not that much larger an airplane, although it appears to be bigger when standing next to it—probably because of the size of the forward fuselage and engine intakes. The F-15 has a wingspan of just under 43 feet, is a little less than 64 feet long, and stands almost 18 1/2 feet high. With full internal fuel, four missiles, and three 600-gallon external tanks, it weighs in at 57,400 pounds. It is a single-seat aircraft that is powered by two Pratt and Whitney turbofan engines, each rated at 23,930 pounds

Fig. 14-1. McDonnell Douglas F-15 configured with missiles for the air-to-air mission. The 20mm Gatling gun is located in the right wing root, just outboard of the engine inlet duct. (courtesy McDonnell Douglas Corporation)

of thrust with afterburning. These engines give the Eagle performance figures that are truly outstanding: maximum level speed of over Mach 2.5, and ceiling of 100,000 feet.

As mentioned earlier, air-to-air combat engagements are rarely conducted at that speed and at that altitude. However, the ability to reach these extremes translates into something more meaningful when you are twisting and turning behind an opponent as you press in for the kill. Power like that means that you can lay four or five Gs on the bird while chasing your quarry and not only maintain your Mach, but also have the capability to accelerate and close to weapons launch range.

Normally when a bird is designed to reach these speeds, it has undesirable characteristics at the other end of the airspeed spectrum, such as high stalling speeds and instability problems. Not so with the Eagle, which can be slowed down to about 110 knots in a wings-level attitude. Here the stick is held full aft, yet the aircraft barely indicates any buffeting, although it does begin to lose altitude if kept in this condition. The noteworthy thing here is the aircraft's stability at this speed, with no tendency toward yawing, Dutch roll, or falling off on one wing. This type of low-speed controllability also makes for a comfortable speed on final approach, with touchdown being at about 130 knots.

Another demonstration of its superior slow flying characteristics was given to a representative of *Aviation Week and Space Technology* magazine. The aircraft was cruising at 8,000 feet when the test pilot chopped the throttles to idle. He then pulled the nose up into a 60-degree climb and held it there until the airspeed had bled off to 250 knots. At this point he gave it full aft stick and pulled the nose up and over into the remainder of the loop. At the top of the loop the airspeed had dropped to zero, yet despite this, there was enough elevator authority left to pull the nose through and complete the maneuver.

There are some other features of the F-15's engines that are particularly important in a combat situation. The first of these is that they don't smoke. A fighter with engines that produce a black smoke trail is at a definite disadvantage in an engagement—especially one that takes place over a solid white undercast. The smoke plume shows up like an arrow pointing directly at the bird creating it, a factor that can be easily exploited by an alert foe. (This was a chronic problem with the F-4 until recently, when the combustion chambers in the engine were modified to make them burn clean.)

Another plus for the F-15's powerplants is that their total thrust is greater than the aircraft's weight in a combat configuration. The resulting 1.3:1 thrust-to-weight ratio allows the Eagle to climb straight up, which is a tough act to follow in a hassle. The F-15's tremendous rate of climb allowed it to set eight world records for time-to-altitude from a standing start on the runway. During these runs it went from brake release to over 39,000 feet in less than a minute, and was through 65,000 feet in just over two minutes. Numbers like that are enough to make an old fighter pilot cry.

The high thrust-to-weight ratio pays even greater dividends when it comes to acceleration. With all this power available, the pilot really has to be on his toes to keep up with things during a zero-G acceleration maneuver. This tactic is resorted to when you need a large jump in airspeed almost instantaneously, such as when you're bounced while cruising along at subsonic speeds. It is accomplished by plugging in the burners and pushing forward on the stick until the G meter reads zero, and holding it there. In this weightless condition, all of the engine thrust is being used to increase velocity, with none being wasted to counteract gravity or create lift. Using this technique, the F-15 would accelerate so fast that the tiger in the cockpit might feel that he is hanging on more than flying the bird.

Aircraft performance is only half the reason why the Eagle is so awesome at the air-to-air business. The other half must be attributed to the advanced design and capabilities of its weapons system.

The heart of the avionics package is the lightweight APG-53 pulse-Doppler radar built by Hughes Aircraft. This radar can detect and track small high-speed targets at ranges beyond 100 miles. Even more important, it has an excellent "look down" capability because of its Doppler circuitry. This specialized type of radar eliminates ground clutter and allows the pilot to see targets at treetop heights. After lock-on, the system provides accurate tracking information to the on-board computer, which delivers steering directions and other target data to the pilot's displays. The radar is also used to provide guidance for the Sparrow missiles after launch. Should the pilot decide to press on in for a gun attack and maneuvers into his opponent's six, the radar acquires the target automatically and presents range and steering information on the Heads Up Display.

Other parts of the avionics package include an inertial navigation system that is coupled to a horizontal display indicator. This latter piece of gear presents a symbolic picture of the terrain below on a cathode ray tube, with a depiction of the aircraft's present position. Additional unique features of this system are an interrogator receiver-transmitter that tells the pilot whether the aircraft he picks up on the radar—or the one his bird is pointing at—is friendly or not, and an internal countermeasures system that automatically jams enemy radar signals.

Navigation and target finding by radar ground mapping is also enhanced by the Doppler beam, which sharpens up the radar return presented on the scope until it almost resembles a photograph. Special circuitry in the APG-63 allows a picture to be shown that clearly reveals objects on the ground that are separated by 59 feet or more. This high degree of resolution is invaluable for locating aiming points on radar bombing runs, and as the mission progresses, this radar picture is updated every six seconds.

The rest of the avionics package contains the normal communications, navigation, and RHAW gear found in any fighter. The radios do have a rather unusual feature that has been needed for quite some time. The communications sets have cryptographic capabilities, which prevents the enemy from monitoring transmissions between aircraft and with ground stations. This allows pilots and controllers to "tell it like it is" without having to talk around mission tactics or sensitive subjects, or clip their transmissions to the point where little or no information is passed.

The armament carried by the F-15 is well adapted to its multi-role mission. When configured for air-to-air, it carries four Sidewinders and four Sparrows, as well as a Gatling gun with 940 rounds of ammunition. This doesn't sound like very much ammunition for a gun that fires 6,000 rounds per minute, but it must be remembered that even a short burst from this weapon can do an incredible amount of damage.

When the name of the game is air-to-ground, there are five hard-

Fig. 14-2. F-15 Eagle with air-to-ground load and conformal fuel tanks installed. (courtesy McDonnell Douglas Corporation)

Fig. 14-3. General Dynamics F-16. The gun port for the 20mm cannon can be seen on the fuselage side, just below the rear arch in the canopy. The missiles on the wingtips are AIM-9 Sidewinders. (courtesy General Dynamics)

points beneath the wings and fuselage where a total of 16,000 pounds of bombs can be hung. If a fighter of the last generation had to carry this many bombs, it would have to give up at least a part of its air-to-air capability. This is not the case with the Eagle, since these bombs are carried *in addition to* the full complement of missiles mentioned above. At this time, the F-15 is the only Air Force fighter that is authorized to carry and release bombs at supersonic speeds. The fact that it can even go better than Mach 1 with all this weight and drag hanging out in the breeze is mind-boggling.

Even with all of the above going for it, the F-15 still has great legs. Without using air-to-air refueling, its normal range is better than 2,800 miles, and this is increased to over 3,400 miles when the bird is fitted with low-drag conformal tanks attached to the outboard side of each engine duct. In this latter configuration it has flown nonstop and unrefueled from the United States to Europe.

Not too long after the Eagle made its debut, another bird sprang from the nest, and was aptly named the Fighting Falcon. The F-16 was first flown in 1974, and was primarily designed as a lower-cost alternative to the F-15 for both ourselves and our NATO and Middle East allies. From the very beginning it was quite obvious that we had another winner on our hands, and this General Dynamics bird was a fitting stablemate for the Eagle.

Although it uses the same engine as the F-15, the Fighting Falcon is a considerably smaller aircraft. It has a wingspan (including the tip-mounted missiles) of just under 33 feet, and an overall length of a little more than 49 feet. The bird stands about 16 1/2 feet high, and with full internal fuel and wingtip missiles, weighs only 23,600 pounds. This weight, being pushed by an engine with 23,930 pounds of thrust, gives the aircraft about a one-to-one thrust-to-weight ratio.

Where all this really makes a difference is in the F-16's truly phenomenal ability to turn. It is the first production fighter to have a placard limit of nine Gs, and will sustain seven Gs at sea level with an entry speed of only 300 knots. If you boost this entry speed up to 375 to 400 knots, nine Gs can be held indefinitely. What is even more amazing is that the aircraft will actually *accelerate* during this turn—another pause for the old heads to wipe away a tear.

How about the pilot during all this high-G maneuvering, which at times will cause a 160 pound jock to weigh over 1,400 pounds? Naturally, good physical condition and getting accustomed to flying in this environment do help, but after six Gs, things start to hurt. In order to give the pilot a little assistance in this area, the F-16 has a seat that is tilted back 30 degrees. This simple change allows the pilot's weight to be distributed over a larger portion of the body, and considerably reduces fatigue and discomfort. This slightly unusual position doesn't take much getting used to, and it has no adverse effect during landing or instrument flying.

Probably the most unique feature of the F-16 from a pilot's standpoint is the side-mounted stick. There is no conventional control stick coming up from the floor between the pilot's knees. Instead, there is a stick grip mounted on the right console at arm level, which only moves a very slight amount in each direction. This stick does nothing more than transmit electrical impulses to the airplane's computer to indicate what control actions the pilot desires. The quad-redundant computer then analyzes just about everything that has any bearing on the contemplated maneuver, such as airspeed, altitude, gross weight, rate of movement desired, etc. It then calculates the correct amount of deflection needed for each control surface to optimize these parameters and sends the appropriate electrical signal to that surface's servo-actuator.

This "fly by wire" system allows the pilot to fly along the feather edge of the performance envelope of the airplane without fear of exceeding the bird's limits and getting into an out-of-control situation. As might be expected, this system causes pilots new to the airplane some problems during close formation and landing due to overcontrolling. However, this tendency disappears after building up some time in the bird.

The Fighting Falcon was designed to replace the F-4E throughout the Air Force, and a quick look at some comparison figures will show the merit of this plan. Although it only weighs half as much as the F-4, it has twice the combat radius and a 50 percent better turning capability. It can accelerate twice as fast as an F-4 and carry the same load as the Phantom twice as far, and

Fig. 14-4. A pair of F-16s in a vertical climb. (courtesy General Dynamics)

in regards to weapons delivery, it can accomplish the air-to-ground mission with greater accuracy because of its superior avionics.

The turning ability just mentioned was dramatically illustrated when an F-4E and an F-16 flying side by side each started a maximum-performance turn. Both birds were in the contrail layer, and the resulting condensation trails showed the F-16 as having completed a 360 degree turn, which tightened as it progressed, before the F-4 had finished three quarters of a much wider, constant turn. The combat implications of such a capability are self-evident. With maneuvering potential like this, Mach 2 plus speed, and a standard armament load of two Sidewinders and a Gatling gun, the Fighting Falcon is a force to be reckoned with in any air superiority situation.

The radar system in the F-16 is also a pulse Doppler type, and has similar look-down capabilities and enhanced navigational mapping displays as previously described for the F-15. In keeping with the latest philosophy for air-to-air combat, a Heads Up Display is also incorporated into the system.

When configured for the air-to-ground role, the bird has a total of seven stations on which to load a variety of weapons and/or external fuel tanks. At the present time, the F-16 is serving with the air forces of Belgium, Denmark, the Netherlands, Norway, Israel, and Egypt, and is on order for Korea, Pakistan, and Venezuela— truly a multi-role, multi-national fighter.

The last friendly aircraft to be discussed here as one of the new generation of fighters is the AV-8A/B Harrier. In reality, it is hardly correct to call the Harrier a member of the new generation, since the first model entered squadron service with the RAF in 1969. These original birds were built by Hawker Siddeley Ltd. in England, and were intended for the close air support mission, working from small clearings close to the front lines by utilizing their VTOL capability. This was just the type of weapon the Marine Corps was looking for to support their traditional role of taking and expanding a beachhead. They conceived of it initially operating from small carriers; once the battle pushed inland, they could use cleared areas, partially damaged airfields, or roads. Accordingly, the Marines procured 110 Harriers from the British in 1971.

The new American fighters coming out about this time had some very impressive numbers: speeds better than Mach 2 and altitudes over 65,000 feet—definitely high and fast. The Harrier, on the other hand, was the epitome of the low and slow. Its max speed was only .88 Mach at sea level and .98 Mach at altitude—

Fig. 14-5. Hawker-Siddeley Harrier. (courtesy National Air and Space Museum, Smithsonian Institution)

certainly not the stuff to draw much attention!

However, what *did* get everyone's attention was a new concept of in-flight maneuvering that added a fresh dimension to the air-to-air game. This radically different idea was thought up by the Marines, who modified their birds to try it out; when perfected, the Harrier became just about unbeatable in a low-altitude, hard-turning fight.

The new technique was called Vectoring In Forward Flight, or VIFFing. To understand how this works it is necessary to take a look at the bird's Pegasus engine, which is rated at 21,500 pounds of thrust. The engine gases, instead of rushing through a conventional tailpipe, are directed to four rotatable nozzles located on the sides of the aircraft. In the original Harriers, these nozzles were pointed downward for vertical operations, and then rotated aft for forward flight.

The modification tried by the Marines was to bypass the device that locked the nozzles in the rearward position. This allowed the pilot to control the thrust vector of his engine in all phases of flight. What this meant was that a Harrier jock could dramatically increase his rate of turn by rotating the nozzles toward the downward position and use his engine thrust to push him around the turn quicker. This really comes in handy if you have a bad guy in your six whose bird could turn just a little better than yours. It would not be long before he was pulling the proper lead to hose off a burst, but in a Harrier, you could ruin his tracking solution by VIFFing to a new flight path that puts his pipper quite a bit behind you.

To visualize what happens when the thrust is vectored downward, consider a Harrier in a tight turn where the flight path can be thought of as describing a circular arc through the sky. When the VIFF is applied, the aircraft is literally translated from the original arc to another one parallel to the first, but above it in the plane of the turn. ("Above" here means in relation to the aircraft, and not to the actual horizon or the true vertical.)

Such a maneuver must really water the eyes of the attacker, who by this time is probably getting ready to paste another victory flag on the side of his bird. One minute his quarry is right where he wants him—in the bottom corner of the gunsight combining glass—and in the next instant the bird suddenly jumps to the top of the windshield bow, where no amount of pulling will bring his pipper even close. While trying to figure out what happened to his tracking solution, he also notices that his closing rate on the bird in front of him has increased considerably, and he is starting to slide out in front of his foe. Unless prompt corrective action is taken, an overshoot will occur, and the attacker quickly becomes the attackee.

This rapid deceleration is another aspect of VIFFing. When the exhaust nozzles are turned downward, the bird loses a substantial amount of its forward thrust vector. This has the same effect on slowing down the airplane as opening the speed brakes. However, in a hassle it is a little more effective because you don't telegraph your intentions to the guy in your six by something as obvious as a speed brake extension. The subtleness of the action causing the rapid deceleration, coupled with the increased turn rate, will undoubtedly cause the attacker to overshoot and thus lose his advantage.

On the other hand, if a Harrier is chasing someone in a tight turn and has to VIFF to get his pipper on the bad guy, this deceleration characteristic might work to his disadvantage. If the VIFF is held too long, the decrease in forward velocity may cause the Harrier to slip out beyond effective gun range.

Physically, the Harrier is not a big airplane, being a few feet smaller than an F-16 in all dimensions, and a little lighter. Because of the requirements for a vertical takeoff capability, the maximum allowable weight of external stores is only 9,200 pounds, which includes weapons and fuel tanks. The normal combat load consists of two or four Sidewinders, plus various combinations of bombs, missiles, or rocket launchers. The bird also has two gun pods built into the underside of the fuselage, which house multi-barrel, rapid-firing cannons. The weapons delivery system uses TV and a laser, linked to a computer and a Heads Up Display, to detect and track

Fig. 14-6. AV-8B Harrier II built by McDonnell Douglas for the Marine Corps. (courtesy McDonnell Douglas Corporation)

Fig. 14-7. MiG-23 Flogger. (courtesy National Air and Space Museum, Smithsonian Institution)

targets. Other equipment and avionics are similar to that used in the typical modern fighter.

The Opposition

The three aircraft just described have some fairly impressive vital statistics, and when the normal Mk. 1, Mod 0 hungry tiger straps one on, the combination would seem to be unbeatable. However, the opposition has not been idle during the years these birds were being developed. Assuming comparable skill levels, the guys in the white hats will need every bit of performance capability that these airplanes can deliver if they are to hack the mission against the current generation of MiGs.

The first of these to appear on the scene was the MiG-23, which has the NATO code name of Flogger. This bird was produced in quantity by the Soviets and now forms the backbone of their tactical and air defense forces, as well as those of the Warsaw Pact countries. It incorporates a swing-wing design for optimum performance at all speeds. However, the sweeping action is not done automatically in response to flight conditions, but must be accomplished by pilot-initiated action.

The MiG-23 is equipped with an engine that develops 27,500 pounds of thrust with afterburning, resulting in a top speed of Mach 2.35 and a service ceiling of 61,000 feet. It is also capable of Mach 1.1 at sea level. The radar set in the MiG-23 has a search range of 53 miles and a tracking range of 34 miles—very modest when compared to fighters in the Free World of the same vintage. This system represents the first Soviet aircraft with a demonstrated (although rudimentary) ability to track and engage targets below its own altitude. Armament on the Flogger consists of a twin-barrel 23mm cannon in a belly pack and five pylons for carrying radar and IR-homing air-to-air missiles or other types of external stores. As of December 1982, there were approximately 1,400 Mig-23s in service with the Russian and Warsaw Pact Air Forces and their Middle East allies.

The reigning top gun in the communist arsenal is the Mig-25 Foxbat. This airplane is just a tad larger than the F-15 and resembles it in many respects, with its twin tails, yawning, slab-sided intakes, and large, fixed-sweep wings. In an engagement involving F-15s and MiG-25s, it would be a tough job to visually identify one from the other at the speeds and altitudes involved.

The Foxbat is powered by two engines, each with 24,250 pounds of thrust in afterburner, which give the bird a top speed of Mach 3.2 in a clean configuration. However, when it is armed with its usual load of two radar and two IR missiles, the airplane is limited to Mach 2.8—still not too shabby!

After it was first spotted by western observers, the MiG-25 was shrouded in mystery, being touted by the Russians as the world's fastest combat aircraft. Their claims were reinforced in May 1975 when a special version of the Foxbat (using engines with 30,865 pounds of thrust) recaptured two time-to-climb records from the F-15. It also set additional records of 4 minutes, 11.7 seconds to

Fig. 14-8. MiG-25 Foxbat. Note the similarity of this design with the F-15. (courtesy National Air and Space Museum, Smithsonian Institution)

238

114,829 feet, and an absolute altitude reached of 123,524 feet.

The veil of secrecy around the MiG-25 was broken when a defecting Russian pilot brought one to Japan. He reported that the aircraft took considerable time to accelerate, and then had trouble maintaining sustained high speed. Our investigators found that the fire control system was bulky and lacking in advanced technology. Of particular note was the fact that it used vacuum tubes throughout. The radar had a very high power output, but this feature was devoted to anti-jamming, rather than to increasing the detection range, which was only 62 miles. The aircraft had a good airborne computer installed, along with RHAW gear and ECM equipment that included decoys and jammers.

Another interesting side note was that the Foxbat has only half the cockpit instruments of the F-4E, and a gunsight that is less versatile than the one used in the Phantom. The lack of instruments might have some advantages in a few situations, but considering the entire gamut of today's operational requirements, it probably imposes quite a number of limitations. The defecting pilot also mentioned that an improved version of the MiG-25 was under development. This model had the bigger engines used on the record-breaking flights, a strengthened fuselage to permit flying supersonic near the ground, improved avionics, and hardpoints for two more missiles, plus a gun. Subsequent improvements since that time have upped the armament load to eight air-to-air missiles and increased the radar search and track ranges to 190 and 167 miles respectively.

The Soviets have also developed their own version of the Harrier, which has been observed operating from carriers/cruisers since 1976. The Yak-36MP, however, is not quite the airplane that the Harrier is. The thrust vectoring arrangement on the aircraft permits only vertical takeoffs, thus precluding the heavier armament loads made possible by the Harrier's Short Take Off and Landing capability. This same problem also rules out the possibility of VIFFing.

AWACS

Although fighters and their employment are the end-all and be-all of the hungry tiger's world, another factor has gained an almost equal status in the overall scheme of things. This is AWACS, and despite the near-magical capabilities of the F-15 and F-16, it has become an essential ingredient in nearly all tactical operations.

The scope, speed, and complexity of modern aerial warfare

Fig. 14-9. Boeing E-3A Sentry. The midair refueling receptacle is located on the top of the fuselage, just aft of the cockpit. (courtesy National Air and Space Museum, Smithsonian Institution)

established a requirement for information on enemy activity far beyond visual range, and far beyond the relatively limited range of fighter radars. In order to plan intelligently and react properly, today's commanders must have the ability to look deep inside enemy territory to monitor air activities and determine their intent. AWACS provides this long-range eye in the form of the Boeing E-3A Sentry, which is a 707 airliner converted into an airborne GCI site—and much more.

The most distinguishing feature of this conversion is a large antenna housing, perched above the aft section of the fuselage, that rotates six times a minute. The system requires no separate height finder, since the main antenna electronically scans in elevation as it searches in azimuth. The radar can be operated in the normal pulse mode, the pulse Doppler mode, or both together. This latter mode provides the means to look down and detect low-flying targets against rugged background terrain. Using normal radar, the ground would reflect such severe clutter that all targets within it would be lost. Using pulse Doppler and a sophisticated filtering system, this masking clutter is removed, leaving only valid target returns on the scope. Inside the radome is another antenna, mounted on the back side of the radar antenna. This is part of the IFF (Identification-Friend from Foe) system, which helps to separate our fighters from theirs once the engagement is joined. It also receives data from various sensors that provide the same kind of information from ground sources.

While cruising at 30,000 feet, an E-3A can detect low-flying aircraft out to 250 miles in the pulse Doppler mode, and even farther than that in the normal mode. Along with the surveillance and control needed for the aerial situation, the system can simultaneously detect and display surface and maritime information. From the coded sensors mentioned above, the position of friendly ground forces can be depicted, as well as the status of key facilities such as airfields, fuel dumps, bridges and storage depots.

The mass of information flowing into the AWACS and to and from the fighters until its control is staggering. Yet to be truly valuable, this information must be given to the decision-makers on the ground—both military and political. One of the big pluses, and a prime *raison d'etre* for the E-3A, is its ability to transmit a comprehensive air and surface situation picture via TV to decision centers on a near real-time basis. *For the first time in history, commanders have the ability to see beyond the enemy's borders and view the battlefield itself from above.* This makes possible timely tactical decisions and coordinated international actions based on high-confidence data.

Attempts by the enemy to deny information to AWACS by jamming are for the most part unsuccessful. Its radar circuitry is specially designed to allow the controllers to work with clear scopes against jamming that completely saturates ground radar stations.

In order to accomplish its normal mission, the Sentry requires a crew of 17, which includes a flight crew of four. If an extra flight crew is provided, the E-3A's time on station is almost unlimited because of its in-flight refueling capability.

During the time the Sentry was being developed for the Air Force, the Navy saw the need for a similar aircraft to use with its carrier task force. The only problem here was one of size, since it had to be capable of operating from a flight deck. The Grumman E-2C Hawkeye was the answer, and although it is smaller and cheaper than the Sentry, it is no less potent. It too has a large discus-shaped radome (24 feet in diameter) mounted above the fuselage, feeding a radar and sensor system that performs the same functions as those on the E-3A. The reduced overall size of the radar in the Hawkeye necessarily limits its effective range to a little less than that in the Sentry.

With its clutter-free look-down capability, the E-2C can

simultaneously control 40 interceptors or strike missions, even in a heavy jamming environment. Its computer memory contains an intelligence library listing the radar signatures of every type of radar set in the world. Incoming radar signals from as far as 400 miles away are analyzed, compared, and identified almost instantly, and an appropriate symbol on the scope is assigned to the emitter. If it is a hostile aircraft and is within range of the Hawkeye's radar, the controller assigns a fighter to attack it merely by touching the enemy blip with a light stick. Instantly, information starts flowing to the friendly fighter, vectoring him in for the kill, which is quickly registered—probably before the enemy pilot even knows he is under attack. Again because of its size, the E-2C does not have the capability of transmitting a TV picture of the real-time situation to ground commanders.

The discussions in this chapter of the various aircraft flown by the good guys, illustrating their wide range of capabilities, should leave no doubt as to the enormous complexity of these machines. The giant strides made by technology has put systems and devices in the hands of today's hungry tigers that were viewed as Buck Rogers stuff only a few years ago. There can also be no doubt that all these new things have given us a formidable weapons system with which to gain aerial supremacy. However, what about the troops in maintenance? Do the high-technology components that make today's birds so potent require high-tech supermen to maintain them?

In the past, when quantum leaps in fighter development oc-

Fig. 14-10. Grumman E-2C Hawkeye. (courtesy National Air and Space Museum, Smithsonian Institution)

curred, this was pretty much the case. Exotic electronics and novel, one-of-a-kind systems required very sophisticated ground support and test equipment to keep these birds in commission. This apparatus in turn demanded a high order of skill to operate it effectively. In a nutshell, these aircraft were a nightmare as far as maintenance was concerned. It was a very common experience to crank up a bird, turn on the radar, and then sit in the chocks for what seemed like an eternity while specialists replaced major units or tweaked voltages in an attempt to bring the set on the line. The multiplicity of systems needed to make the airplane function properly required specially trained maintenance people from quite a few disciplines.

And even if everything went okay and the bird got airborne, these same unique maintenance requirements restricted the number of bases where it could land. Before single-point refueling equipment came into widespread use, a bird could sit at a strange field for days waiting for a fuel truck with the proper nozzle on its servicing hose to be driven from the closest location. The same problem could arise as a result of incompatible ground power carts, or air compressors. If the airplane needed maintenance requiring any of the aforementioned specialists, it usually necessitated flying in these people and their gear while the aircrews twiddled their thumbs at base operations. After the problem was diagnosed, it was a sure bet that a part had to be flown in from some distant depot, installed, and flight-tested. All in all, it was not unusual to spend a week nursing a sick bird back to health.

Apparently the planners in the Puzzle Palace (Pentagon) learned something from these trying years during the '50s and '60s. The new fighters are much more self-sufficient, and can be turned around at strange bases with little or no ground equipment. The intricate avionics in these birds still develop problems; however, because of miniaturized solid state circuitry, failures are not as common as in the old school.

Even repairs made after engine start take less time than before. This is because the new weapons systems have built-in test features that inform the maintenance crew where the problem is located. But in each section of the system there are zillions of parts and components that could be the source of the difficulty. Since most of these parts are mounted on circuit boards, a solution was found by a mechanism that flagged the malfunctioning board. The corrective action is simply to remove the faulty board and replace it with a good one, and the bird is off and running in a minimum amount of time. The same amount and level of skills are needed in maintenance, since all these broken circuit boards must eventually be analyzed and fixed, and some failures will occur that cannot be corrected by so easy a process. But in the long run, the fault isolation feature and the self-flagging components have helped considerably in reducing ground time and getting the bird airborne—where the hungry tiger can put it to work.

There is another problem (which might be more properly named a requirement) of modern tactical air forces that has not diminished over the years. This is the need for tankers for just about every mission that involves going more than 500 miles from the home drome. Today the need is probably more urgent than in the past, because, due to costs, there are fewer fighters available to cover our worldwide commitments. Given the ever-shrinking number of bases available to us overseas, the importance of tankers assumes even greater proportions. A responsive tanker force allows us to deploy a considerable amount of tactical airpower to just about any spot on the globe in no more than a day or two. Such a move can have a decisive impact on the balance of power in any theater where aggression might crop up.

Improved Weaponry

The frontline aircraft in the inventory at the beginning of the '80s were certainly prime examples of future technology. While their systems were as modern as tomorrow, the air-to-air weapons they carried had been around for many years. The Sidewinders and Sparrows found on the F-15 and F-16 are merely improved versions of missiles that have been used since before the Vietnam War.

The improvements in the third generation Sidewinder include better maneuverability, which will help correct a long-standing difficulty with this weapon. With earlier versions, it was possible for the target aircraft to outturn the missile if the pilot reefed it in at just the right moment. The newer weapon has improved tracking stability, along with an annular blast fragmentation warhead for increased lethality. It is also less susceptible to countermeasures by the target aircraft.

The Sparrow has been updated as well, with solid state circuitry, a larger motor, and Doppler guidance, which improves its performance at both medium and dogfight ranges. This latter area is where the Sparrow came up short in the past. During a close-in hassle, the weapon could not be expected to guide properly if an attacker launched it too close behind his foe. A short firing range did not allow sufficient time for the missile's radar to acquire the target, and thus a miss was almost guaranteed.

The 20mm Gatling gun mounted in the F-15 and F-16 is the same one used in the Phantom II during the Vietnam era, and it is still an awesome weapon for close-in work.

The air-to-ground game picked up a new wrinkle during the last decade in the form of the "shoot and leave" missile. Just before launch, such a weapon is fed information about the target that is retained in its on-board computer to provide guidance after it is launched. Once on its way, it gets no further help from the delivery aircraft, which is then free to leave the area or look for other targets.

Since the war in the Falkland Islands, probably the most famous of these weapons is the French built Exocet. This devastatingly effective missile can be launched from an altitude of 30,000 feet at a range of 45 miles from the target. Before firing, the Exocet is given information on the target's range and heading, and also told how high it is to fly over the water. After launch, the missile dives steeply to a cruising altitude, and then begins a series of steplike descents, 50 feet at a time, until it is about six miles and 31 seconds from the target. It then maintains an altitude of six feet over the water by means of a radio altimeter. Also at the six mile point, the missile's own radar picks up the target and provides final guidance.

Traveling this close to the surface, the Exocet is very difficult to detect on defensive radar because of reflected false images and clutter created by the waves. Even if it was picked up, it would be a tough target to bring down because of its size and speed. The Exocet is a little over 15 feet long, 13 3/4 inches in diameter, has a wingspan of about 3 1/2 feet, and travels at .93 Mach. The warhead it carries is 352 pounds of high explosives.

The "shoot and leave" missile that the U.S. is betting on is the Maverick, which was designed primarily as an anti-tank weapon. The missile uses either TV or infrared for target acquisition and weapon guidance, with the newer models using the latter. The image of the target is transmitted from the detector in the nose of the missile to a scope in the cockpit, where the pilot centers the crosshairs on the target and locks this picture into the weapon's guidance system. Once locked on, the only thing left to do is squeeze the trigger and leave the area. The Maverick is a little smaller than the Exocet, being eight feet long, a foot in diameter and having a two foot wingspan. Since it is intended for use against armor, it has a hefty warhead of 462 pounds of explosives in the form of a shaped charge.

The Maverick, however, has been running into a lot of criticism from Congress and the General Accounting Office, both of whom doubt its effectiveness in combat. Their contention is that in any scenario except masses of armor moving in waves across Europe, target acquisition and discrimination is much too difficult for the present system—and they may just have a point.

Consider a pilot flying over relatively unfamiliar terrain trying to pick out a well-camouflaged column of tanks hiding in a wooded area. He will also be weaving back and forth to keep from becoming an inviting target for ground fire. Spotting a well-concealed tank under these conditions would be tough, but let's suppose that this is his lucky day and he gets an eyeball on the armored column. Even if he can get a picture of the target through the missile, the problem now becomes one of sufficient contrast between the camouflaged tank and its surroundings. Unless the system can distinguish between the mottled green and brown tank against a mottled green and brown background, it will not guide properly. On top of this, throw in poor light conditions, precipitation, fog, or smoke, and you are further reducing the possibility of the TV Maverick flying well.

Given these very real and very common battlefield problems, it is easy to deduce that the TV Maverick is strictly for clear days against targets that are pretty much in the open. To counter these limitations, the IR version of the weapon was developed. Although the missile can now be used under conditions of poor target/background contrast and in darkness, the question of proper target identification becomes paramount. In a shifting battlefield scene, how can the pilot be sure he is not shooting at one of ours but one of theirs? Overall, it seems as if there are still a few bugs to be worked out of the Maverick before it can hack the specs of its extremely difficult mission—that of killing tanks in Europe.

As of the end of 1982, the Soviets are not reported as having the "launch and leave" type of missile.

Probably one of the cleverest and most needed innovations to hit the fighter business in quite some time is the "Heads Up Display" or HUD. Pilots flying birds of the same vintage as the F-4 had to be content with a gunsight that projected only the pipper, concentric circles for estimating windage, and some indication of aircraft roll. If the jock needed any other information pertaining to his flight situation—such as heading, airspeed, altitude, Gs, etc.—he had to look into the cockpit and scan the instrument panel for the required readouts. This meant taking his eyes off his opponent, and even though this was only for the briefest of instants, it almost guaranteed losing contact with a maneuvering target whose range was a mile or greater.

A pilot's eyes are his best weapon, but he has to keep them on the target to be effective. The HUD was the perfect solution to this problem, presenting both target and flight information to the pilot in such a way that his eyes never have to be refocused into the cockpit during an attack. It does this by projecting on the gunsight combining glass all essential data for the type of attack under way, be it either air-to-air or air-to-ground. The amount of data and the method of presenting it varies with each aircraft, but whatever the format, this type of display represents a significant milestone in the development of fighters. Aiming and target data are usually centered on the combining glass, and portray such things as weapons impact point, projected flight path of the airplane, time to target, and missile status. Farther from the center is shown flight information such as altitude, airspeed, G loading, heading, etc. Superimposed on all these data may be a projected artificial horizon that depicts both the angle of bank and the degrees of climb or dive.

The numbers and lines used to present all this information to the pilot are light images on the combining glass, and thus are always in his field of vision. A unique feature about these images is that although they appear to be on a glass only about two feet in front of the pilot's eyes, they are really focused at infinity. The pilot, whose eyes are also focused at infinity, therefore has no trouble reading them since he does not have to refocus his vision on a spot a few feet away. This system probably takes a little getting used to, particularly for the old heads who have trained themselves over the years to sneak a quick look in the cockpit every now and then to see how things are going. But once they become believers, it would be possible to fly all but the most precise instrument maneuvers just by using the HUD.

Lessons of the Mideast and Falklands

High-performance aircraft such as the F-15 and F-16, with exotic weapons systems feeding data through a Heads Up Display, firing missiles with improved capabilities, and the whole ball game controlled by AWACS, may seem like a winning combination. In many respects it is, and a quick look at the results of the Mideast and Falkland Island Wars will show what can and can't be done with such a team. The Israelis have given both these aircraft a real workout in all types of combat situations, and their operations offer probably the best example of how to effectively employ these advanced aircraft.

A good illustration of how well these birds do in combat occurred in July 1979 over southern Lebanon. A flight of four F-15s were flying top cover for some fighter-bombers who were working over a ground target. The Syrians scrambled eight MiG-21s to intercept the Israelis, and once contact was made, it was all over in three minutes. Five MiGs were shot down and the rest headed for home, while the F-15s suffered no damage.

During Israel's invasion of Lebanon in June 1982, a massive aerial battle took place that was reminiscent of the titanic slugfests between the RAF and the Luftwaffe during the Battle of Britain in 1940. On June 9th, 90 Israeli jets engaged 60 from Syria, and once again the F-15s and F-16s were the stars of the show. That day the Syrians lost 29 birds, and again the Israelis came away unscathed. While accomplishing all this great air-to-air work, the Israelis *also* knocked out all the SAM sites the Syrians had emplaced in the Bekaa Valley.

During the next two days this scenario repeated itself, with 50 more MiGs being shot down and no Israeli losses. These incredible statistics seem almost too good to believe; however, the Israelis had three major advantages over the Syrians that made this a "no win" situation for the latter.

The first of these was that just about all of the Syrian force was made up of MiG-21s. While this bird is a good match for the F-4, it is completely outclassed by the F-15 and F-16. The superior performance, armament, and weapons systems of the American-built aircraft resulted in a turkey shoot for the Israelis, as the score suggests.

Another equally important factor in these lopsided battles was the skill of the pilots involved. Because of their long involvement in a series of wars, Israeli pilots are superbly trained, and consistently have the edge over their Arab rivals in this critical area.

The last—and perhaps the most important—element that turned the tide against the Syrians was AWACS. This was the prime catalyst for these stunning victories, since it was responsible for skilled crews in first-class fighters being vectored to the right place at the right time. Undoubtedly, a good percentage of the kills were made possible by the fact that AWACS controlled the intercept to the point that the Israelis were brought in below and behind their opponents. With an initial advantage like that, it was like shooting fish in a barrel for the F-15s and F-16s. It must have really watered the eyes of a Syrian MiG pilot to suddenly realize he has a flight of F-16s in his six with a bunch of hungry tigers at the controls. About all he could do here is rely on a tight turn to save his hide. But when he's pulling six to seven Gs and looks back to see an F-16 *loafing* through the turn at eight Gs *and closing*, there's not much left for him to do but consign his soul to Allah.

In the air-to-ground war the Israelis fared much the same, with superior equipment and excellent training again being the winning combination. Their raid against the Iraqi nuclear reactor at Osirak on June 7th, 1981, was a perfect example. This strike was made up of eight F-16s: two carrying just camera gear to record the results, the lead aircraft with two smart bombs to punch through the concrete reactor dome, and the rest carrying two 2,000 pounders each. Fighter protection was provided by six F-15s. The strike force covered the 600 miles to the target at low altitude, and each bird made a pop-up maneuver for one pass on the reactor complex. The raid encountered no SAMs or interceptors, but did pick up some flak, and their route was planned to keep them just out of range of the Saudi's AWACS.

The flight was, however, detected by Jordanian radar, who interrogated them in Arabic for the proper identification. Equal to the task, the Israelis answered in Arabic, and convinced the GCI site that they were either Jordanian or Saudi aircraft. The Jordanian controllers also dropped the ball at this point because they did not cross tell these targets to Saudi or Syrian radar. The results of the raid are history, but the entire mission points up what can be accomplished by bold planning and even bolder execution. The foresight of timing the flight to avoid the AWACS and having pilots who could speak Arabic on the mission bear the stamp of the hungry tiger. In just about every engagement over this troubled area, the combination of modern fighters controlled by AWACS has proven to be the decisive factor in winning and maintaining control of the air.

Turning to the Falklands, we see an entirely different picture. Critical mistakes in planning on both sides made this war a very touch-and-go affair, where the scales of victory could have swung to either side at any time. Britain's success was quite a close call, and only occurred because of the resolve of her political leaders, the professionalism of her troops, and modern equipment. Good luck and a lot of last-minute improvisations were also major factors in their win.

As far as equipment went, the Brits were delighted with the performance of their Harriers. The jump jets flew 1650 sorties (all but 150 from two carriers) that encompassed just about every type of mission you can do in a fighter. They did particularly good work in the air-to-air role because when they engaged the Argentines, they were in their element—a low-altitude turning fight. Although not designed as an air superiority fighter, the Harriers ran up an impressive score against the A-4 Skyhawks and Mirages flown by the Argentine Air Force. They knocked down a total of 27, most of which were accounted for by the improved version of the Sidewinder.

Another potent weapon in the British arsenal was their sea and land-based air defense missile systems, which were credited with 40 kills. All in all, the Argentines lost 109 aircraft from all causes, including 31 Skyhawks and 26 Mirages, while only five Harriers were lost—all to ground fire.

Judgements about such a one-sided score—and about the fact that the Harriers did so well against aircraft more adapted to the air-to-air role—must be tempered by the realities of the Falklands situation. Argentine aircraft were operating at about the absolute limit of their combat radius, having to carry a load of bombs 400 miles to the target, fight their way in for one pass, and then dash for home. It is very probable that these birds were at or below Bingo fuel when the pickle button was pressed, and thus could not afford to hang around and tangle with the Harriers.

The Argentine pilots also showed that the tiger's stripes are not worn by just the good guys. They pressed home their attacks against British ships and installations with determination, daring, and skill. Argentina's air effort, however, was dogged by bad luck. Although their pilots scored many hits on British ships, the fuses malfunctioned and they failed to detonate. They might have employed their famous Exocet more liberally, but they had only five on hand when the fracas broke out. Their misfortunes continued when they tried to locate the QE II. A reconnaissance mission was mounted using a Boeing 707 flying at 18,000 feet, but they never did locate the plum of the invasion fleet. All they got for their trouble was a chance to evade a barrage of British SAMs.

What lessons can be learned from these widely separated wars with their distinctively antipodal methods of operation, as far as the employment of fighters is concerned?

The most glaring fact that relates fighter operations in these wars is the absolute essentiality of AWACS. The Israelis had it over Lebanon and completely dominated the aerial scene. Neither the British nor the Argentines had it in the Falklands, and it was like blindman's buff. With a Grumman E-2C Hawkeye patrolling the 400 miles of open water between the Falklands and the mainland, it would have been a piece of cake for the Harriers. The enemy could have been intercepted at about the halfway point, and losses to the fleet could have been reduced considerably. In all probability, the embarrassingly easy Exocet attack against *HMS Sheffield* could have been met and thwarted.

Although not a factor in the Mideast, where short-range missions are the usual order of business, the lack of a tanker force was a serious deficiency on the part of the Argentines. Their Mirages and Exocet-launching Etendards were not even equipped for midair refueling, thus severely limiting the tactics for these "big guns." They did have two KC-130s that were used to refuel the Skyhawks, but this was simply not enough.

Another conspicuous shortcoming on both sides was the lack of an ECM capability. The British Navy never detected an Argentine GCI site on top of Mt. Stanley, which kept their fleet under surveillance and helped to guide incoming fighter-bombers to their targets. If the British had placed the proper emphasis on electronic warfare, this radar would have been discovered immediately and made a prime target early in the game. About the only countermeasures they did use was chaff. This was dispensed in huge quantities in an attempt to create an "umbrella" over the British fleet whenever Argentine aircraft were on the attack. Despite being old-fashioned and somewhat unsophisticated, it worked, and the only ships that were hit by missiles were those outside the chaff "umbrella."

The fighter pairings in the Falklands raises the natural question: "What if the Mirages had had a midair refueling capability? Would the Harriers have fared so well?" Both aircraft are roughly of the same vintage, but the Mirage was designed for the air-to-air role, while the Harrier's forte is ground support. The answer to the question depends on what type of fight evolves once the engagement starts. If the Mirage jocks get suckered into a low-altitude turning fight, the superior maneuverability of the Harrier will quickly put them at a serious disadvantage. However, with a Mach 2-capable aircraft, the Mirage drivers would be foolish to play the

Harrier's game and try to turn with it. High-speed hit-and-run tactics are called for, followed by a rapid climb for altitude and repositioning. Faced with this type of an attack, the Brits would be in for some tough sledding.

The moral taught by the Mideast and Falkland Island Wars is patently clear when it comes to fighter operations: Don't get in the game unless you have advanced aircraft, well-trained aircrews, an adequate tanker force, good ECM capability, and—most important—AWACS. Getting in the game is only the first step; *staying* in it is another matter entirely. The latter requires continual development, improvement, and refinement of your capability in all the areas mentioned above.

Next, we'll look at some new devices and ideas that are being worked on to make our current fighters even more versatile and effective.

Part III:

The Near Future

Chapter 15

The Potential of Future Weapons

As with any highly competitive business in today's world, the firm that does not continually improve its product soon loses out to the competition. This is a fact of life whether you're dealing with automobiles of fighter planes. By yesterday's standards, the capabilities of today's aircraft smack of wizardry and black magic. Items that were being developed just a short time ago—and viewed with the old adage: "It'll never get off the ground!"—are now operational and in squadron service.

However, in the development labs around the country, these very same things are being looked on as pretty much old hat. Technology is progressing at warp speed, and is producing systems and devices today that are still considered in the realm of science fiction. Undoubtedly, after a few refinements, these too will become commonplace in very short order.

The hungry tigers will most likely have to burn a lot of midnight oil to keep up with all these innovations; however, it will be time well spent. All of these gadgets are engineered with one thing in mind—increase the effectiveness of the fighter as a weapons system. They do this by relieving the pilot of peripheral functions, increasing the accuracy of his weapons, and simplifying the decision-making process covering mission essentials.

Innovative Airplanes

Although the F-15 and F-16 are slated to be in the inventory well into the 1990s, improved models of both aircraft are either in production (F-15C/D), or have prototypes flying (AFTI/F-16 and F-16XL). The most exciting developments with respect to the air-to-air mission are occurring in the latter. AFTI stands for Advanced Fighter Technology Integration, and its purpose is to combine and test in the F-16 a number of maturing technologies. It is not intended to introduce AFTI as an operational system by itself, since current testing is directed toward the next generation fighter.

The AFTI version of the F-16 can be distinguished from production models mainly by the twin canards jutting out at an angle beneath the engine inlet. These canards are activated by the fly-by-wire system, and, in conjunction with the flaps and horizontal tail, permit the AFTI/F-16 to execute six maneuvers that cannot be done by any other aircraft. Through various combinations of these controls, it is able to make small, precise changes in the aircraft's flight path or attitude. It can move sideways (lateral translation) while continuing to point its nose straight ahead, or make a "flat" turn (direct sideforce) without rolling into a bank. The nose can be pointed in a different direction than its flight path in a skid-like maneuver called lateral pointing. This nose-pointing can also be done in an up or down direction without changing the flight path (pitch axis pointing). The bird can also fly up or down without raising or lowering its nose (vertical translation), or without changing its angle of attack (direct lift).

These maneuvers are intended to be held for just a few seconds, but this is ample time to fire a missile or hose off a good burst with a gun. All these moves really amount to a new way to fly, and the implications of being able to do all this fancy footwork in a combat situation are almost too much to grasp at first blush.

This F-16 test bed is also earmarked for the evaluation of voice controls in the cockpit. The purpose of this system is to redistribute the pilot's workload by reducing the number of hand and eye actions needed to perform various cockpit functions. With this device, the pilot can keep his hands on the stick and throttle and his eyes on the target while activating certain flight and weapons control subsystems. Switching fuel tanks, inserting target data, and calling up missile status displays are examples of commands that could be adapted to voice controls. Eliminating the manual actions needed to accomplish routine tasks is especially important in low-altitude high-speed flight. The system is set up by the pilot loading a cassette recording of his voice into the computer, which tells it how this particular pilot pronounces each of the words in its vocabulary. At present, the computer understands 36 words and incorporates a synthesized voice to answer the pilot, confirming that the requested action has been accomplished. Tests were conducted in the early '80s to evaluate the effect of voice changes under stress and high Gs against a background of cockpit noise.

There is another idea under development that will help to free the pilot from all but the most crucial tasks. This is the helmet-mounted sight, which projects a half-inch size image of crosshairs on the pilot's visor. He then simply turns his head until the crosshairs are centered on the target, presses a button on the sidestick controller, and the airplane's sensors slew toward the target and lock on. This system could work well with another innovation in the works called the radar-aimable gun. Once the radar is locked onto the target for a gun attack, tracking information would be sent to a mechanism that controlled the alignment of the gun in its mounting. This is turn would move the gun as much as plus or minus three degrees in elevation and azimuth to bring the bullet impact point right on the target. Something like this would be especially helpful if you were chasing an aircraft that was maneuvering violently, or who could turn just a little better than your bird. In tests, this setup resulted in getting three times as many hits on a target as with a fixed gun.

The system also has an add-on feature that may or may not have to much application in a combat situation. This is an autopilot connected to the throttle and speed brakes so these can be actuated automatically to keep the aircraft at the optimum gun firing range. This gadget provided 30 to 50 percent more hits than the manual control method.

From an old fighter pilot's point of view, all these clever devices that react instantly to the pilot's slightest whim might be carrying things a bit too far. Consider the situation where a flight leader in a bird with AFTI, voice controls, a helmet-mounted sight, and a radar aimable gun turned to look at his wingman to give him a hand signal, and inadvertently hit the acquisition button. The aircraft would translate laterally, point its nose, turn the gun, and zap!— no more wingman. Seriously, all these technologies installed in an airplane like the F-16 would make it one of the most potent aerial weapons ever to leap off into the blue.

It is easy to visualize what an order of magnitude improvement these systems would give to the present model of the Fighting Falcon. A real stretch of the imagination is required to conceive what these and other innovations could accomplish if incorporated in the newest version of this bird, the F-16XL. The first of these enhanced capabilities demonstrators rolled out of the hangar in mid-1982, and the most obvious change is the larger, cranked arrow wing. This graphite composite wing has over twice the area of the standard F-16 airfoil; along with a fuselage that has been lengthened by almost five feet, the internal fuel capacity has been increased 82 percent. The new wing also reduces drag by 53 percent, resulting in supersonic penetration speeds in a strike configuration.

This version of the F-16 still retains the Mach 2 speed and nine G turning capabilities of the original, but it can carry twice the payload for the same distance, or can go twice as far with an equal payload. The F-16XL will have a weapons carriage system that provides 17 stores stations beneath the wings and fuselage, arranged in a semi-conformal configuration. This concept offers less weight and drag, and also reduces the aircraft's radar cross section.

The improved performance realized by the redesigned wing and longer fuselage can be adapted to the existing F-16 fleet by simply bolting the new components in place. It is expected that these advanced technologies will give us a viable air superiority force through the year 2000.

Another mind-boggler dealing with wings is also on the way in the form of the "mission adaptive wing." This concept will feature a wing that can alter its shape in flight for better range or maneuvering as the situation demands. It will do this by changing its camber from the wing root to the tip, and varying it from the leading edge to the trailing edge. Computers and sensors will shape the flexible material of the wing to the contour required for the existing flight conditions. This is just about what a bird does, and the resulting gains in performance will mainly come from increased aerodynamic efficiency and the reduced weight of the overall system. The new-technology wing began initial testing in the fall of 1983, and will certainly be a candidate for inclusion in the design of the next generation fighter.

Upgraded Avionics

Aircraft are not the only things being improved for the foreseeable future. Avionics, as might be expected, continue to make giant strides toward a *"Star Wars"* type of weapons system.

The F-16C/D entered service in 1984, and it features a radar that has twice the range of the set in the older aircraft. This additional range is needed to enable the radar to be compatible with the upcoming AMRAAM (Advanced Medium Range Air to Air Missile). This is a launch-and-leave weapon that will have inertial midcourse guidance and active radar terminal homing. However, for it to be effective, the airborne radar must be able to reach out a long way and pick up the target.

A modification for the F-15's radar has also been developed that increases its target discrimination ability by a substantial amount. This improved system is now capable of distinguishing objects and terrain features as small as eight and a half feet square, and separated by the same distance, at a range of *ten miles.* It wasn't too many years ago that you considered yourself lucky to pick up an airborne target the size of a B-52 at ten miles, to say nothing of an object on the ground.

Another mod in the works is a programmable signal processor that will have the ability to analyze the radar energy reflected by the compressor stage of the unknown aircraft's jet engine. By comparing this signal with known patterns stored in the computer, the system will be able to assess the identity of the aircraft.

Infrared devices will also play a significant role in the up-and-coming weapons systems. One of the Air Force's priority development programs is LANTIRN, which stands for Low Altitude Navigation and Targeting Infrared for Night (they really reached for *that* one). This uses forward-looking infrared sensors housed in two pods, one for navigating and one for targeting. The system will allow a fighter to drop below the clouds at night to approach the target area at low level utilizing terrain-following radar and IR sensors. Once individual targets are detected, they are classified and prioritized according to the pilot's mission plan, and each is assigned an IR Maverick missile. The system then waits for the pilot's consent to fire. Once this is given, it locks on to each target in the priority sequence, fires a Maverick, and then goes on to the next.

Since lasers and infrared detectors are affected by cloud cover and precipitation, LANTIRN is not intended to be an all-weather attack system. Nonetheless, these IR sensors that look ahead of the aircraft are amazingly sensitive. A test of one type in the spring of 1982 involved a mock attack on a civilian airport. During the run-in, the IR detector picked up the emissions from the exhausts of a taxiing twin-engined business aircraft. From that point on there was no difficulty in keeping the crosshairs of the weapons delivery system centered on *either engine* of the bird on the ground.

The defensive side of the avionics package has not been neglected, either. The latest trend is toward very sophisticated jammers that are paired with computers to make them "receiver/processors" or "power management systems." These work by analyzing incoming signals, identifying their source, and determining which are hostile. They prioritize the ones that need to be jammed and select the jamming mode that capitalizes on the weaknesses of the attacking radar, and then concentrates the power of the system against the priority targets. Since all of this is done by the computer, it can be reprogrammed in minutes to react to updated intelligence about the threat.

All of the information detected by the radar and gathered by the sensors must be presented to the pilot in easily understandable form so that it can be reacted to instantaneously. This is where the advanced cockpit displays of tomorrow's aircraft will play a vital role. Even in today's birds, the electronic display panels have assumed a dominant position among the instrument clusters. Their importance to the tactical portion of the mission has relegated the usually sacrosanct primary flight instruments to less prominent locations. They are now found on sub-panels, which in the past were usually reserved for nonessential instruments such as pneumatic pressure gauges or utility hydraulic system pressure.

Some new ideas being worked on in this area will offer considerably more information on aircraft systems, flight conditions, and enemy activity than those in use at this time, and will even show this data in color. One such item is a map display with the aircraft at the center, encircled by several large colored rings indicating range capability at the present throttle setting. As the power is changed, so would be the circles. These indications would also be offset from the center of the display to take into account the last known wind speed and direction. Such a presentation would be invaluable in helping the pilot make the necessarily quick decisions on recovery under minimum fuel and bad weather conditions. The cumbersome and time-consuming calculations involving time, distance, and fuel remaining would thus be eliminated.

Another approach in this same vein would be a planform drawing of the airplane that shows the fuel system status pictorially. Numeric overlays would give the pilot time and distance figures based on the available fuel state and current flight conditions. Again, color would be used, with empty tanks being shown in yellow and fuel remaining in blue; failed boost pumps would be indicated by a red X, and color-coded bars could show which fuel valves were open or closed.

Three-dimensional terrain maps could also be simulated that would give the pilot a representative display of the ground features over which he is flying. Radar information would be converted into a pictorial projection of ridgelines and contour lines that resemble what the pilot would see through the windscreen.

Probably the most dazzling of the new displays being developed is the Pictorial Format Program, which is intended for introduction into service in the mid-1990s. This system will take information from multiple sensors and produce a full-color picture for the pilot. The picture will show the key elements of the mission and the operational environment the aircraft is flying through. The ground and the sky will be depicted accurately and in perspective, with the pilot's own aircraft superimposed in the correct attitude and position and colored black. Nearby friendly aircraft such as wingmen will be shown in green, and located accurately in relation to the pilot's airplane. Enemy fighters will be presented in their correct spot in space, and will be colored according to the degree of threat they pose. One that is turning away from the flight or is out of range would be in yellow, while one coming at the flight head-on would be colored red. Ground threats would be depicted in a similar fashion and would be shown to scale. A SAM site in the line of flight would obviously be a hazard and thus would be colored red, while one that was out of range but should be avoided would be in yellow. The projected flight path of the pilot's bird is shown as a green ribbon extending out in front of the black aircraft symbol. The Pictorial Format display is an excellent example of how advanced avionics will make the pilot's job *easier* rather than more complicated, as did new features in the past.

While all of these marvels of electronic warfare certainly sound like the answer to a fighter pilot's prayers, they are not achieved without exacting a penalty. The electrical equipment that is planned for the new fighters all requires a considerable amount of power for operation. This in turn demands more air conditioning to keep these systems cooled to proper operating temperatures. The physical size of the exotic equipment, plus that of the cooling systems needed to keep it running, establish a requirement for more space in existing fighters, which even today is fairly limited. The F-15 is in better shape than the Fighting Falcon in this respect, since it has more room and engine power available for these systems. The latter is going to require some fancy engineering to fit all the new mission equipment within the airframe and keep it operating efficiently.

Better Bullets

The armament fired by these ultra-sophisticated weapons systems of the future will be improved versions of today's missiles, or entirely new ones. In order to capitalize fully on the system's potential, radar missiles will have to have the capability of operating in a heavy ECM environment. And IR missiles will need an increased sensitivity and a larger look angle so that they can be employed on a front quarter attack, where the IR signature of the target aircraft is considerably reduced.

A gun attack, even in present-day fighters, is still initiated from behind while attempting to fly a path identical to that of the target. Firing on another fighter with a gun from the front quarter is pretty much of a "by guess and by God" situation. It was called "deflection shooting" during the Second World War, and only the very lucky achieved any significant results using this method. Once the lead-computing gunsight was developed, the traditional high-side gunnery pass proved to be the most accurate. Now even that hoary bastion of old fighter pilots seems to be destined for the archives of ancient tactics. Tests have already proven that an F-15 with its flight control system coupled to the fire control computer can shoot down a maneuvering F-102 drone from the front quarter. Both aircraft were in sharp right turns at more than three Gs, and closing at 760 knots. The F-15 fired a two second burst from its gun and that was all she wrote for the drone.

How will all this near-magical equipment affect the way that the hungry tigers of tomorrow will earn their living? Will these science-fiction devices alter the tactics of air-to-air engagements of the future? Probably not to any marked degree. Mutual radar coverage at extended ranges will most likely have opposing fighter forces still coming at each other head-on. Long-range fighter radar and long-range missiles will certainly result in the first volleys being exchanged before either side has a visual on the other. If the AMRAAM missile is perfected and fighters are able to lock on to the target and launch the weapon at around 100 miles, there may even be time for a second frontal attack. Once the AMRAAM was on its way, the pilot could lock on to another target, select one of his Sparrows, and launch it when the target closed to the proper distance. Or, depending on what he feels the chances are for a kill with the first missile, he could stay locked on to the original target and fire the Sparrow only if the AMRAAM missed.

Once the opposing flights of fighters passed each other, things would revert to standard dogfight tactics. But with improved, all-aspect IR missiles, pointable guns, and advanced fire control systems, it will probably be more of a wild, free-shooting melee than before. These new technologies will preclude the necessity of getting into someone's six before launching armament. People will be hosing off missiles and taking shots with the gun from every angle, which could result in quite a hassle.

The development of fighter designs since the First World War seems to prove one immutable law: The more the aircraft is designed for speed, the less maneuverable it becomes. Normally, this could be expected to continue into the foreseeable future, as maximum speeds start approaching Mach 4. Birds in this class would be great for straight-and-level work, but the small, razor-thin wings needed for these speeds would not allow much high-G turning. Given the usual progression of things, dogfighting might evolve into a series of high-speed level attacks, with little or none of the close-in maneuvering that typifies today's engagements.

However, this too will probably not come to pass, mainly because of the variable camber wing. As soon as the "Tally ho!" is called and it is time to start bending it around, the wing would change from the high-speed to the high-lift configuration. The instantaneous added maneuverability this allows will let the pilot quickly swing into his opponent's six.

Another possibility to give these super-fast birds a better turning ability would be some adaptation of the VIFFing principle used on the Harrier. This could be in the form of fixed nozzles pointing downward in the belly of the aircraft through which exhaust gasses could be vectored when a tight turning capability was needed.

Any future scenario involving the employment of fighters must include as one of the givens the use of AWACS by both sides. With such extended-range radar coverage, it would hardly be possible for either side to vector their fighters in for a surprise kill. One-sided engagements such as the Israelis had over the Syrians in 1982 will become few and far between. When all aircraft are given sufficient information to turn so as to meet the opposition head-on, the positioning odds are equaled.

Add to this missiles and fire control systems that just about guarantee a hit with every shot, and who would be the winner in such a confrontation? Of course, the scales would tip to the side with a significant superiority in numbers; however, if they are both about equal, electronics is again the key to victory. Here, in both the initial head-on slash and the ensuing engagement, ECM will be the deciding factor. The fighter that has the capability to deny the enemy information as to its position, and can jam or decoy missiles fired at it, will undoubtedly have the upper hand in any contest.

The ECM equipment carried on tomorrow's fighter must have broad-band coverage so as to be effective against the radars used in SAMs, interceptors, and enemy fighters and missiles. It also must be able to selectively jam the most immediate threat, and above all, it must be powerful enough to overcome countermeasures used against it.

Assuming a parallel development of ECM and offensive capabilities by both the good guys and the bad guys, it is possible to envision an actual regression of fighter tactics in the future. With no one on either side being able to see anyone on their radar—even if they did, having their missiles jammed into impotence—eyeballs may come back in fashion. Tactics will revert to those used in WWI—locate the enemy visually, maneuver to get behind him, and hose him down with the gun. Maybe even silk scarves, cloth helmets, and goggles will make a comeback!

The visual air-to-ground mission will probably not change too much in the future. Dive-bombing will still be a learned art, although improvements in smart bombs and the dive-toss function will probably bring these techniques into more common use. The most likely improvement areas will be low-level, all-weather navigation and off-set bombing.

The LANTIRN system described above will certainly be the first major step in this direction, since it is already under development. At this time, LANTIRN is designed primarily for use against tanks and armored vehicles, but once it becomes operational, its capacity could be expanded to include other types of target complexes.

The three-dimensional terrain map mentioned earlier could also be a part of this system to simplify getting to and from the target area. The combination of these devices will permit a night weather approach to the general locality of the target, even though the actual attack must be made in VFR conditions. Perhaps the laser and IR mechanisms used to locate and designate targets will be improved to the point where they can function acceptably in clouds or precipitation.

The sharpness of the pictures available by using the new high-resolution radars will definitely increase the accuracy of offset bombing. Even the fine-tuned image on an F-4's radar was a bit fuzzy and diffuse, and the placement of the tracking cursors was pretty much of an educated guess. The picture-like quality of the newer radars will permit these cursors to be locked on with much more precision, which will in turn yield bombs with better CEPs.

This same clarity and definition will also produce superior results when launching standoff weapons. More accurate target parameters can be set in the missile guidance system before it is fired, thus ensuring that it will have a better chance of acquiring the target on its own for terminal guidance. Since the trend is toward "shoot and leave" weapons, this factor assumes an even greater importance, especially in the heavy ECM environment that is expected in future conflicts.

A new development that is on the drawing boards for the air-to-ground game is the "Wasp" mini-missile. These will be fired in clusters of ten or more, at night or in any kind of weather, and will be of the "fire and forget" type of weapon. The aircraft's computer will direct each missile in the "swarm" to a different target as long as there are more targets than missiles. Another weapon, the Tomahawk II, is being perfected for attacking heavily defended high-value targets. This will be initially intended for runway cratering attacks on hostile airfields.

However, it must be remembered that no matter how advanced and how perfect each of these new items of equipment appear, they will only reign a short while before an effective counter is devised.

Chapter 16

The Advanced Tactical Fighter

The new technologies for the near future talked about in the preceding chapter represented the leading edge of innovative thinking during the late 1970s and early '80s. At the midpoint of this later decade, follow-on improvements and new prototypes started to appear as earlier concepts were translated into hardware. This was not the result of a random developmental approach, or the accidental discovery of some technological breakthrough. Rather, it was all part and parcel of a general plan designed to progress through an orderly succession of steps toward the weapons system referred to earlier as the next generation fighter. As more and more pieces of this futuristic puzzle fell into place, even the name of this project was changed from the nebulous, far-off-sounding "next generation fighter" to the more concrete and tangible "Advanced Tactical Fighter."

Also, by this time, the original models of the F-15 and F-16 had been in the inventory for ten years and six years respectively. During the lifespan of any fighter, improved models are routinely introduced throughout the production run. In the past, these subsequent models incorporated a series of small improvements over the basic design that were dictated by operational use and/or emerging technologies. But, in the main, such changes only affected the type aircraft concerned, and could not be applied across the board to the entire fighter fleet. Nor did they have much direct applicability to fighter designs coming off the drawing boards in the near future.

This was not the case when the F-15C/D and the F-16C were delivered to operational units. The improvements found in these newer aircraft not only enhanced the performance and capabilities of each, but more importantly, they were essential building blocks in the road toward the Advanced Tactical Fighter. During the intervening years between their introduction and the projected date of the ATF's first flight in 1991, these devices and concepts will be continually modified and improved upon until they meet the requirements for inclusion in the new fighter.

Some of this hardware is intended for immediate use, while other new developments will be tested in demonstrator aircraft. Only a few of each aircraft in this latter category will be built, since their purpose is to test some radical concept that is not quite ready to be introduced fleetwide. Two such demonstrators, the AFTI/F-16 and the F-16XL, have already been described in the previous chapter, and each has a specific mission. The AFTI/F-16 is an advanced *technologies* demonstrator that will be used to investigate the mission-oriented applications of the new way of flying described previously. Other jobs this aircraft is intended for is the testing of the integrated digital fire/flight control system, high-level systems automation, and the automatic maneuvering and attack system. The longer fuselage and cranked arrow wing of the F-16XL make it ideally suited for the role of an enhanced *capabilities* demonstrator. As such, its primary mission will be to prove concepts for increased range and payload, better survivability and operational capabilities, and a feasible method for the precision attack of ground targets at night, under the weather.

The other big gun in today's fighter force is also slated for a demonstrator role. The F-15 has been designated as the vehicle to develop a Short Takeoff and Landing capability for the fighter of the future. Current plans call for the installation of two dimensional thrust directing engine nozzles on this bird, and these will be utilized for STOL purposes, in flight vectoring, and thrust reversal on landing. In order to gain increased stability and control of the aircraft at the lower speeds associated with STOL operations, movable canards will be fitted on the sides of the engine intakes just forward of the wing root. The goals of the F-15 STOL program seem astounding given the capabilities of even present-day fighters. What they are shooting for is a demonstrator that will be able to land successfully on a 1,500 by 50-foot runway, with a zero braking coefficient in a 26-knot crosswind. This amounts to putting an airplane weighing over 40,000 pounds on a strip smaller than most lightplane airfields *when the runway is covered with glare ice—and in a strong crosswind.*

Once this capability becomes a reality, the tactical advantages it offers are not just limited to ice-covered runways not aligned with the wind. It will also allow fighters equipped with this modification to take off and land from bomb-damaged runways that would have otherwise been rendered useless for normal operations by one or two well-placed cratering bombs. The ability to work out of just about any airfield that is not totally destroyed will increase the sortie generation potential and allow these aircraft to stay in the fight.

Other test items that will be a part of the program are integration of the engine nozzles and flight controls, a new landing guidance system, and a soft-field landing gear that will permit operations from a soft, wet runway. Flight tests of the STOL demonstrator are expected to start in 1987.

Operational Improvements

As mentioned earlier, demonstrators are but one side of the concurrent development picture. Improvements are also taking place on the operational side of the coin that are directly benefitting the fighter pilots of today.

The C model of the F-16 is now in service; however, a casual glance shows little to differentiate this bird from the earlier A models. All the major changes in this aircraft have been internal, and include a 2,000-pound increase in maximum takeoff gross weight capability, upgraded cockpit and avionics, better electronics cooling, expanded memory, speed and reprogrammability of onboard computers, and significant improvements in the radar system. This last item represents the big difference between the modified aircraft and its predecessors. The new features that are now available include a 40 percent increase in detection and tracking ranges, the ability to track ten targets while scanning, raid assessment capability, increased resolution in ground map mode, and the ability to track fixed and moving ground targets. The weapons system on the F-16C is now compatible with the AMRAAM, LAN-TIRN, Airborne Self Protection Jammer, and the radar warning receiver.

F-15 squadrons have also benefitted from an upgrading of the original A model of the Eagle. The F-15C has increased its maximum gross weight for takeoff from 56,000 to 68,000 pounds, has an additional 2,000 pounds of internal fuel, and provisions for the conformal fuel pallets. The improvements to the radar and avionics systems are essentially the same as those listed above for the C model of the Fighting Falcon.

Another stepping-stone on the way to the Advanced Tactical Fighter is the concept of the dual role fighter. The objective of this program is to have an aircraft that is equally at home in either the air-to-air or the air-to-ground type of mission. This is not an easy task, and involves quite a bit more than simply hanging bombs on a good air superiority fighter. This was the approach taken in the past, and just about always resulted in less-than-optimum performance across the board. The hardpoints, pylons, and other paraphernalia needed for carrying bombs added considerable weight and increased the overall drag of the airplane, even after the ordnance was dropped.

In addition to these problems, the dual role fighter prototype will also explore the difficult job of night ground attack and low-level navigation in and under the weather. The testing of the F-15 is pretty well along, and will culminate in December 1986 with the delivery of the first E model. One really outstanding feature that will be incorporated in this aircraft is a low grazing angle, which is the ability to acquire ground targets at long range while at low altitude. The improved radar that is earmarked for the F-15E has the capability of picking up individual oil tanks in a refinery at a range of 70 nautical miles while flying at 7,500 feet AGL. Something like that wasn't even dreamed of a dozen years ago in the heyday of the F-4 and the F-106.

This simultaneous, two-pronged approach in the development of the hardware that will influence or become a part of the ATF is absolutely essential. Any significant program slippage would be disastrous, since the Advanced Tactical Fighter is already further behind the F-15 than the F-15 was behind the F-4. With the advances in Russian fighter designs proceeding at a brisk pace, the ATF must be ready by the mid-1990s to meet their very real challenge.

ATF Requirements

The long lead times that are inherent in the design of any modern weapons system dictate that the required elements of that system be established well in advance. The ten years remaining before the ATF becomes operational may seem like more than enough time, given the progress already made with the new versions of the F-15 and F-16. The performance and capability of these aircraft are indeed dramatic; however, there is much work yet to be done. A review of the criteria established by the Department of Defense for the ATF, clearly shows that time will not be hanging heavy on our hands during the next decade. The things that the ATF will be required to do are absolutely mind-boggling to fighter pilots of the late '60s, even if they were flying the most advanced and sophisticated birds of that period.

While the maximum speed of the Advanced Tactical Fighter will only be a little beyond that of current aircraft, it will operate at this speed far more efficiently, and with less fuel consumption. It will be able to cruise at supersonic speeds without the use of afterburners, and will have a longer range on just internal fuel. The good turning ability that is so important in any fighter-vs.-fighter engagement will be a prime requisite, as shown by the following G requirements. The bird will have overall G limits of plus nine and minus three, with 80 percent of internal fuel on board. Within these parameters, it must be able to pull the Gs listed below for the various airspeed and altitude combinations:

9G at 10,000 feet and .9 Mach
5G at 30,000 feet and Mach 1
6G at 30,000 feet and Mach 2.5
2G at 50,000 feet and Mach 1.5

The new aircraft will be able to step out and move rather smartly, with the requirement for a sea level acceleration from .6 Mach to better than Mach 1 in 20 seconds.

The low-speed end of the spectrum will also be addressed with the inclusion of a STOL capability and thrust reversing. In-flight thrust vectoring is another feature that will be incorporated in some models. However, this thrust vectoring will be only that which can be achieved with the two dimensional nozzle that is planned for the F-15 demonstrator. Current requirements do not call for a full-fledged vectoring system like that found in the Harrier. Apparently, the weight and performance penalty paid for the fully rotatable nozzles and a vertical liftoff capability preclude them from being in the cards for the ATF. The most likely reason for this is that the vectoring nozzles on the engines can produce enough thrust in the vertical direction to give the turning rate needed for a close-in dogfight. However, these nozzles will not give the ATF a

VIFFing or vertical translation ability, but when you can pull nine Gs in a fight, this item might not be worth the extra weight needed to have it available. Like the F-15 STOL demonstrator, the Advanced Tactical Fighter will have a thrust reversal feature on its engines. Aside from the obvious advantages of this device on slick or short runways, it is something that will be used on each landing to help reduce tire and brake wear. Thrust reversing will also eliminate the need for a drag chute system, which was so common on fighters up through the '60s.

Another requirement for the ATF will be that it incorporate the "Stealth" technology, or "low observability," as the Air Force prefers to call it. The most promising ways of reducing the apparent radar image of an airplane are all being considered for the ATF program. The first of these is a relatively small size, although the stealth advantages achieved by this will not be the overriding design criteria for this new aircraft. Rather, the optimization of the engineering factors involved in meeting the specifications will most likely result in the ATF being about the same size as the F-15.

One of the primary offenders on any jet aircraft as far as reflecting radar energy is concerned is the face of the engine compressor. Since the design of this unit is fixed by other aircraft requirements whose importance outweigh any stealth considerations, other means must be found to neutralize this undesirable feature. Of course, the solution to this problem will only reduce the radar cross sectional area of the ATF by a given amount. The remaining parts of any aircraft make up the majority of its radar signature; therefore, some additional methods must be utilized on the new fighter to diminish its overall reflectivity. Large rudders, pylons for weapons carriage, and outsized engine pods have to be eliminated or reduced considerably to meet this criterion.

Another factor in the stealth area that must be considered is some method of countering the enemy's infrared detection systems. The turbine section and exhaust plume of all jet aircraft generate an enormous amount of IR radiation, which can be detected and tracked by ground and airborne systems much the same as a reflected radar signal. It is doubtful that these emissions can be eliminated entirely without undesirable design changes being added to the ATF; however, some way must be found to veil this radiation so that its presence is minimized.

The final major requirement for the ATF will be an increased sortie generation rate. What this means is that the new aircraft will be able to earn its keep by being a more productive combat weapon.

This is achieved by increasing the flying hours on each airframe, which in turn dictates that the bird must be less prone to malfunctions, easier to maintain and repair when it does break, and be capable of a quick turnaround between missions. The goal in this area is to produce a weapons system that will spend substantially less time in the maintenance hangar.

All of the foregoing requirements add up to an imposing piece of machinery, and the obvious question arises: "Will the pilot be able to handle all this hardware, or will he just be along for the ride?"

During the design process to meet all these specifications the pilot will not be forgotten. Rather, the various systems are being put together in such a way that the throttle-bender will not be overtaxed. Even though the Advanced Tactical Fighter will be more capable than any previously built fighter, the pilot's tasks will be more manageable and his cockpit less cluttered and disconcerting. Because of the demands of the multi-mission role envisioned for the ATF, the pilot will be provided with a tremendous amount of highly compressed real-time information from a variety of sources. Instead of having to wrestle with a multitude of decisions affecting all facets of the mission, the system will be able to synthesize all mission and target data, and let the pilot know where his targets are, and his threats in the area, and which of the latter demands his immediate attention.

Combining all the requirements for the ATF in one bird without a great deal of compromise between them seems like an impossibly large order. But, like most other problems, the needed solutions will be found through the proper application of resources. For many years, seven aircraft companies have been actively engaged in finding the answers to the myriad questions associated with designing, building, and flying the ATF. The firms involved in the competition to produce the ATF are Boeing, General Dynamics, Grumman, Lockheed, McDonnell-Douglas, Northrop, and Rockwell International. Eventually three of them—or three teams from this group—will be chosen to design and build the Advanced Tactical Fighter. So far, each of these companies has spent an estimated $10-20 million on this project, which will undoubtedly be followed by more as the selection deadline draws near.

About 85 percent of what each of the seven companies are doing in relation to designing the ATF is known to the other firms. However, the remaining 15 percent represents very closely held industrial secrets by each company involved. A majority of this latter area has to do with how each manufacturer plans to integrate all the varied technologies needed for the ATF. With the scheduled first flight less than six years away, the competition will most surely heat up and the pace will quicken considerably. Even after the bird flies, the operational test phase allows for no idle time, since current plans call for the ATF to be in squadron use by the mid-1990s.

Meeting the Requirements

Now that the players are known and the game plan is pretty well defined, it's time to take a look at how the stiff requirements for the Advanced Tactical Fighter will be met. Some of the original problems have been solved, the solution to others are in the last stages of testing, and there are yet others that require additional research. We will discuss some of the "knowns" and "almost knowns" that look like a good bet for inclusion in the ATF design.

Looking first at performance, it is generally accepted that the ATF will have two engines. Along with the increased reliability factor, two engines will be needed to achieve the speed, acceleration, and turning capabilities mentioned earlier.

However, performance such as this is usually not realized just by the installation of multiple and/or more powerful engines. The real secret of the ATF's performance will be its light weight. Extra weight is a curse on any fighter plane, since it always degrades performance, and, for the most part, is not worth the penalty imposed for having to carry it around. Japanese pilots flying the A6M Zero in the Second World War were almost fanatical in their efforts to lighten their birds. They stripped out radios, antennas, self-sealing tanks, armor plate, parachutes, etc., but ended up with an aircraft whose maneuverability and prowess in combat bordered on the legendary. Based on the initial concepts of how the Advanced Tactical Fighter will be built, it is estimated that approximately 60 percent of the airframe will be made from composite materials. This construction technique will reduce the weight of the ATF by 30 percent over a comparable aircraft made from all metal components.

Drag has always been a problem that affects the performance of any aircraft, particularly fighters. A new bird comes off the drawing board, and the initial, stripped-down version usually exhibits good performance in the air-to-air mission. Then someone decides that this capability can also be applied in the air-to-ground role. Pylons and ordnance-mounting racks are added to the airplane, and these, along with the bombs they carry, increase total drag by a tremendous amount. Even after the bombs are dropped, the high drag index of the pylons and racks diminish the bird's performance in all other areas. The once nimble and quickly accelerating bird has become a dog. However, as the cost of new fighter designs increased, this was the fate of just about every tactical fighter because it was uneconomical to develop separate air-to-air and air-to-ground forces. The close air support mission was an integral part of tactical air doctrine; therefore, compromises in overall performance had to be made.

Until recently, little was done on designing a new weapons carriage system that had less of an adverse impact on all tactical roles the bird had to perform. Fighter planes had to carry bombs, and pylons were the best way to do it, and that was that! But a few years ago, tests conducted with the F-16XL resulted in a brand new approach to carrying bombs on a fighter plane. This concept was known as the semi-conformal mounting of munitions, and did away entirely with pylons, as well as multiple and triple ejector racks needed to mount the bombs.

In this system, the bombs are snugged up close to the under-surface of the wing with only the ejectors protruding from the wing, and are stored in-line, fore to aft. The reason for this is that when bombs are mounted directly behind one another, the second has only half the drag of the first, and the third only half that of the second. Also, by staggering rows of bombs inboard-to-outboard, interference drag between the rows is reduced as well. The combination of these two principles results in the total drag of this carriage system being 60 percent lower than that of conventional mounting methods. It also allows the bird to fly at supersonic speeds with a full load of bombs.

Another major contribution in both weight-saving and in the improved electronics needed for the ATF is a concept being developed at this time known as the Very High Speed Integrated Circuit (VHSIC). These revolutionary "chips" have a greatly increased capability over integrated circuits currently in use. In addition, the power requirements for components utilizing VHSICs is quite a bit less than that needed for similar items in today's fighters. This in turn would call for smaller and lighter generators, thus producing another considerable saving of weight. Along with needing only 20 percent of the power now required for like items, and being one quarter the size and weight of existing circuits, the cost of VHSICs will be one-tenth that of present day components, yet they will work ten times faster. These qualities will offer great promise in the area of launch-and-leave weapons, better on-board computers, and more effective electronic warfare capabilities.

An example of the potential to be realized in VHSICs is shown by a comparison of how their use would affect the present day F-15. The existing radar signal processor in this bird weighs 50 pounds, has 5,000 integrated circuits, and needs 1,600 watts of power to operate it. By incorporating the VHSIC technology, this same unit would be reduced to one printed circuit board with 45 VHSICs weighing three pounds and only requiring 50 watts.

Overall, it is estimated that if the VHSIC technology does not mature, the aircraft will be 5,000 pounds heavier. This fact alone will have a direct impact on the eventual cost of the ATF, since the price tag on any airplane is directly proportional to airframe weight. If the high-tech weight-saving approach is not utilized in building the ATF, the bird will probably end up running about $60 million a copy. This figure could be reduced by one third if these new concepts are employed to lighten the airframe and equipment wherever possible.

Electronics are truly the key to success in meeting the tough mission requirements of the ATF. Nowhere is this exemplified more than in the systems designed to allow the Advanced Tactical Fighter to attack ground targets at night. The original hardware built for the LANTIRN system described earlier did not really live up to expectations. Consequently the entire package was redesigned, and at this time the bugs in the navigation pod have been pretty well eliminated. However, there is still some work to be done on the targeting pod, which will eventually make possible night attacks against small, single targets such as a truck or a tank. But even with this current limitation, LANTIRN is still a very impressive weapons delivery system.

The navigation pod of LANTIRN acting alone will enable a single-seat aircraft to bomb area targets at low altitude in the dark more safely and effectively than any past aircraft. Any large target that the pilot could see in the daytime could be hit at night using just the nav pod. This revamped piece of gear was tested in the fall of 1984, and it proved to be very capable of doing the job. Pilots were able to fly at night over unfamiliar terrain at speeds of 610 mph at an altitude of 200 feet, and at 550 mph at 100 feet. The infrared navigational displays on the HUD enabled them to fly with as much confidence as if in daylight. However, since it relies on optics and infrared systems, LANTIRN will only make an aircraft capable of attacking at night under the weather, not *in* the weather.

Another factor in the design of the ATF that will enhance its performance is its engines. Each of this bird's two engines will provide more than twice the thrust, in relation to its weight, than any present-day fighter engine. Both Pratt and Whitney and General Electric are already working on the design of this new engine; however, the details are highly classified. Such a lead time is necessary because modern high-performance engines take longer to develop than airframes. It is predicted that the number of compressor and turbine stages in the ATF engine will be about half those found in today's engines. Also, it is expected that the total number of parts in this powerplant will be 50 percent less than the amount in current models.

Electronics again play a key role in that engine operation will be governed by the Digital Engine Electronic Control System, which fine-tunes the various stages of engine operation in order to deliver optimum performance at all times. The pilot's inputs to this system are given by the position of the throttles. This precise control, and the new turbine components, will allow the engine to operate in the 1,800 degrees Fahrenheit range, which is 300 to 400 degrees higher than engines of the '60s and '70s. By the time the ATF becomes operational, it is expected that the technology of molecular composites will be developed to the point where engine parts can be made that will permit temperatures above 2,000 degrees.

Meeting the stealth requirements for the Advanced Tactical Fighter will be a tough nut to crack. Information about the techniques that will be employed on the ATF are understandably a closely guarded secret, since a breakthrough in this area by either side would seriously alter the balance of power throughout the world. Some of the more obvious methods of approaching this problem were alluded to earlier, such as eliminating the pylons for carrying bombs. If the semi-conformal weapons carriage system described above were used, a great deal of the radar reflectivity associated with present-day systems would be done away with. Although this is a significant improvement over the pylon system, it is not the perfect answer. The bombs themselves add to the total cross sectional area of the airplane, and would increase the size of its radar return. A possible alternative here would be to have the weapons carried internally, but this would present an additional design requirement of building in a bomb bay that would accommodate enough bombs to make the mission worth the effort.

The other big problem in reducing the radar signature of the ATF is how to diminish the effect of the compressor face on each engine. Current research indicates that there is a way to engineer this undesirable feature out of the final design. Instead of affording enemy radars a direct look at the compressor face, the Advanced Tactical Fighter will incorporate engine inlet ducts that are specifically designed to nearly eliminate such reflections. This is accomplished by building a series of gentle curves in the walls of the duct. These curved surfaces, in combination with the compressor face, act like a series of mirrors that reflect incoming radar energy from side to side within the duct. Instead of being reflected directly back out of the duct, it is, in effect, bounced back and forth until it dissipates, and thus is effectively "swallowed" by the duct.

Even with these clever innovations, when all is said and done, you still have a sizable piece of metal traveling through the air that does reflect radar energy. The real hush-hush efforts of those working on the stealth problem center around the possibility of coating the entire aircraft with a radar-absorbing material. A substance such as this would soak up most—or all—of the radar transmissions that are directed at it. Even if the material was not perfect, and allowed a small amount of energy to be reflected back to the transmitter, the desired effect still might be achieved. A weak return such as this will produce a diffuse and dim "paint" on the enemy's radar screen; therefore, it is a good possibility that it would be overlooked on a screen cluttered with electronic jamming, ground returns, and countermeasures. With the aerial battle moving at supersonic or near-sonic speeds, only a moment's hesitation or confusion on the enemy radar operator's part may be all that it takes to allow the good guys to hit the target before the opposition really knows what's up. There are undoubtedly numerous problems dealing with strength, flexibility, bonding, and resistance to heat and cold that must be solved before this material becomes an operational reality. What little has been said about this absorptive material seems to point toward a coating of glass fibers embedded in plastic and bonded to a titanium skin.

The solutions to the vectored thrust requirement of the ATF will most likely be found when the F-15 STOL demonstrator flies in 1987. The technologies for movable engine nozzles and thrust reversing are fairly well developed at this time, thus the major problem will be to determine just how much capability can be achieved with a nozzle that is not deflected to the full straight-down position. The ATF will not have the ability to take off and land vertically like the Harrier; therefore, some thrust component must be maintained in the rearward direction in order to sustain adequate flying speed. However, with the integration of the movable nozzles, the variable camber wing, and possibly canards, the ATF will have excellent maneuverability and low-speed flight characteristics. Deflecting the nozzles in an upward direction will allow the pilot to really bend this bird around in a hard turning engagement. This extra edge gained by having the ability to generate high rates of turn by using vectored thrust will certainly be a key factor in the survivability of the ATF in a combat situation.

The requirement for the ATF to be capable of more sorties per aircraft will be accomplished in two ways. First, the incorporation of the LANTIRN system will permit the bird to attack targets at night and in weather conditions that would preclude such a mission with today's equipment. Without LANTIRN, close air support against medium to small targets is normally limited to day VFR in order to gain the higher accuracy needed for targets in this size range. Night dive-bombing under flares is just about out of the question when ceilings are less than 15,000 feet, and this method, like the Combat Sky Spot and Commando Nail techniques mentioned earlier, is usually designed for area targets such as base camps and truck parks. Therefore, the improved electronics destined for the ATF, including LANTIRN, will allow targets to be hit around the clock, thus denying the enemy the respite that darkness and bad weather have usually provided.

The second approach to better sortie generation will focus on designing simpler maintenance procedures for the ATF. Quicker turnaround and less downtime between missions cannot help but improve the airframe utilization rate. Nearly all maintenance functions require the use of special tools and equipment, but the ATF program is working toward a significant reduction of the items needed to maintain the aircraft.

A good example is the paraphernalia required just for the engine. Normally, this includes such things as large screens to cover the intakes during ground runs, special dollies for engine removal, lifting bars, testing and monitoring devices, and specialized tools of all kinds. The engine now being used in the F-15 and F-16 requires 25,000 pounds of unique tools. The goal for the ATF is to bring this figure down to 5,000 pounds. Not only does this presage simpler maintenance procedures, but such a weight reduction will have a dramatic impact on the mobility plans of any unit equipped with the ATF.

Once the VHSIC becomes available, the number of components in the electronics section of the airplane will also be reduced. This in turn will make for quicker fault isolation procedures, where a malfunctioning circuit board or component can be identified and replaced in no time at all. The ability to fix something in a very short time after engine start will turn many potential aborts into productive sorties—which, as far as the ATF is concerned, is the name of the game.

Flying Solutions

All of the above mentioned approaches to solving the myriad problems involved in building the ATF seem to indicate that the firms participating in this venture have a pretty good handle on how to get there from here. With so many of the answers in hand, a more or less obvious question comes to mind: "Is there any new hardware on the ramp to test out these theories?" The follow-on models of the F-15 and F-16 are operational, and are also part of a test program designed to prove out certain concepts for inclusion in the ATF, but their evolution is more the result of our need to maintain superiority in the fighter business rather than a sequence of events intended solely for the ATF. The one *really* new airplane flying today, whose mission is purely experimental, is the Grumman X-29. This aircraft is an exciting blend of technologies

Fig. 16-1. Grumman X-29 forward-swept wing demonstrator. This picture shows the relationship between the canards, wing, and strakes. (courtesy Grumman Aerospace Corporation)

that in all probability will have a direct impact on the design of the Advanced Tactical Fighter. The most striking feature of the X-29 is the rear-mounted, forward-swept wing, and the testing of this concept was one of the major reasons this aircraft was built. While the idea of a forward-swept wing is not new, it is unusual, and a little background on this innovation would perhaps be appropriate.

Aeronautical engineers first recognized the advantages of the forward-swept wing during World War II. Their studies showed that such a design would improve maneuverability, is virtually spin-proof, had better low speed handling with reduced stalling speeds, and produced lower drag across the entire operational envelope, especially at speeds approaching Mach 1. All these pluses would seem to make the forward-swept wing the answer to the designer's prayers; however, it had one characteristic that negated all its good points: As speed increased with this type of wing, it would experience structural failure and tear off. The reason for this was the aerodynamic stresses that cause every wing to flex while in flight. However, in the forward-swept wing, this flexing increased the angle of attack of the outer wing sections, which generated more lift. This in turn increases the air loads and causes further bending of the wing. As speed increases, these forces are also increased, and a point is soon reached where the wing fails.

It would appear that the easiest solution to this problem would be to build the wing stronger so that it could withstand these forces. But tests proved that the additional structure required to stiffen the wing added so much extra weight that all the aerodynamic benefits of the forward-swept wing were nullified. The state of the art of aircraft construction that prevailed in the 1940s prevented finding a solution to this problem, and the concept of the forward swept wing was shelved.

Before the idea was given up as a lost cause, two different designs were built in Germany. The first was an experimental jet bomber made by Junkers in 1944, but its development was not completed. The second was the Hansa business jet, which made it into limited production in 1964. The forward sweep on this latter aircraft was only 15 degrees, and thus was small enough to avoid any serious structural problems.

This type of design remained dormant until a few years ago, when advanced composite materials were adapted to aircraft construction. These amazing combinations of epoxy, fiberglass, and other woven substances provided the needed strength to build a forward-swept wing that would not tear itself loose, and yet these materials are light enough that no major weight penalty was incurred. The reason why this new wing was successful was that it was aeroelastically tailored to resist stress by virtue of its shape, thickness, and the direction of the "lay up" of the bonded graphite and boron composites.

This last item perhaps needs a little amplification, and an analogy can be drawn with the procedures used to fiberglass boats and homebuilt aircraft. When fiberglass cloth is epoxied to the plane or boat, it is most important to lay the cloth on the form with its fibers running in a certain direction. This fiber orientation is critical if the maximum strength of the cured composite is to be attained, and is referred to as the "lay-up" of the glass cloth or other material being used. By carefully designing the lay-up of the forward-swept wing, engineers have actually created a counterforce in the wing that acts to prevent twisting as the wing is flexed upward by aerodynamic loads. The entire wing of the X-29 is a very solid structure indeed, where the thickness of the lower skin varies from four tenths of an inch at the tip to eight tenths of an inch at the root. At this latter point, the wing cover is made up of 156 layers of the composite material. Each of these skins is attached to the six spars by some 1,000 titanium precision fasteners. Despite its size and thickness, each of these skins is surprisingly light, weighing in at 289 pounds.

Another remarkable feature of the wing built for the X-29, is that it is only one third as thick as any previously built supercritical wing. This type of airfoil is different from the classic design used on most aircraft. A supercritical airfoil has a blunter and thicker leading edge than normal airfoils. This design allows the wing to fly faster before developing a shock wave on the upper surface, which causes the boundary layer air to separate from the wing, which in turn creates drag and decreases lift.

Sweeping a wing forward also produces a much more desirable airflow in the spanwise direction across the wing. On a conventional aft-swept design, airflow bends outward toward the wingtips, and at high angles of attack, this is where the stall starts to develop. As the stall progresses, more and more of the outer wing panel is in disturbed air, rendering the ailerons less effective. The airflow over forward-swept wings tends to migrate toward the root, and it is here that the initial stall sets in. Even as the wing gets deeper in the stall, the wingtips and the ailerons remain in smooth air, thus maintaining full roll control and better resistance to spins.

Going from the wing to the rest of the airplane, it is apparent that other parts of the X-29 are just as amazing as the wing itself. Lift generated by the wing of the conventional aircraft tends to pitch the nose downward, and therefore must be countered by a downward airload on the stabilizer. These two forces acting against each other reduce the net aircraft lift. The lift of the rear-mounted forward-swept wing on the X-29 also tends to pitch the nose down, and this action is balanced by the canards. However, in this case, the canards generate lift in the *upward* direction, which adds to total aircraft lift.

These canards also perform another very important function that contributes to the overall performance of the X-29. These surfaces are placed relatively close to the wing, in what is known as a "close coupled" configuration. By being located here, the tip vortex generated by air moving over the canards is carried back over the wing, where it is forced toward the root by spanwise airflow. The rotation of this vortex is such that it helps to hold the boundary layer air close to the wing surface, thus delaying the stall. Since this aerodynamic action takes place where the stall on a forward-swept wing initiates, it, too, enhances the performance of the X-29, especially at low speeds. Strakes leading back from the trailing edge of the wing to the rear of the fuselage are used to augment the canards in situations where efficiency is not critical. These would be most effective to rotate the aircraft on takeoff, or to pitch the nose down from a deeply stalled condition.

Add-On Test Programs

Along with being a demonstrator for a workable forward-swept wing, the X-29 will also be used to conduct further testing on another concept that will most certainly be used on the Advanced Tactical Fighter. This is the mission-adaptable wing that was mentioned in the last chapter. Its smooth surface and ability to vary the camber according to flight conditions make this system a major contributor to the efficiency and maneuverability of the X-29. Like the F-16, the flight controls in the X-29 are operated by a fly-by-wire system, where pilot inputs are converted to electrical impulses that are routed to a computer, which actually directs the movement of the control surfaces. The triple-redundant system changes the position of the canards, the strake flaps, and the three variable camber segments on the trailing edge of each wing 40 times each second just to maintain straight and level flight. This constant updating of the controls is necessary because without it, the X-29 would destroy itself almost instantly in flight. This is due to the severe longitudinal instability inherent in the X-29's design, because both the wing and the canards produce lift instead of balancing each other. This tendency is so pronounced that Grumman's project director compares it to shooting an arrow tail-first. Were it not for the computerized flight control system, the X-29 would not fly at all.

The idea of having a computer integrate and coordinate all control system functions, coupled with the concepts being developed by the AFTI/F-16 that were talked about earlier, introduces a revolutionary theory that will undoubtedly be developed for the ATF. This concerns the ability of the ATF to absorb a large amount of battle damage and still remain flyable. Up till now, taking a hit that destroyed a substantial amount of the control system just about always called for a bailout as the proper emergency procedure. Research is now being done with fast-acting sensors and computers that will take into consideration any damage done to a control surface. Once this damage is sensed, the system will compensate for it instantly and automatically.

For example, if enemy fire destroyed a part of a wing, the flight control computer would reconfigure the other available control surfaces (such as canards, rudders, ailerons, stabilators, and flaperons) to keep the aircraft controllable. In a situation like this, the pilot could not react fast enough to take the proper corrective action, even if he knew what was wrong and what had to be done. Once the problem was diagnosed and fixed, an added feature of this system would be to inform the pilot what had happened, and what the aircraft was still capable of doing.

Ordinarily, one would think that such an ingenious, new, and innovative airplane as the X-29 would cost a staggering amount to develop to the point of having a flyable machine on the ramp. Although getting the X-29 in the air was not a free undertaking, many large-scale savings in both time and cost have been realized since the design work was begun in 1981. These were made possible by utilizing many off-the-shelf components for those parts of the X-29 that did not involve the testing of new concepts. Using items from other aircraft eliminated the time to design and build them, and this proven hardware also did away with one more unknown in the final package. Some of the components that make up this hybrid are a forward fuselage from an F-5A taken from the Air Force boneyard in Arizona; the landing gear, accessory gearbox and flight control actuators from an F-16; and the General Electric engine from the Navy's F-18 Hornet.

Up to its first flight on December 14, 1984, the progress and success achieved by the X-29 was almost too good to be true. The Grumman design team had obviously done their work well, and this airplane offered the promise of a new breed of tactical fighters that were smaller, lighter, and less expensive, yet more efficient than present day designs. Engineers were optimistic to the point of hoping that if all goes well during the two-year testing program slated for the X-29, the need for an ATF prototype will be eliminated.

This would certainly be a boon to the development of the Advanced Tactical Fighter, but like all test regimens, many problems may yet be uncovered and have to be solved before such a quantum leap can be considered. One such stumbling block might be the industry's lack of experience in the use of advanced composites for fighter aircraft. This is particularly true for the heavy load-bearing structures in these birds, such as that needed for weapons mounting points under high G conditions. Another area of potential difficulties that has to be investigated is how the addition of underwing missiles and stores will affect the flexing of the forward-swept wing.

The main job of the X-29 test program will definitely be to evaluate the performance of this wing design, and the operation of the variable-camber wing. However, there are other new technologies related to the ATF that can use the X-29 as a testbed. It is likely that this airplane will be used to explore the potential of a two dimensional engine nozzle that would eventually be integrated with the flight control system. This assembly, designed by General Electric and known as the Aden nozzle, will be movable through plus and minus 30 degrees, and will improve high-altitude, low-speed maneuverability.

Grumman also proposes that the X-29 be utilized for investigating an entirely new approach to the stealth requirement for the ATF. Rather than using the techniques described earlier for hiding an aircraft from enemy radars, this concept will attempt to make it less visible to the naked eye. Known as "active camouflage," it will involve the carefully modulated illumination of the underside of the aircraft so that it blends into the daylight sky.

The 21st Century

Even though it is still quite a few years from fruition, the ATF program seems well on track, with definite goals and a good game plan on how to reach them. Research, as always, continues despite the lack of immediate applications for the concepts under investigation. There are a number of projects that, barring major technological breakthroughs, will probably not mature in time for inclusion in the initial versions of the ATF. However, these will undoubtedly be earmarked for follow-on models as soon as the state of the art permits.

The test program mentioned earlier for voice-controlled cockpit actions has pretty much determined that work remains to be done in this area. Although this system has shown great promise, it has to be *absolutely* foolproof to operate in a combat situation. At a time like this, you don't want armament to be fired because the computer "thought" it heard the correct command. The direction that the development of this technology will most likely take is to concentrate on routine cockpit activities. Such lethal functions as weapons arming/release will in all probability still be done by switch action in the fighter of the future.

The fly-by-wire system of computerized flight controls envisioned for the ATF would still be susceptible to electromagnetic interference, which introduces anomalies into the network. Already on the drawing board is a fly-by-light control system that utilizes fiber optics instead of electrical wiring. Along with eliminating the interference problem, these data links are also faster and lighter than present circuitry.

After the turn of the century, it is expected that progress in the field of amorphous metals will have advanced to the point where they can be used for aircraft. Amorphous metals are those with a random molecular structure, rather than the ordered crystal matrix of today's materials. The absence of defined boundaries between crystals makes these metals highly resistant to corrosion, since there is no place for corrosion to start. This structure also makes amorphous metals three orders of magnitude stronger than steel.

Looking at all the recent developments, and those yet to come, the remaining years to the turn of the century look like exciting ones for tactical air—and those lucky enough to be involved in it. New airplanes and new equipment are on the way that will increase the potential and capability of the fighter jock of the 21st century. But there is no doubt that even when the ATF becomes a reality, new concepts that are only vague theories now will be poised on the drawing boards, ready to push the Advanced Tactical Fighter into obsolescence.

Chapter 17

Conclusions

Looking back over all the previous discussions concerning just what it takes to be a fighter pilot in modern warfare, it is probably an understatement to say that the job is becoming more complex. Despite all the dazzling new concepts designed to lessen the pilot's workload, flying the fighters of today and tomorrow is definitely not a task for amateurs. Whipping along at 500 knots on the deck at night and in the weather demands the utmost in skill and professionalism, to say nothing of intestinal fortitude. The same could be said about wading into a flight of MiG-25s, or pressing on down through a wall of flak to the weapons release point. In the aerial supremacy game today, you're either a hungry tiger or you're dead—or, at the very best, a severe liability to your squadron mates.

The newly minted fighter pilot, just pinning on his wings after graduating from flying school, is only at the threshold. Although it is very deflating to the ego, he must realize that he has only completed the rudimentary entrance requirements for the tiger's world. He can get an airplane off the ground, fly it from A to B, and get it back down again. He still has to learn how to fight with it.

The amount of training it will take to turn this fledgeling into a hungry tiger is enormous, and does not occur overnight, no matter how bright the student. As mentioned before, there are a considerable number of skills that must be mastered before being qualified even to fly as a wingman. Becoming proficient in each one to the point where the flight leader can depend on—rather than worry about—the wingman takes a long time and a lot of practice. The aura of the hungry tiger finally emerges when the mission essentials become paramount, and the mechanics of flying the airplane are instinctive to the extent that the bird becomes a physical extension of the pilot's thoughts and reactions. During any tactical activity a million things flash through a tiger's mind: keeping a jink going to confuse enemy gunners, the position of the bird in relation to the target and the wingman, the correct maneuver to counter the enemy's efforts to escape, anticipating and planning for the next move after that, proper scope interpretation on a low level run, etc. These are the things on which a pilot's attention must be focused. If he has to consciously work at staying in position on the leader's wing rather than flying it naturally as a coordinating team member, he's more hindrance than help. If he must stop to think about or mull over what weapon to select for the attack in progress, the fleeting chance for victory will pass him by.

Today's airplanes—and even more so those of tomorrow—contain a multiplicity of systems to monitor and control. Although expensive and infinitely complex, they are essential if these birds are to successfully meet the tough challenge posed by the enemy. The lightning-fast pace of a modern war dominated by electronics demands offensive and defensive systems of advanced capability if air supremacy is to be won. Knowing how to operate this equipment in the middle of a fight and utilize all of the subtle options it offers will be the key as to who prevails. These systems collect and have available an enormous amount of data concerning the pilot's tactical environment—far too much for the jock to look at and interpret in the short time available. The various new cockpit displays are an attempt to distill this mountain of information to its essentials. These are then presented to the pilot in an easily readable fashion that allows him to manage all the aircraft systems effectively.

This does not mean that the tiger of tomorrow will find time hanging heavy on his hands on a tactical mission. He will probably be just as busy as an F-4 driver during the Vietnam fracas. However, because of the vast increase in the aircraft's potential, his activity will accomplish much more, and he will be considerably more aware of the ground and air picture around him than his Vietnam counterpart. All this exotic equipment and the numerous types of weapons that can be used with it combine to provide a wide variety of options for each tactical situation. Learning *how, when,* and *where* to apply these options effectively is why so long a training period is required to earn the tiger's stripes.

Today's fighter pilot must be a jack-of-all-trades. The unpredictable nature and quickness of modern war, coupled with the expense of the weapons systems required, precludes the use of nearly all specialized tactical units. In the past, certain squadrons were designated and equipped for interception, others for the close air support mission, while still others handled interdiction and the air-to-air role. Not so today, with fighters in the inventory that can "do it all."

Since the plane has all these capabilities, the tiger flying it can have no less. As pointed out before, it is more likely than not that the pilot will have to be highly proficient in each skill area on every mission. A typical sortie in the European theater would, in all probability, require a low-level penetration in the weather, locating the target by radar, a pop-up to a visual delivery, engaging enemy interceptors to fight your way out, and most likely a midair refueling. The birds scheduled to be in the inventory for the next 15 to 20 years are all single-seaters, which means that this multi-role mission will have to be performed by one person.

As new and more advanced equipment appears on the scene that allows these aircraft to do their job even better, the pilot's workload will again approach the saturation point. This may set the stage for requiring the next generation fighter to be a two-seater. Although this might reduce its overall performance somewhat, it is the price that must be paid if the bird is to perform its mission and survive. An alternative to the fighter with a two-man crew is to continue with the current trend of single-place aircraft, but have them accompanied by a highly specialized ECM bird such as the EF-111A.

That tactics for the air-to-air and air-to-ground mission of today will probably not change appreciably in the foreseeable future. Higher performance aircraft carrying systems and weapons with increased potential will undoubtedly expand the engagement arena. Once the fight is joined, missiles and guns will be fired at just about any crossing angle, thanks to all-aspect weapons and advanced fire control systems. But regardless of all the electronics, the victory will ultimately belong to the tiger who can maneuver into his opponent's six and nail him with whatever weapon it takes to make the kill. Increased accuracy and greater safety from defensive fire are the big refinements in the air-to-ground business.

Smart bombs and standoff weapons like the Maverick will be the preferred and most economical way of attacking a target. However, it is improbable that this type of ordnance will ever replace iron bombs entirely, and the direct delivery of slicks and high-drags will continue to be a prime tactical consideration. The remarkable pictures produced by modern radars are without a doubt a tremendous boon to the troops doing offset bombing. They ease the navigational problems of getting to and from the target, and their finer resolution permits a more accurate delivery of the munitions.

The biggest problem to be overcome on these missions is countering the effect of hostile ECM. If the pendulum swings to the defense, the countermeasures could be so severe as to force aircrews to revert to time, distance,and the inertial navigator. This same problem could also negate the effectiveness of the most crucial ingredient of any future air battle, the AWACS bird. As in the '50s and '60s, fighter pilots will still have to learn how to work around and through ECM in order to hack the mission.

Fighter aircraft will continue to develop by leaps and bounds, and their magical electronic components will certainly keep pace. More and more functions will necessarily be assumed by computers because of the mass of information needing processing in any tactical situation. Automated systems are also being used in ever-increasing numbers in an attempt to give the pilot more time for the primary mission activities.

Does this growing trend toward the use of machines point to a fighter force of the future made up of highly sophisticated drone aircraft? Will the hungry tiger be an extinct species in the 21st century? No way! Although mechanical and electronic aids have become an integral part of aerial combat, they are still just that— *aids*. Man remains the essential ingredient.

As pointed out in other portions of this book, a machine cannot perform in a combat environment like a man for the following reasons: It can only report the specifics of a tactical situation, but cannot analyze them and react accordingly. Once launched, its flight plan cannot be quickly altered in order to adapt to changing mission requirements. And, in all probability, it would not be recallable in a brinksmanship situation.

Perhaps the very essence of what it takes to be a hungry tiger and how the new technology impacts on this calling are summed up by a quote from the leader of the Luftwaffe in World War II. General Adolf Galland remarked: "Only the spirit of attack borne in a brave heart will bring success to any fighter aircraft, no matter how highly developed it may be."

Glossary

Glossary

AK-47: A Russian-made light infantry weapon in widespread use among communist forces. It is magazine-fed with semiautomatic or automatic fire capability, and is analogous to our M-16 rifle.

ASL: Above Sea Level; the altitude indicated by an aircraft's altimeter.

bandit: An aircraft known to be hostile.

bingo fuel The amount of fuel that will allow you to make a normal recovery at your home base, plus the amount necessary to divert to an alternate base if required.

bounce: To attack another aircraft, element, or flight, usually taking it by surprise.

CBU: Cluster Bomb Unit, a bomb-shaped container used to dispense small antipersonnel bomblets; also used to designate the bomblets themselves.

CEP: Circular Error Probable, a measure of accuracy given in terms of the radius of a circle whose center is the aiming point, so that on the average half the bombs will strike inside the circle, and the other half will fall outside. In combat, a typical CEP would be about 250 feet.

chaff: Small, thin strips of aluminum foil cut to exact lengths determined by the wavelength of the radar to be jammed. When dropped from an aircraft, the packages are blown open by the airstream, and the chaff disperses to form a "cloud" of the material, which then falls at a very slow rate of descent. This "cloud" is an extremely good reflector of radar energy, thus masking any real targets under the chaff drop.

clock code: A frame of reference used to locate traffic in the area of a given aircraft, with the nose of the aircraft being twelve o'clock and the tail being six o'clock. "High" and "low" are also used with clock code directions to further pinpoint a position. For example, "Bogey at two o'clock high" would mean that this aircraft is approximately 60 degrees to the right of the nose of your aircraft, and above your present altitude.

combining glass: A flat plate of glass that is part of the gunsight mounted in the pilot's line of vision just behind the windshield. Acts as a screen on which aiming and flight information can be projected using light symbols.

EF-111A: A version of the General Dynamics F-111 that has been modified by the Grumman Corporation for the electronic countermeasures mission. It carries no armament.

electric goon: An EC-47 "Gooney Bird" with special equipment and antennas to monitor electronic sensors on the ground and other hostile electromagnetic emissions.

element: A pair of aircraft acting as a unit under the direction of the element leader; also, the number three and four aircraft in a flight of four.

field level maintenance: Major structural repairs on any part of the aircraft. Does not involve complete disassembly such as removing center wing section from the fuselage.

firefight: A situation in which opposing ground forces are actively engaged in shooting at each other.

flight: Four aircraft acting as a unit under the direction of the flight leader.

G: A unit used to express the force of gravity, e.g., a force of two Gs will cause an object to double its weight while the force is being applied due to the doubled gravitational pull on the object.

GCA: Ground Controlled Approach, a procedure by which an aircraft flying in the weather is guided by precision radar through an approach and a descent to the runway for landing.

GIB: Guy In Back, the crewmember in the back seat of some fighters who operates the radar, weapons delivery system, and navigation gear.

G loading: The number of Gs put on the aircraft during a maneuver.

grunt: A ground soldier, as opposed to someone who flies; anyone who doesn't fly.

idiot panel: A grouping of 25 to 30 small light panels that illuminate individually when various aircraft systems fail. Since these are located on a sub-panel, a Master Warning Light on the instrument panel comes on when any failure occurs. This calls the pilot's attention to the idiot panel to determine which system has malfunctioned.

IFR: Instrument Flight Rules, flying in the weather with the aircraft's instruments as the primary reference.

jink: A rapid, random movement of an aircraft, usually at high speed and high G loadings, to avoid being shot down by another aircraft or by ground fire. In the former case, it is referred to as a "last ditch maneuver" to shake an opponent off your tail.

Jolly Greens: Nickname for the HH-53 helicopter used for rescue work in Vietnam.

klick: A kilometer, or 1,000 meters.

mamasan/papasan: Terms that became popular during the Korean War, anglicized corruptions of the Japanese suffix meaning "little," i.e., little mother and little father. Became almost a universal term to denote any oriental woman or man of middle age or older.

mark: A pyrotechnic of some kind used by the FAC to pinpoint the location of the target to be attacked. Usually a cloud of white smoke from an exploded white phosphorous rocket (daytime), or a long-burning flare called a "log" (nighttime).

MER: Multiple Ejector Rack, an ordnance mount that can carry up to six weapons, usually unguided bombs, at once.

pipper: A dot of light at the center of the image projected on the combining glass by a gunsight. Used as the primary aiming reference for air-to-air or air-to-ground weapons delivery.

pucker factor: An arbitrary designation to depict the degree of nervousness or anxiety associated with a given mission. The term is derived from the human reaction—voluntary or involuntary—to tighten the lower intestinal tract in situations of stress or danger. Heavy flak, low bombing altitudes, and difficult targets all produced a high pucker factor.

punch out: To use the ejection seat to abandon a crippled aircraft.

R&R: Rest and Recuperation, an officially granted respite from the area of hostilities, usually at a well-known vacation spot.

ROK: Acronym for Republic Of Korea. Commonly used to identify a member or a unit of Korea's armed forces.

Sandys: Call sign for the Douglas A-1 Skyraiders used to sterilize an area before a rescue effort, and which patrol the area during the actual pickup to keep the enemy's heads down.

SAM: Surface-to-Air missile.

shack the target: To score a direct hit.

six: The most commonly used clock code term. Six always refers to the area behind an aircraft. Examples: "Check your six," meaning keep an eye peeled behind you, or check the area immediately to the rear of your bird; "I'm in his six and closing," meaning you are behind an opponent and have an overtake rate established; and "He's in your deep six," meaning another aircraft is behind and below the aircraft you are calling.

spread formation: An arrangement of aircraft where individual planes are about 100 feet from one another. Used in VFR conditions going to and from the target area. A little more relaxed than close formation, yet not spread out as far as tactical formation.

sterilize: To clear an area of hostile activity, particularly with respect to preparations for rescuing downed aircrews.

stroking the burner: Lighting the afterburner, usually only for a few moments, to increase airspeed slightly or to prevent it from bleeding off too rapidly.

TER: Triple Ejector Rack, an ordnance mounting with three stations.

TDY: Acronym for Temporary Duty, a tour of duty, usually of short duration, at a base other than your permanently assigned station.

UHF/DF: Ultra High Frequency Direction Finder, an electronic device that homes in on and indicates the direction to a signal in the ultra high frequency band, usually another radio transmitting in that spectrum.

VFR: Visual Flight Rules, flying in clear or partially cloudy weather when the ground or a lower cloud deck can be used as a reference.

VTOL: Acronym for Vertical Takeoff and Land, usually refers to airplanes like the Harrier, or various research aircraft with the same capability.

Bibliography

Books

Frizzell, Colonel Donaldson D. and Bowers, Colonel Ray L., editors. *Air War: Vietnam.* New York: Arno Press, 1978.

Gunston, Bill, ed. *The Illustrated History of Fighters.* New York: Exeter Books, 1981.

Taylor, John W. R., ed. *Jane's All the World's Aircraft 1970-71.* London: Jane's Publishing Co. Ltd., 1971.

_____. *Jane's All the World's Aircraft 1980-81.* London: Jane's Publishing Co. Ltd., 1981.

_____. *Jane's All the World's Aircraft 1982-83.* London: Jane's Publishing Co. Ltd., 1983.

Periodicals

_____. "Aerospace World News, Views and Comments." *Air Force Magazine,* October 1984, pp. 34-35.

_____. "ATF Project Stresses Range Supportability." *Aviation Week and Space Technology,* November 19, 1984, p. 53.

Berry, F. Clifton, Jr. "The Current Avionics Approach: Rational Standardization at Work." *Air Force Magazine,* July 1980, pp. 62-75.

_____. "The Revolutionary Evolution of the F-16XL." *Air Force Magazine,* November 1983, pp. 50-56.

Browne, Malcolm W. "A Ship Killer Comes of Age." *Discover,* July 1982, pp. 18-23.

_____. "Video Warfare Over Lebanon." *Discover,* August 1982, pp. 90-92.

Canan, James W. "Coming On and Coming Up." *Air Force Magazine,* January 1985, pp. 34-42.

_____. "Forward Sweep." *Air Force Magazine,* January 1985, p. 61.

_____. "Toward the Totally Integrated Airplane." *Air Force Magazine,* January 1984, pp. 34-41.

Carroll, Captain Robert G. H. "F-16: Swing-Force Fighter for the '80s." *Air Force Magazine,* April 1976, pp. 30-35.

Corddry, Charles W. "Britain's Near-Thing Victory." *Air Force Magazine,* December 1982, pp. 50-53.

Correll, John T. "The Future Forms Up at ASD." *Air Force Magazine,* January 1983, pp. 40-50.

_____. "The Many Battles of Maverick." *Air Force Magazine,* March 1983, pp. 98-103.

_____. "Where TAC is Heading." *Air Force Magazine,* June 1984, pp. 50-58.

DeMeis, Richard. "Forward-Swept Wings Add Supersonic Zip." *High Technology,* January-February 1983, pp. 33-40.

Deming, Angus. "Mideast Dogfight." *Newsweek,* July 22, 1981, pp. 24-38.

Edwards, Captain Wayne C. "The F-16: Not Like Any Other." *Air Force Magazine,* August 1980, pp. 34-39.

Healy, Melissa."Futuristic X-29 Plane Fashioned for Artful Advances in Agility." *Defense Week,* September 4, 1984, pp. 6-7.

Hendrickson, Walter B. Jr. "Wrong Way Wings." *National Defense,* March 1983, pp. 41-42.

Hermann, Robert J. "Electronics in Warfare: A Look Ahead." *Air Force Magazine,* July 1980, pp. 76-80.

"Integrated Control System Aids Delivery of Weapons." *Aviation Week and Space Technology,* June 8, 1981, pp. 407-409.

"Iron Bombs Used in Iraq Attack." *Aviation Week and Space Technology,* June 15, 1981, p. 32.

_____. "Jane's All the Worlds Aircraft Supplement, August 1983." *Air Force Magazine,* August 1983, pp. 78-79.

Klass, Phillip J. "Improved Version of F-16 Radar to Undergo Testing." *Aviation Week and Space Technology,* June 8, 1981, pp. 149-150.

Marsh, General Robert T. "A Preview of the Technology Revolution." *Air Force Magazine,* August 1984, pp. 42-49.

_____. "McDonnell Douglas to Develop STOL F-15." *Aviation Week and Space Technology,* October 8, 1984, p. 21.

Milton, General T. R. "Drawing Lessons From The Falklands War." *Air Force Magazine,* July 1982, p. 89.

_____. "Too Many Missing Pieces." *Air Force Magazine,* December 1982, pp. 48-50.

Ritchie, Steve. "An Eagle for All Arenas." *Air Force Magazine,* November 1983, pp. 43-49.

Robinson, Clarance A. "USAF Reviews Progress of New Fighter

Programs." *Aviation Week and Space Technology,* November 28, 1983, pp. 44-51.

_____. "U.S. Upgrading Its Strategic Arsenal." *Aviation Week and Space Technology,* March 9, 1981, pp. 23-33.

Ropelelewski, Robert R. "F-15 Fighter Abilities Evaluated." *Aviation Week and Space Technology,* April 26, 1982, pp. 39-46.

Russell, George. "Attack and Fallout." *Time,* June 22, 1981, pp. 24-38.

Schefter, Jim. "Invisible Bomber." *Popular Science,* February 1983, pp. 60-63.

Scott, William B. "Display Designs Advanced for One-Seat Combat Role." *Aviation Week and Space Technology,* March 8, 1982, pp. 217-223.

Skantze, General Lawrence A. "How the E-3A Gives the Big Battle Picture." *Air Force Magazine,* July, 1977, pp. 58-65.

Stein, Kenneth J. "AWACS Capabilities Tested in Europe." *Aviation Week and Space Technology,* January 30, 1978, pp. 60-61.

Sweetman, Bill. "Advanced Fighter Technology," *Interavia,* November 1983, pp. 1197-1199.

_____. "Forward-Swept Wing Technology Integration for the ATF." *International Defense Review,* February 1984, pp. 25-27.

Taylor, John W. R. "Jane's Aerospace Survey 1985." *Air Force Magazine,* January 1985, pp. 62-70.

_____. "Jane's All the World's Aircraft Supplement, December 1981." *Air Force Magazine,* December 1981, pp. 137-144.

_____. "Gallery of Soviet Aerospace Weapons." *Air Force Magazine,* March 1982, pp. 95-110.

_____. "Jane's All the World's Aircraft Supplement,

October 1982." *Air Force Magazine,* October 1982, pp. 89-92.

The International Institute for Strategic Studies. "The Military Balance 1979/80." *Air Force Magazine,* December 1979, pp. 61-135.

_____. "The Military Balance 1980/81." *Air Force Magazine,* December 1980, pp. 62-131.

_____. "The Military Balance 1981/82." *Air Force Magazine,* December 1981, pp. 53-125.

Young, Susan H. H. "Gallery of USAF Weapons." *Air Force Magazine,* July 1982, pp. 153-169.

Index

Index